CLARK CC

THIS BOOK PROVIDED BY
VOTERS
LAS VEGAS - CLARK COUNTY LIBRARY DISTRICT
1991 BOND ISSUE ELECTION

APGAR ... MAP ... IOWA TESTS ... BRIGANCE K & I ...
SAT TESTS ... MMPI ... STANFORD ACHIEVEMENT TEST
SERIES ... STRONG-CAMPBELL INTEREST INVENTORY ...
WESCHLER SCALES ... EEG ... MRI ... BLOOD TESTS ...
LEAD SCREENING ... TB TEST ... ADT

Between the Apgar Test, given immediately after birth, and the
SATs, required for college admission, your child will probably take
dozens of tests. Some are routine developmental tests or medical
screenings. Others may determine the quality of your child's education, whether a serious illness is diagnosed correctly, or if your child
needs special supportive services. This complete, one-volume parents' guide tells you what you should know about 150 of the most
common tests: what each test measures—and doesn't; how reliable
it is; what you have a right to know about test results; and more. Designed to help busy parents navigate through a sea of acronyms and
professional jargon, this essential reference provides vital information that allows you to become your child's best advocate.

TESTING AND
YOUR CHILD

VIRGINIA E. McCULLOUGH has published more than 300 articles
on subjects ranging from family living to health care. Her previous
books are *TMJ Syndrome: The Overlooked Diagnosis* and *Touch: A
Personal Workbook*. An active member of the National Writers
Union, she is the editor of *Entrepreneur Life*. She lives in Chicago,
Illinois.

TESTING AND YOUR CHILD

What You Should Know About 150 of the Most Common Medical, Educational, and Psychological Tests

VIRGINIA E. McCULLOUGH

A PLUME BOOK

PLUME
Published by the Penguin Group
Penguin Books USA Inc., 375 Hudson Street,
New York, New York 10014, U.S.A.
Penguin Books Ltd, 27 Wrights Lane,
London W8 5TZ, England
Penguin Books Australia Ltd, Ringwood,
Victoria, Australia
Penguin Books Canada Ltd, 10 Alcorn Avenue,
Toronto, Ontario, Canada M4V 3B2
Penguin Books (N.Z.) Ltd, 182–190 Wairau Road,
Auckland 10, New Zealand

Penguin Books Ltd, Registered Offices:
Harmondsworth, Middlesex, England

First published by Plume, an imprint of New American Library, a division of Penguin Books USA Inc.

First Printing, October, 1992
10 9 8 7 6 5 4 3 2 1

 REGISTERED TRADEMARK—MARCA REGISTRADA

LIBRARY OF CONGRESS CATALOGING IN PUBLICATION DATA:

McCullough, Virginia.
    Testing and your child : what you should know about 150 of the
most common medical, educational, and psychological tests/
Virginia E. McCullough.
        p. cm.
    Includes index.
    ISBN 0-452-26840-0
    1. Child development—Testing. 2. Children—Medical examinations.
3. Psychological tests for children. 4. Educational tests and
measurements. I. Title
HQ767.9.M39 1992
153.9′3—dc20

                                                                    92–53540
                                                                        CIP

PRINTED IN THE UNITED STATES OF AMERICA
Set in Times
Designed by Leonard Telesca

A NOTE TO THE READER
The ideas, procedures, and suggestions contained in this book are not intended as a substitute for consulting with your physician. All matters regarding your health require medical supervision.

With love to my children,
Laura Kathleen and Adam David,
who continue to fill my life
with wonder and joy.

CONTENTS

DEVELOPMENTAL TESTING 98

EDUCATIONAL TESTING   156

PSYCHOLOGICAL TESTING 237

Acknowledgments

So many people helped with this book that a separate volume would be needed to list them all. The librarians at the Ronald Williams Library at Northeastern Illinois University in Chicago were particularly generous to me, a nonstudent who was totally unfamiliar with their collection.

I'd also like to thank Ann and Jim Kepler and Lyle Steele for their early perception of the need for this book and for finding a publisher for it, and my editor, Alexia Dorszynski, who asked the right questions and helped me clarify the information. Thanks also to Marcella Dillard, Susan Polodna, Kathleen McGovern-Luckritz, Lois Long, Julia Schopick, Maureen Clark, Hal Wright, my sister, Marifran Carlson, and my parents, Lucille and Arnold Carlson, for their advice and support. A special word of appreciation and love goes to Lu Buckmaster, a dear friend and the best assistant a writer could ever have.

Finally, professionals in many fields agreed to help me choose the tests I've included, provide information about testing procedures and terms, and review test profiles. While I take full responsibility for any unintentional errors, they have been valuable consultants and have kept me on track. The consultants are: Daniel Cukier, M.D.; Molly Jacobs, M.D.; Nancy Sidon, Psy.D.; Pamela Olson, M.A.; Irwin Heller, D.C.; Linda Wait, Ph.D.; Pamela Fleege, Ph.D.; Ronald Rosenthal, Ph.D.; and Holly Johnstone, Ph.D.

A Word to Professionals

Doing the research for this book was a fascinating adventure, made far easier than it might have been because so many professionals have spent their lives researching and writing about issues that involve the well-being of all our children. I am well aware that a book of this nature can barely scratch the surface of the fields mentioned, let alone do justice to the complexity of the topics. However, I also realized that there is simply not enough information available to parents that provides even the most basic discussion of testing and all of its ramifications.

It is my hope that health care providers, mental health professionals, classroom and special education teachers, school counselors, speech and language clinicians, and child development experts will make this book available to the parents of the children they serve. I trust that the questions the book generates will add something to the communication between parents and the professionals whose assistance they seek.

Preface

Testing is a part of life that most of us simply take for granted. Blood is drawn during a routine physical exam, an x-ray is ordered for a knee that is mangled on the volleyball court, achievement test time rolls around again, a reading or math group is assigned after classroom assessments. Then one day an adolescent behaves in an unusually troublesome manner, and testing is suggested, or a child falls behind in classwork and a round of testing is done. Suddenly, testing takes on new importance.

Which tests are chosen and why? What do the scores mean? What, exactly, are the tests measuring? As a parent who has been confronted with situations in which testing has been suggested, I know firsthand that the entire issue can be both reassuring and frightening. Testing can both produce and relieve those apparently universal parental reactions—worry and guilt.

My own daughter and son, ages 23 and 22, respectively, have managed to survive my ignorance, but I am still astonished by how little I knew about the various types of testing, or the potential influence of test results on their lives. While researching and writing this book I found myself saying, again and again, "If I had only known what questions to ask."

Over the years, I was deprived of valuable information because I didn't know enough about testing to ask the right questions. I didn't have a clear understanding of the context in which the testing was taking place, nor did I grasp the consequences of the results and interpretations. And because I now know how complex testing can be, my personal goal for this book has become clear and concise. Simply put, I hope to provide enough information about testing in general, and some specific widely used tests, to help parents ask the "right" questions. What does this test measure? How does it do it? Can the results be confirmed? How important are the results? Is the testing itself stressful? If my child has a known disability, is this test valuable?

The ultimate goal of testing should be to help a child in some way—physically, developmentally, educationally, or emotionally. If this is not the case, why do it in the first place? Therefore, when the testing is over and the results are in, the most important question a parent can ask is, "Now what do we do?" I believe that a better understanding of testing can help us become full partners in our children's treatment plan, educational goals, counseling, and so forth. The more information we have, the better we are able to work with the professionals we rely on to help us with the often overwhelming job of being parents. I hope this book can be one tool to help you make your way through the increasingly complicated maze of testing.

Virginia E. McCullough,
1992

INTRODUCTION
Welcome to the World of Testing

About a minute after the arrival of a baby is heralded, he or she is also welcomed into the world of testing via the Apgar scores. While not, strictly speaking, a test, the Apgar evaluates the overall condition of a baby shortly after birth, using a numerical scoring system. Specifically, it can identify a newborn who is "at risk" so that emergency procedures can be immediately initiated. In this sense, the Apgar is a valuable tool, one which, no doubt, saves lives.

Although I am the mother of two children, I didn't learn about the Apgar until I began researching the general area of evaluation, screening, assessment, measuring, and grouping of children. Was ignorance bliss? I'm not sure, but I have learned that all testing has both an emotional upside and a downside. A labor and delivery room nurse recently told me that today's sophisticated, well-informed parents know enough, in the midst of all the post-birth excitement and exhaustion, to ask, shout, or demand, "What's the score?" And from that moment on, a number becomes the basis on which to feel good or to worry.

This book makes no attempt to settle the debate over the proper place of testing of children. In no way can it be considered an advocacy book. Rather, what we are attempting to do is acknowledge that physical, developmental, educational, and psychological testing is a fact of our children's and our lives.

We also proceed with an assumption that knowledge is power. The more you know about the various tools that are used to evaluate your children's physical, emotional, and educational development and progress, the better able you are to make intelligent, sound choices. Despite the existence of the seemingly powerful "experts," it is you, the parent, who will ultimately decide what is best for your child.

There's no denying that testing is a part of every child's life. Every year, more than 100 million standardized educational tests are administered to school children in the United States; the vast majority are administered to fulfill local or state testing mandates. That is, depending on where you live, your child will take particular standardized achievement tests because the local or state laws have required them. In some localities, children are given a battery of tests at some point in every grade. In others, particular school years are chosen as the testing grades. Some states have developed their own tests, which are administered to the state's students at particular educational junctures. Other states rely heavily on the myriad tests developed by professionals or testing services. School districts within each state may use some "customized" state or local tests along with published tests of their own choosing. The various combinations are based on educational policies that develop and change rapidly.

The 100 million figure doesn't include developmental, vision, and hearing screenings; individual psychological evaluations; or tests given to identify those children considered gifted or learning disabled. Nor does it include the various medical tests that your child might need for one reason or another. If a child has difficulties—a learning disability, for example—he or she could undergo several dozen tests in a single year. Many of these tools will be used to rule out particular causes so that a diagnosis can be "fine tuned." Furthermore, the testing could fall into all four broad categories— physical, developmental, educational, and psychological.

As any educator or clinician will note when looking at the title of this book, we have included many procedures and tools that are not, by strict definition, tests. A screening procedure is not considered a test; nor is a developmental evaluation or a child-behavior inventory. Yet devices and procedures that fall into these categories are included. For the sake of simplicity, we are using the word *test* to include those tools and procedures used to identify a child's physical, developmental, psychological, and educational strengths and weaknesses. And by this we mean abilities, aptitudes, achievement, emotional development and adjustment, and organic health or disease. Obviously, this covers a lot of ground; we have tried to include the types of tests that you are most likely to encounter during your child's first eighteen years or so.

While there are numerous critics of such extensive evaluation of children, few people seriously harken back to the good old days when kids "just grew up." Many of us probably wish, at least at times, for the era when life seemed more simple. However, before we romanticize the pretesting days, it is good to remember that in education alone, screening and diagnostic testing have revolutionized education for children with learning disabilities and other impairments. In the "good old days," many of these children were ignored, held back, labeled "slow," or otherwise ostracized. Unfortunately, this still can occur, even with extensive evaluation processes available. The development of sophisticated medical testing and psychological/educational evaluations have helped millions of young people, who otherwise might be institutionalized, to reach their potential. In some cases, testing has even saved lives. Few people deny that testing has a valuable place in a society that values its children's development.

The controversial areas of academic testing usually focus on the following questions: Do today's tests actually measure what they claim to? Do standardized tests tell us what we need to know about a child's true ability? Are test scores used to group or label children either prematurely or unfairly? Currently, the answer to each of these questions tends to be yes, no, maybe, and sometimes. However, if you are aware of the debate over testing methods and the limitations of testing, you will have an advantage when considering options for your child.

Among the liveliest debates in educational circles today is that going on over the group of achievement tests known as *standardized*. The majority of men and women who are parents today were given numerous standardized tests as young people. Who among us didn't know at what grade level we were reading and how we compared to every other kid in the country? We could either brag or hide, depending on our grade equivalent score, and of course, our percentile rank.

Standardized testing has, in a very real sense, been the foundation upon which our children are promoted, retained, tracked, and identified for further testing. When scores are in the broadly defined average range, we sleep a bit easier because presumably the school system, the teachers, and our children are all doing their respective jobs.

It's only when some disparity seems to occur that most parents get involved in the nitty gritty of the score. You know, for example, that your second grader reads very well. You have proof of this because she reads stories to you at night and seems to understand them. She even checks her own books out of the library on a weekly basis. Furthermore, her teacher tells you that she reads well and gets As in reading—and always has. Why then is her score on the standardized test so low? Why is her placement in a new reading group being discussed? When you decide to investigate, you find out that your second grader answered questions on only one page of the test. Somehow, she missed the instruction to turn the page and complete the section. I know this can happen; it happened to me. Almost every family has at least one "testing" story.

By definition, standardized tests are norm-referenced, meaning that individual scores are compared with other children taking the test. This type of testing is called *objective* because only one right answer is possible on each question. Therefore, scores can be mechanically tabulated rather than individually interpreted. Statistical concepts such as percentile and stanine enter the picture because each score is placed on a scale, with an average range determined by the scores of all children taking the test. Percentile and stanine groupings can be further broken down into school districts and even the individual school. In other words, it is possible for your child to be simultaneously "average" in math ability nationally, "above average" in your state, and "below average" in a particular school.

Critics of standardized testing claim that while the tests purport to have been developed using scientific methods, to be free of cultural or gender bias and highly reliable, these contentions are, upon examination, simply not true. For example, the critics argue that a multiple-choice or true/false format does not measure what children actually know. They also argue that this type of testing does not take into account such things as the different ways children learn, the complex, multifaceted nature of intelligence, or the variation in dialects and language used in homes and communities across the country. Critics also argue that the tests are objective only in that they are scored uniformly once the test key has been determined. In other words, subjectivity has already been built into the test prior to establishing the scoring norms. And, because of the necessity of norms, the law of averages must apply. Some children *must* fall above or below average or the test isn't valid.

Some states and school districts across the country have already begun exploring alternative ways to evaluate educational progress, particularly of young children, for whom developmental variation is often marked. It has long been acknowledged that young children are not particularly good test takers.

Authentic evaluation is one term currently being used to describe the methods employed in what could be called an alternative or an adjunct to standardized testing, at least in some situations. It includes such things as observation, portfolios of work, special projects, noting methods of problem solving, and so on. For example, in authentic evaluation, a portfolio of the actual work a child produces is evaluated throughout the school year to see if a child is actually learning the skills necessary to move to another grade. Teacher observations are also recorded. In this way, individual differences—strengths and weaknesses—can be observed and noted.

This method takes into consideration that not all children learn the same skills at the same time, and, proponents say, it honors that difference rather than punishing it. It also eliminates the need to try to fit young children into a uniform testing environment, a must if a standardized test is to be considered valid.

Included in the concept of authentic evaluation is a method of testing known as *criterion-referenced,* meaning that actual mastery of a skill is evaluated but results are not norm-referenced; that is, compared to others who have taken the same test. Criterion-referenced evaluation eliminates the need for a "bell curve," in which above- and below-average groups must be identified. This type of testing is also said to be more efficient at spotting individual strengths and weaknesses, thereby allowing more specific solutions to identified problems. Individual progress is also more easily evaluated using criterion-referenced testing. Periodic tests to establish that a learning goal has been reached is an example of this type of test. The child's results are used only for the purpose of moving on to more difficult material or repeating the same lesson plan until the skill is mastered.

A category of testing known as *readiness testing* is part of the current debate over the legitimate uses of test results. Permission to enter kindergarten or first grade, placement in early reading groups, or placement in special education classes may depend on the results of a test given to children ages 4 to 6. However, this age group typically changes rapidly and has widely varying rates of development. Many young children simply don't do well on tests, especially when they know or sense that the adults around them place great importance on the results. Educators have actually identified "test anxiety" among children in this age group. Furthermore, the conditions under which these tests are given may not be uniform, making the results suspect anyway. Generally speaking, you should feel free to challenge any placement decision based on a "readiness" test. On the other hand, if you investigate and can see that your child is having difficulties in particular areas, you may want to ask for more in-depth evaluations.

I mention this controversy not with the intention of examining all positions in the debate, but to alert you to the changes that may well be taking place in your child's school district. You may want to learn the direction in which your child's school is heading and become part of the decision-making process. At the very least, awareness of the trends in testing will help you to be a better-informed parent. And in practical terms, you will have a foundation on which to base questions you want to ask.

Nowadays there are numerous reasons that your child might encounter psychological testing. Among these are: suspicion of a learning disability; a disorder that seems to have no obvious cause (e.g., speech/language problems, frequent headaches, bed wetting, or fainting spells); behavioral problems at home or school; possible clinical depression; diagnostic evaluation for severe, long-term unmanageability; as part of child custody arbitration; or if your child is in trouble with the law. As with all other testing, it pays to be aware of the reasons psychological evaluation is being suggested—or even ordered—as often happens in child custody cases or other legal situations. Full-scale psychological evaluations tend to be very expensive and are not necessarily needed every time a problem is suspected. If you are taking your child to a therapist and testing is suggested, find out what the therapist expects to find from the testing.

The field of psychological evaluation also gets a bit fuzzy when it begins to overlap with medical, developmental, and educational testing. Parents whose children are having academic or developmental difficulties might be sent to various physicians, education specialists, or psychologists. The terminology parents encounter—attention deficit disorder (ADD), hyperactivity, minimal brain dysfunction or disorder, and so on—can be confusing as well as alarming. When possible, it is best to have one person act as "stage manager" or director. It is this person's job to help coordinate test results in all of the fields and to try to integrate and interpret the information. (Pediatricians, school guidance counselors, private therapists, or education specialists are examples of professionals who can act in this capacity.)

You will also do well to acquaint yourself with the purpose and method of all tests your child may be taking, no matter which discipline they happen to fall under. For example, you may learn that some psychological tests are always done as part of a battery of tests and are not considered valid when done alone. A developmental test given at intervals to your premature infant is done to track progress and to note any developmental lag as early as possible. You might learn that an ominous-sounding medical test is done—99 percent of the time—to rule out a serious pathology, rather than to confirm a hunch. The medical practitioner often tries to eliminate possible diagnoses in order to narrow down the field—a method referred to as differential diagnosis.

It's also important to remember that some tests are more complex than others and require highly trained, highly skilled examiners. In some cases, specific professional credentials are required. An untrained person might not, for example, be aware that the child doesn't understand the directions or is intimidated by the examiner. The results of a test given under these conditions would be suspect. (Obviously, graduate students, student teachers, and interns learn how to perform tests as part of their training. In most cases, this works well because other professionals confirm test interpretations.)

Perhaps the single most important advice any parent can receive when trying to make his or her way through the complex world of testing is: Ask questions; don't be afraid and be a pest if you have to. *Assume that you have the right to know everything.* Why is a test necessary? How will it benefit your child? What will it confirm or rule out? Is there an alternative test (less stressful, less invasive, less expensive)? In short, ask anything you want to know.

In many, if not most cases, testing is used in conjunction with other evaluation tools. Observation and both structured and unstructured interviews are also used to gather information. Using these other methods helps those evaluating a child determine what specific areas to test and may also determine which parts of a test— *subtests*—should be given. (It is often far more efficient, not to mention economical, to use only specific portions of a lengthy test.)

It is also important to put testing in perspective. Yes, it is a fact of life. Yes, it serves a valuable purpose; if fulfills many needs; it is a systematic way to gather information. However, testing is not an exact science in any field. Tests reveal ambiguous results: false positives/false negatives, suggestions that a problem exists, but no conclusive diagnosis, and so on. Each tool has limitations. Screening is not the same as diagnosing; ability measurements and achievement tests are two different things. Nor do intelligence tests measure creative ability.

A good rule of thumb to follow is to recognize that the greater the impact a decision is going to have on your child, the more information you need to make it. Therefore, think of testing as one way to gather information, and use test results to evaluate your choices. Seldom is one test going to reveal all of the information needed.

Ultimately, you are going to sort through various opinions and impressions, some of which may be based on test results. But testing, valuable as it is, can be but one part of a decision.

What Are Your Rights?

Regulations, statutes, and common practices governing testing vary from state to state, but there are some general statements that can be made about parents' rights. Parents should always assume that they have the final say in all decisions made about their children. Furthermore, parents should always feel free to ask questions about *any* test. To get the best results when questioning teachers, school officials, counselors, and so on, operate on the premise that your child's academic records and psychological profiles are open to them, the same way you automatically assume that your child's medical history is always available. Parents should operate on the premise that they have the following rights:

• Parents have the right to see their child's school records. In some states, this right is guaranteed by specific statute. In other states, school records fall into the category of other public records, thereby making educational records open. In theory, this applies to both custodial and noncustodial parents. In practice, however, a noncustodial parent may have to be assertive because some school districts have excluded the noncustodial parent from school conferences. (Numerous court cases have established the right of parent access to records, and it is unusual for a parent to be denied this information. However, a parent must *ask* for access; few school districts routinely make them available.)

• Parents have the right to challenge information they believe is inaccurate. Let's say that your child has scored poorly on a test that was later discontinued because its validity was questioned. As a parent, you can ask that the test result be removed from the permanent record. The results of any evaluation should be removed when later reports show that the original information is incorrect.

You also have the right to challenge any placement made based on testing that is out of date. Simply put, this means that a child's high-school track, for example, should not be made on the basis of testing performed in fifth or sixth grade. If you believe your child is being incorrectly placed, you have the right to request a review.

As an aside, the right of removal also applies to such things as pejorative remarks about a child or information that could be used in an adverse way. For example, the state of New Hampshire recently ruled that statements made about a student's political views should not be part of the school record.

- Parents have the right to challenge any educational decision made about their child on the basis of a test score. If the child is being denied entrance to school, is retained in a grade, placed on a specific track, or otherwise placed in a special grouping, be sure that you have access to all of the information on which such a decision was made. Find out what other tests or evaluation tools can be used to verify the decision or change it. The "squeaky wheel" principle applies here. Those parents who are firm in their requests for justification of any educational decision are the most likely to get the best results.

- Parents have the right to request testing. If you are puzzled by your child's performance in school, or suspect that an undiagnosed learning disability might be contributing to some academic difficulties, start by approaching your child's teacher and requesting an evaluation. The procedure for carrying out your request varies from school district to school district.

- Parents have the right to know what tests are scheduled, how and when they will be given, and what the scores will be used for. Many schools give certain tests at predetermined intervals. Your permission is generally not required for these tests. However, permission is generally needed for any non-regularly scheduled, individual test. For example, your child should not be given an individual psychological test without your knowledge and permission. If your child is enrolled in a program that is tracking development or evaluating progress on a regular basis, your permission for retesting may be implied by initial enrollment agreements. You might want to check this out if you object to frequent retesting.

- Parents have the right to obtain private testing for the purpose of amassing more information, confirming or challenging a diagnosis or placement, and the like. This issue doesn't come up often, but when it does, it can be crucial. Court cases involving educational placement have been resolved in part because of private testing that parents introduced as evidence.

- Parents have the right to know who has access to their child's records. Some states allow law enforcement or other governmental agencies access to school records. Some schools ask parents to sign a blanket agreement allowing their child's records to be released without parental permission. In that foresight is better than hindsight, it may be better not to sign a general release. It is advantageous to have the school get your permission each time records are requested. Your child's school records should be looked at in a similar way as medical records; that is, they are private until you decide that authorized parties should see them.

  Some states and schools acknowledge the right of young people to have access to their own records and give permission for their release (age 14 in Delaware, for example); in other locales, parents, but not students, can request them.

- Parents have the right to insist on anonymity when their child's test scores are going to be turned over to research organizations. Research can obviously be considered a legitimate use of test scores, but a child's identity should never be revealed.

- When a child has a disability, a parent has the right to have the child tested with instruments designed to test children with that particular disability. For example, a child with impaired hearing should not be given a test in which the instructions are given orally. A paper-and-pencil IQ test may be invalid when a child has a learning disability that limits reading skills.

- The Education for All Handicapped Children Act (P.L. No. 94-142) mandates an appropriate public education for all children, regardless of disability. This federal law includes the right to proper evaluation and testing.

These parental rights may seem quite logical and based on simple common sense. However, it should be noted that some school districts—or even individual teachers—are not necessarily operating under the common, generally accepted practices of the day simply because old habits are hard to break. Therefore, don't hesitate to assert yourself.

How to Use This Book

This book is designed to help you quickly locate individual tests by name in four basic groups: medical, developmental, educational, and psychological. The tests within each group are listed in alphabetical order.

In some cases, the line between the test categories is a fine one. Intelligence tests are an example of this. My criterion for deciding how to classify a specific test has been the setting in which the test is taken. Those IQ tests given in groups, usually in a classroom setting, are included in the educational testing section. However, IQ tests that are given individually, usually as part of psychological assessment, are included in the psychological test listings. On the other hand, whereas many vision and hearing screenings are done in a medical or clinical setting, they are included in the educational testing section because they are frequently done in school settings. However, these screenings may identify problems treated by professionals who specialize in fields that may not be available in school environments. Students are then referred to outside resources.

The information presented about each test is meant to (a) inform parents about the nature of the test and, when necessary, to help prepare their children for the testing procedure and (b) provide information that will allow a parent to form questions after test results are received. The test profile isolates and highlights the most important facts about each test:

1. The name and edition or form of the test. This information could be important because tests are frequently updated, and because revised and otherwise different forms of some tests may be used with different age groups. Similarly, some tests have both a screening version (usually shorter) and a diagnostic version (usually longer).

2. The person or persons whose recommendation and or permission is needed (i.e., parents, school psychologists, physicians, judges, teachers, and so on).

3. What the test actually tests. Every test seeks to explore specific areas and has limitations, boundaries, and scope. A screening tool is not a diagnostic tool; intelligence tests do not measure artistic ability; achievement tests tell you only what a child knows at that particular time, but can't predict future performance.

4. Which tests, especially those classified as medical, require preparation. For example, a GTT (glucose tolerance test) is valid only if specific instructions have been followed prior to taking the test.

5. How a test is performed and what to expect during the procedure. This portion of the test profile explains the "setup" for the procedure. Some tests are administered to large groups; others are given individually and the child is alone with the examiner. Some medical tests inevitably bring some discomfort; others are painless, but involve the use of intimidating-looking high-tech equipment. By knowing something about the environment in which a test is performed, you can help prepare your child for it, and in some cases, ease any "test anxiety" that may develop.

6. How a test is scored and the ways in which results are interpreted. This is crucial to putting any test in perspective. When discussing your child's test results with a professional who is attempting to explain the significance of any particular result, it helps to have an understanding of the lingo of testing—stanine, percentile, inconclusive, borderline, and so on. This section should help you understand the methodology used in the scoring system for that particular test.

7. Whether a test can be used diagnostically. Tests vary in reliability and it is always important to understand that testing is only one way to identify and diagnose both difficulties and strengths. Much of the medical testing your child is given is used to rule out problems, or to put a name on a difficulty and treat it. Some tests are more "delicate" than others, and false positives are common. Retesting is then recommended. Certain educational test results are considered invalid when the conditions under which the test is given are different from those mandated by the test publisher. There are numerous situations in which this important information could lead to either retesting or additional testing.

When addressing other professionals, reliability is often expressed in statistical terms. However, for purposes of this book, we have chosen to discuss reliability in a more general way. Does a test generally measure what it claims to (technically known as validity)? Do the results yield information that is useful in a particular way? What factors might influence reliability or usefulness? It should also be noted that professionals vary widely in their opinions about how useful any particular test is.

8. What it doesn't test. At one time or another, most parents misinterpret the results of a test because they don't understand its limitations. A low reading score, for example, may arouse alarm because you assume that this problem reflects on your child's intelligence. Similarly, you may think that a test result that shows an aptitude for a particular skill means that your child is good at it. A test that reveals an emotionally based problem is not, with any appreciable accuracy, measuring intelli-

gence, creativity, and so on. In medical testing, the same principle applies.

9. Whether the test is generally given as part of a group or battery of tests. Many psychological studies, for example, are considered valid only when the test results are evaluated within a group of tests. Screening tests, by definition, can only point to problems. Therefore, diagnostic tests will be recommended. We've tried to provide a general idea about the type of follow-up testing that may be recommended for your child.

To help you make your way through the maze of testing, an extensive glossary is included. The developmental, medical, psychological, and educational fields are well known for their jargon. Thus, even those who consider themselves reasonably well-informed are likely to encounter confusing terminology. The glossary will also help you when you are compiling a list of questions you want to ask your child's physician, teacher, guidance counselor, psychologist, and so on.

The appendices include information about prenatal testing, a group of procedures becoming increasingly common. This section is meant to be a guide to help you ask questions in order to weigh the pros and cons of this relatively new type of testing. We have also included a brief discussion of paper-and-pencil preemployment testing that your teenagers could encounter when they are screened by potential employers.

The basic premise of this book is that the more you know about testing and its ambiguities, the more thoroughly you will be able to understand and evaluate your child's progress, difficulties, and growth and the various decisions that must be made along the way.

MEDICAL TESTING

O f the various types of tests discussed and listed in this book, medical tests are probably the most familiar to parents. Beginning at birth and continuing during the early years, our babies and toddlers receive any number of tests, mainly to monitor their development or to rule out early problems that may not be apparent by observation alone. Many of these tests fall under the heading of routine well-baby or well-child care.

However, sooner or later, most children fall ill, and medical testing takes on a new purpose. Blood tests, throat cultures, urinalysis and x-ray testing may be necessary even if the illnesses are considered routine or "normal" childhood events, and CAT scans, ultrasonography, EEG, and MRI may be performed when more sophisticated diagnostic techniques are necessary.

Parents sometimes assume—erroneously—that the more "high tech" the diagnostic procedure, the more serious the problem must be. This simply isn't true. Many sophisticated procedures are used to *rule out* the most serious conditions so that the more likely possibilities can be explored. For example, a father told me that when his 11-year-old daughter, who suffered from persistent headaches, was being scheduled for an MRI, he assumed that the physician believed she had a brain tumor. (Clearly, communication between the parents and the physician was not optimal in this case.) In fact, the doctor ordered the MRI to eliminate from consideration this very slight, but serious, possibility. Once a brain tumor had been ruled out, other causes for the problem were explored. And in this case, it turned out that the headaches were caused by food allergies, a far less frightening diagnosis. (Some would argue that this case illustrates *over-testing,* that allergies should have been considered first. Reasonable people strongly disagree about the role and amount of testing in medical practices today. However, a debate of this issue is outside the scope of this book. I use this example only to point out that as medical technology continues to advance, parents are faced with an increasing number of decisions.)

Even in this age of technology, however, many tests that we consider relatively simple continue to be used to screen for or to diagnose relatively serious problems. For example, the Glucose Tolerance Test (GTT), a test that has been widely used for decades, is still the most reliable procedure to diagnose diabetes; in fact, there is no high-tech test to replace it. Relatively simple blood studies are still used to screen babies for the sickle cell trait, for iron deficiency anemia, and for elevated lead levels, and urinalysis can confirm the presence of a bladder infection when symptoms prompt a parent to take the child to the doctor.

The tests listed in this section are generally recommended by physicians and nurses or nurse practitioners (nurses with extensive training in a medical specialty). Many are also performed and interpreted by these professionals. Others are recommended by physicians, but are actually administered by medical technologists. Interpretations are then made by physicians in medical laboratories or in departments within hospitals and clinics, and the results sent to the primary care physician. For example, a radiologist will interpret the results of an x-ray, but it is likely that your pediatrician or family physician will report the findings to you.

The tendency toward specialization we all experience in medicine also applies to the care of children. Many problems are referred to specialists, with the pediatrician or family physician remaining in charge of the case. He or she is the person who coordinates testing and test results and oversees the course of treatment. Most of the time, it is this physician who maintains the most complete health history and test records. (However, it is a good idea to maintain your own test records.)

Particular tests are performed routinely in hospitals and medical practices throughout the country. Some are mandated by state or local statute. For example, before a newborn leaves a hospital or birthing center, its blood will be drawn and tested for galactosemia, phenylketonuria (PKU), and hypothyroidism. Black newborns will most likely be screened for sickle cell anemia, and they and babies of Asian parents will be tested for G6PD deficiency. The blood will also be typed and checked for signs of anemia. Bilirubin levels may also be monitored if an infant shows continuing signs of jaundice, a normal occurrence that generally disappears within a few days following birth. (See individual listings for information about all of these tests.)

Throughout the first year, babies are generally seen by pediatricians or pediatric nurses on a monthly or bimonthly basis. During these visits, immunizations are performed and the growing baby is monitored for developmental milestones. Orthopedic screening is also performed, and some blood tests may be done even if no particular symptoms are present. For example, some pediatricians recommend performing a complete blood count (CBC) between nine months and one year. Children who are suspected of being exposed to lead in their home or day-care environment may be checked for lead levels in their blood. (Lead screening may be done periodically throughout early childhood, especially if lead levels were once elevated.) In urban areas, where tuberculosis infection is common, a skin test for the disease may be performed at about one year. Some pediatricians perform this screening on all one-year-olds. Other children are screened for the disease when they begin school.

Some pediatricians recommend periodic urinalysis or a urine culture for girls over the age of five because a small percentage have bacteria growing in the urine, even if symptoms of an infection aren't present. However, if left untreated, this bacteria can later lead to kidney disease. Urinalysis is also recommended for children at about ages 10 and 15 years, for the purpose of detecting diabetes.

Preschoolers may be given vision and hearing screening in physicians' offices or pediatric clinics. However, all children are given these screening tests at the time they enter school, and they are generally done in that setting. (See Educational Testing, page 156.) In addition, orthopedic screening is done throughout childhood, and overall development is monitored. Other tests are performed when symptoms warrant.

The tests listed in this section include procedures done in medical settings for a variety of reasons: screening, diagnoses, and monitoring treatment. Blood studies, urinalysis, cultures, common x-rays and those tests using x-ray technology, orthopedic screenings, allergy testing, and some tests for parasites and fungal infections are listed alphabetically within the individual categories. (Tests that are considered developmental can be found in Section II, even though they are often done in a medical setting.)

In a child's early years, observation, routine screening, and immunization may be the primary reasons that you take your well child to the doctor. However, it is often during these routine visits that a potential problem is first spotted, which may then lead to one or more of the tests listed. Then again, the presence of symptoms may necessitate a visit, which leads to testing.

Most medical tests have numerous uses, too numerous to list in a book of this size and scope. However, the information provided should help you interpret the general results of tests and should also help you prepare your child for the procedure when necessary. The information should also help you to form the questions to ask your physician when you are puzzled by the need for a test, any risk factors, the "workings" of a procedure, or test results. Remember, it is as important to know the ways in which a medical test becomes invalid as it is to understand accurate results and what they may mean. You should also be able to tell your child what to expect in a testing environment. The world of doctors' offices, hospitals, and laboratories can be frightening to a child. And while some procedures may be painful or uncomfortable, many are not; they may appear forbidding but are actually pain-free.

At one time or another, all parents are faced with the dilemma of how much to tell a child about a test. Is it going to be mildly uncomfortable or quite painful? Is the discomfort going to be over in a matter of seconds or will the pain last longer? You know your child better than anyone else, so ultimately you must decide how much "emotional" preparation is needed. And, of course, this varies enormously with the age of the child. Generally speaking, however, most professionals agree that it is best not to lie to a child who asks questions about the possible discomfort involved in a test. Honest answers to questions such as "Will it hurt?" and "How long?" establish trust and avoid the anger children invariably feel when they believe they have been betrayed by adults. For the most part, pediatricians support this approach.

Children with known disabilities that require special care also need routine pediatric care. Medical testing may need to be adapted to accommodate such children. Parents' self-help groups are valuable resources for parents who need advice and support not readily available elsewhere.

Finally, it is assumed that all medical rests require parental permission, either given directly, as in signing a specific consent form, or indirectly, as happens when one gives birth in a particular hospital in a state that requires specific blood tests for every newborn. If you have questions or objections, it is wise to raise them before a procedure is ordered.

Allergy Testing: Skin Tests (Scratch, Patch, and Intradermal), RAST Test, Elimination Diet

The Elimination Diet is not, strictly speaking, a test.

WHOSE RECOMMENDATION AND/OR PERMISSION IS NEEDED?

Physicians recommend and perform allergy tests. Nurses and technicians may assist in the testing process.

WHAT DOES THE TEST TEST?

Allergies are a result of a malfunction of the immune system, which causes it to overreact to substances normally considered harmless (pollens, certain foods, dust, dander, and so on). Numerous symptoms are associated with allergies, from wheezing, itching, and sneezing to fatigue and moodiness.

Testing may or may not be necessary. In some cases, the allergen is easily identified and can be eliminated from the environment or the reactions to it controlled (e.g., cat dander or cosmetics). Symptoms that can be linked to certain foods can be investigated using a food diary and an elimination diet.

WHAT, IF ANY, PREPARATION IS NECESSARY?

Skin Tests: The child will not take particular medications (e.g., antihistamines) for a few days prior to the test.

RAST: No preparation.

Elimination Diet: No preparation.

HOW IS THE TEST PERFORMED, AND WHAT SHOULD BE EXPECTED?

Skin Test: Scratch tests are the most common type used, once the need for testing has been established. The risk of a severe reaction (an anaphylactic reaction, in which the blood pressure drops and breathing becomes difficult) is minimal when scratch (or patch) tests are performed. An entire scratch test takes 30 to 40 minutes, including the waiting period during which "reactions," if any, occur.

A very small amount of the suspected allergens (called dilute solutions) are placed on the skin of the arms or back. The skin is then scratched lightly with a sterile pin. This causes a slight pricking sensation, which, depending on the age of the child, should be explained ahead of time. Reactions take place in 20 to 30 minutes. In intradermal testing, small amounts of suspected allergens are injected into the skin of the back or arms.

In patch testing the samples are placed on pieces of filter paper and taped to the skin. They are left in place for a day or two. The child will not bathe during this time. Exercise is discouraged because sweating may loosen the patches. The child goes back to the physician's office to have reactions evaluated. Patch tests are often done when a chemical allergy is suspected (e.g., from rubber or perfumes).

RAST Testing: A blood sample is drawn and examined in a laboratory. The child is not involved in the testing.

Elimination Diet: The concept behind the elimination diet is to remove certain foods, commonly associated with childhood allergies (eggs, milk, wheat, soy, and so on), in both their obvious and "concealed" forms—eggs in meat loaf or noodles, for example. The physician gives you directions for carrying out the predetermined protocol. It must be carefully followed to produce results. There is also a protocol for use with infants in which a milk substitute is used. Particular grains and other foods are carefully chosen. An elimination diet is generally done for 2 to 3 weeks, and if it is showing success by eliminating foods that caused allergic reactions, it is continued.

Foods suspected of being "offending" foods are reintroduced one at a time and reactions, if any, are closely watched. Over time, a diet that either eliminates certain foods or allows them in limited quantities every few days can be constructed. It is assumed that environmental reasons for allergies (dust, dander, and so on) have been evaluated before the elimination diet is tried.

HOW ARE RESULTS RECORDED, EVALUATED, INTERPRETED, AND COMPARED?

Skin Test: Inflammation, itching or swelling, or a rash that develops at the skin site is considered a positive reaction to a specific allergen. Reactions to patch tests may take several days to appear.

RAST Test: The blood sample is analyzed to see if antibodies to various allergens are present (20 to 30 allergens are tested at one time).

Elimination Diet: A child's symptoms are expected to improve in 2 to 3 weeks if there are allergies to the foods that have been removed from the diet. When the foods are introduced, reactions are monitored. A food may then be added gradually.

HOW RELIABLE IS THE TEST?

Reliability of allergy tests varies. Reactions to certain allergens on skin tests does not mean that a specific allergen is responsible for the symptoms the child has, and tests may need to be repeated.

The RAST test is not considered as sensitive as the skin tests, but it involves no discomfort. It is possible that skin tests would still be needed following RAST testing. The elimination diet may be quite reliable when food allergies are common and easily removed. It is much trickier when many foods cause reactions. It also requires careful monitoring.

Apgar Test

WHOSE RECOMMENDATION AND/OR PERMISSION IS NEEDED?

The Apgar is routinely done in delivery rooms around the world, and because it is not invasive, permission is not required.

WHAT DOES THE TEST TEST?

The Apgar is not, strictly speaking, a test, but more closely resembles a screening procedure using observation as its method. The Apgar system is used to quickly evaluate a newborn's postnatal adjustment.

WHAT, IF ANY, PREPARATION IS NECESSARY?

No preparation is needed.

HOW IS THE TEST PERFORMED, AND WHAT SHOULD BE EXPECTED?

Approximately one minute and then five minutes after delivery, a medical professional—generally a delivery room nurse, pediatrician, or anesthesiologist—evaluates the newborn in the following five categories: appearance, pulse, grimace, activity, and respiration.

HOW ARE RESULTS RECORDED, EVALUATED, INTERPRETED, AND COMPARED?

Each feature is separately and quickly evaluated, using a score of 0 to 2. For example, if the baby's skin color is completely normal, the observer will record a score of 2. If the newborn's body is blue, the score is 0. The examiner quickly moves to the other features. A typical total score is between 7 and 10. This means that the baby is able to cry vigorously, has a strong pulse, and is breathing well and is rapidly losing any bluishness in the extremities (a common occurrence during birth that by itself is not considered serious). Babies with lower scores are generally given help immediately—are placed on a mechanical respirator, receive suctioning to the throat, and so on.

The second score, taken five minutes after the first Apgar recording, indicates how rapidly the infant is improving. For example, slow, irregular breathing given a score of 1 at the first Apgar may have strengthened and become more regular with strong crying also present. The Apgar score then becomes a 2 on the respiration feature. Most newborns with Apgar scores slightly on the low side show marked improvement by the second scoring period. Emergency measures will be continued for babies who do not show rapid postnatal adjustment.

HOW RELIABLE IS THE TEST?

In the case of the Apgar, the score itself is not as important as what is immediately done for a baby in distress. The test is somewhat subjective in that one observer is initially assigning a numerical score. Therefore, the experience of the individual in the delivery room who performs the Apgar can make a difference. However, the test is considered a very reliable way to identify a newborn who is at risk because the important indicators of distress are quickly noticed.

WHAT DOES THE TEST *NOT* TEST?

In and of itself, the Apgar does not test anything other than the efficiency of the newborn's own life support systems immediately after birth. It does not diagnose specific conditions.

WHAT FURTHER TESTS MIGHT BE RECOMMENDED?

No one test can be considered to directly follow the Apgar. If a newborn is considered at risk, a wide variety of tests might be ordered.

Apnea Monitoring (Sleep Study)

WHOSE RECOMMENDATION AND/OR PERMISSION IS NEEDED?

Pediatricians or nurses and nurse practitioners generally recommend apnea monitoring.

WHAT DOES THE TEST TEST?

Apnea, a short period in which breathing stops, is considered one of the underlying reasons for sudden infant death syndrome (SIDS). While it is normal for a baby to hold its breath for 10 seconds or so, a more prolonged time (20 seconds or more) is considered a high-risk situation and may also be linked to a serious underlying condition such as a heart defect. Prolonged apnea can lead to death because it interrupts the flow of oxygen to the brain. Apnea monitoring may be recommended if a baby is thought to be at risk. Prematurity and a family history of SIDS are two common risk factors.

HOW IS THE TEST PERFORMED, AND
WHAT SHOULD BE EXPECTED?

An apnea monitor—a device similar to a small radio—is provided for home use, usually rented to you by a physician or a hospital clinic. A sensor is attached to the baby's stomach or to the crib mattress. An alarm goes off if the baby does not breathe for a period of time predetermined and preset on the monitor.

HOW RELIABLE IS THE TEST?

The device may give off "false alarms," so, in a sense, apnea monitoring must be "managed." The monitor itself is one part of a home regimen designed to alert parents to a potentially serious episode. Parents should be given specific instructions about stimulating the infant to start breathing as well as monitoring other vital signs.

WHAT DOES THE TEST *NOT* TEST?

Apnea monitoring does not, by itself, diagnose specific defects of the heart or respiratory system. The decision to stop monitoring can be a difficult one because it involves so many factors. However, when a premature infant shows signs that the respiratory system is developing normally and episodes of apnea have stopped for a period of time, it is an indicator that monitoring is no longer needed. If a baby is monitored because he or she is considered at risk for SIDS, the precautionary measure is usually stopped at age 1 year, when the risk is greatly reduced.

ASTHMA TESTS

Asthma is often, but not always, associated with allergies. Therefore, if your child has had what is diagnosed as an asthma attack, allergy tests may be recommended (see page 22). It is also likely that a pulmonary function test (see page 67) may be ordered. In addition, routine blood and urine studies may be ordered to rule out infection. A sweat test (see page 69) may be ordered to check for cystic fibrosis, and a chest x-ray (see page 93) may be ordered to rule out pneumonia.

Professionals differ widely in their opinions about how dangerous asthma is. As with many conditions, severity varies, and how your child is treated depends on many factors, including frequency of attacks, severity of attacks, and number of allergies. Although asthma is usually treated successfully, and the child's day to day life is quite normal, the condition should never be taken lightly. Despite popular misconceptions that asthma is psychological in origin and not physically threatening, it is a potentially fatal illness.

BLOOD TESTS

WHOSE RECOMMENDATION AND/OR PERMISSION IS NEEDED?

Blood tests may be recommended by physicians or nurses. The blood is obtained by physicians, nurses, or medical technicians.

WHAT DOES THE TEST TEST?

Blood tests that measure levels of various dissolved substances in the blood are called *blood chemistries*. These substances are contained in the liquid portion of unclotted blood (the plasma) and number in the hundreds. They fall into several main categories: sugars, gases, hormones, antibodies, fats, proteins, vitamins, minerals, and traces of ingested drugs.

Another group of blood tests examines the size, shape, and other characteristics of the blood cells: the red cells, which carry oxygen to the body tissues; the white cells, which fight infection within the body; and, platelets, the cells that help blood clot. These tests are called *hematologic* tests.

A third blood test group is called *serologic* testing; these tests include those procedures that analyze the blood for antigen-antibody reactions, antibodies, and immune reaction and function.

WHAT, IF ANY, PREPARATION IS NECESSARY?

No special preparation is needed to draw blood. However, **some blood tests** may require fasting for a period of time, or eat**ing or avoiding** certain foods.

HOW IS THE TEST PERFORMED, AND WHAT SHOULD BE EXPECTED?

Blood is drawn for testing in one of three ways: (1) venipunc**ture**, drawing blood into one or more vials through a needle inserted into a vein (generally in the arm or in the back of the hand); (2) the "stick" method, where a small sterile needle pierces the skin (in the fingertip, earlobe, or, in infants, the heel) to obtain a small quantity of blood; or (3) the arterial stick, in which blood is taken from an artery (generally from the wrist; sometimes from the leg).

HOW ARE RESULTS RECORDED, EVALUATED, INTERPRETED, AND COMPARED?

Some test results can be obtained immediately in the doctor's office; others require that the blood be sent to an outside lab. It may take 24 hours or more for the results to be reported, and some blood studies take longer. Blood test results are generally expressed in terms of the relationship to established "normal values": lower than normal or higher than normal. A result may also be expressed in terms of the presence or absence of the substance or element being tested for. Laboratories vary in testing methods and in the range of values considered normal. Physicians may also interpret the results of the tests in different ways.

HOW RELIABLE IS THE TEST?

Any number of factors can affect the results of an individual blood test, including mishandling of the blood at any stage in the process. Numerous drugs will affect blood chemistry and cell proportion and therefore may skew results of a test. This in turn can lead to difficulty in establishing a diagnosis. Generally speaking, blood tests are repeated when there is a question about the validity of the results or when diagnosis of a serious condition is dependent, at least in part, on blood studies. For this reason, it is important to inform the health care provider about any medication your child is taking at the time the blood is collected, including such common medications as aspirin.

WHAT DOES THE TEST *NOT* TEST?

Blood tests may or may not be a definitive factor in the diagnosis of a particular disease or condition. They also do not predict the future course of a condition. Blood tests are usually but one diagnostic tool used in a series of processes or procedures. Similarly, blood tests *alone* do not confirm a positive health status, just as they do not, by themselves, necessarily pinpoint an illness. In other words, a sick child or one with an undiagnosed problem is not declared well simply because blood studies are "normal." Likewise, abnormal results of blood studies may not allow a name to be put on a condition. Other testing may be necessary before the diagnostic process is complete.

WHAT FURTHER TESTS MIGHT BE RECOMMENDED?

Depending on the purpose of the blood test, many other types of medical testing could be recommended: other, more specific blood tests; urinalysis; x-ray testing; cultures, and so on.

Arterial Blood Gases (ABGs)

WHOSE RECOMMENDATION AND/OR PERMISSION IS NEEDED?

Physicians recommend this blood study and may perform it, although specially trained technicians and nurses may draw the blood.

WHAT DOES THE TEST TEST?

An ABGs measures oxygen, carbon dioxide, and acid levels in the blood. The test may be ordered when lung diseases of any type are suspected, or when asthma is being diagnosed. It is sometimes performed prior to surgery to determine lung function in order to guide the choice and amount of anesthesia used, or when lung damage is suspected—after smoke inhalation, for example.

HOW IS THE TEST PERFORMED, AND WHAT SHOULD BE EXPECTED?

The blood specimen for ABGs is taken from an artery, rather than a vein, and is a more painful and difficult procedure than other blood studies. Blood is taken from the radial artery (found in the wrist) or the femoral artery (in the groin area). The age and condition of the child will be a determining factor in whether a parent is present. The exact location of the artery may be difficult to determine, and the child may be "stuck" with the needle more than once.

HOW ARE RESULTS RECORDED, EVALUATED, INTERPRETED, AND COMPARED?

The level of each of the blood gases is expressed as being within or outside a normal range. The amount of acid in the blood is called the pH of the blood.

WHAT FURTHER TESTS MIGHT BE RECOMMENDED?

If a child is being checked for asthma, a pulmonary function test may be ordered, along with allergy tests and a chest x-ray.

Bilirubin Test

WHAT DOES THE TEST TEST?

Bilirubin, a substance produced when the body breaks down red blood cells, can be measured at any time of life. However, destruction of red blood cells occurs very rapidly after birth, when the newborn's liver is not mature enough to adequately handle the process. The increased levels of bilirubin cause jaundice. (About 99 percent of newborns will become somewhat jaundiced, characterized by a yellowing of the whites of the eyes and the skin.) Newborns' blood levels are monitored to prevent the condition, which is normal, from becoming severe. A bilirubin level is considered part of a neonatal screen.

WHAT, IF ANY, PREPARATION IS NECESSARY?

Bilirubin levels can be monitored both in the hospital and at home, in the case of home birth, or if the baby is brought home shortly after birth, an increasingly common trend.

WHAT FURTHER TESTS MIGHT BE RECOMMENDED?

Bilirubin testing continues until jaundice disappears. (See also Blood Typing, page 34.)

Blood Typing (ABO and Rh Blood Typing)

WHOSE RECOMMENDATION AND/OR PERMISSION IS NEEDED?

Blood typing is done for a variety of reasons, and is a standard test in a neonatal screening. Blood typing of the mother is done as part of prenatal care.

WHAT DOES THE TEST TEST?

A blood type is determined by the presence or absence of specific proteins (antigens) found on red blood cells. There are four major blood types (A, B, AB, and O) and two subtypes (Rh positive and Rh negative). Blood type is important because blood received in a transfusion must be of a compatible type; if it isn't, the body's immune system creates antibodies, which can result in serious illness or death. This is even more dangerous if the body has previously been exposed to a foreign blood type. Type O is the universal donor blood type.

Rh type is of concern during pregnancy. Most people (80 percent) have Rh proteins in their blood and are called Rh positive. Those who do not have these proteins are called Rh negative. If an Rh negative mother has a first child who is Rh positive, a few of the baby's blood cells may enter the mother's bloodstream during childbirth. (This does not *always* happen, but the odds are high that it will.) The mother's immune system will begin producing antibodies to the Rh positive blood. In itself, this is generally harmless. However, a future Rh positive fetus can be affected by the mother's antibodies, which can pass into its blood, causing prenatal injury or death. (A treatment to prevent this is now available, but the possibility of this occurring still exists and is evaluated with every pregnancy.)

Blood typing was once commonly used in court cases for which parentage was in question, particularly in paternity suits. It has been replaced by tests that more accurately identify genetic markers.

Chromosomal Analysis (Karotype)

WHAT DOES THE TEST TEST?

A chromosomal analysis is performed to help determine if a disease or condition (often a developmental problem) is caused by an abnormality in the chromosomes. In children, the test is usually performed to investigate suspected birth defects, delayed growth, mental retardation, or abnormal sexual development (e.g., delayed puberty).

HOW IS THE TEST PERFORMED?

The chromosomes in a blood cell are photographed through a microscope. When the photograph is studied, each chromosome is isolated and arranged in what is called a standard order (a karotype) and then individually analyzed.

HOW ARE RESULTS RECORDED, EVALUATED, INTERPRETED, AND COMPARED?

The normal human karotype contains 22 pairs of autosomal chromosomes and one pair of sex chromosomes (females have 2 X chromosomes, males have 1 X and 1 Y). Chromosomes also have a shape, size, and structure that is considered "normal." An abnormal karotype may include missing or extra chromosomes as well as those abnormal in structure. Down's syndrome, for example, is characterized by three, rather than two, chromosomes in the twenty-first pair of chromosomes. Klinefelter's syndrome and Turner's syndrome, conditions related to sexual development, are characterized by abnormalities in the sex chromosomes.

WHAT DOES THE TEST NOT TEST?

Chromosomal analysis does not measure the severity of the conditions resulting from the abnormality.

WHAT FURTHER TESTS MIGHT BE RECOMMENDED?

Chromosome analysis is sometimes done on cells taken from other parts of the body, most frequently the skin or the bone.

Complete Blood Count (CBC)

WHAT DOES THE TEST TEST?

The CBC is usually a hematologic screening test for anemia or infection. However, it is also used as a tool to help diagnose many other conditions. The CBC includes separate studies. They are:

Hematocrit (HCT, Packed Cell Volume, PVC): The portion of blood volume composed of red blood cells. Commonly used in diagnosing anemia.

Hemoglobin (Total hemoglobin, HGB): The protein in the blood that contains iron. The hemoglobin level indicates the capacity of the blood to carry oxygen to cells. Also used to diagnose anemia.

Red blood cell count (RBC): The number of red blood cells in one cubic millimeter of blood. Also used to diagnose anemia.

Red blood cell indices: The size, weight, and hemoglobin in a red blood cell. These indices help to diagnose and differentiate two types of anemia: iron-deficiency and pernicious.

White blood cell count and Differential (WBC, Differential): The white cells (leukocytes) are a key part of the immune system, in that they can recognize and attack foreign organisms or substances. This is why the white cell count is higher during bacterial infections. There are numerous types of white cells, each of which has a specific role in immune response. The WBC measures white cell volume in a cubic millimeter of blood. The Differential establishes the percentage of each type of white cell present.

Platelet count (thrombocyte count): Platelets (thrombocytes) play a major role in blood clotting. The platelets are produced in bone marrow. The number of platelets in a cubic millimeter of blood is measured. (Used to investigate spontaneous or prolonged bleeding or to test the clotting mechanism before surgery.) The prothrombin time (PT) and the partial thromboplastin time (PTT) are used to screen for clotting disorders. The latter is used to screen for hemophilia.

HOW ARE RESULTS RECORDED, EVALUATED, INTERPRETED, AND COMPARED?

These studies are performed by machine. The result of each study is recorded and compared with established normal values for that laboratory. Values for each study are listed separately. Less or greater than normal values may suggest a variety of conditions.

HOW RELIABLE IS THE TEST?

Numerous things affect results of the CBC studies. They include such diverse factors as vigorous exercise, leaving the tourniquet used to draw the blood on for too long, and interference by certain drugs. Therefore, depending on the purpose of the test and other diagnostic factors (such as symptoms or a known condition), retesting may be recommended because of the possibility of false positives and false negatives. The CBC is considered a valuable test because so much information can be gathered quickly; conditions suggested by the results can then be verified with further testing.

WHAT DOES THE TEST *NOT* TEST?

The CBC does not measure substances in the blood (cholesterol, glucose, and so on).

WHAT FURTHER TESTS MIGHT BE RECOMMENDED?

The CBC may be done periodically to monitor conditions such as anemia. The range of other tests recommended following abnormal results of a CBC varies widely. Most of the time, a CBC is ordered for children as part of a routine, periodic checkup.

Electrolytes

WHOSE RECOMMENDATION AND/OR PERMISSION IS NEEDED?

Physicians and nurses or nurse practitioners generally recommend this blood study.

WHAT DOES THE TEST TEST?

Electrolytes is the term used for four minerals found in the body: sodium, potassium, chloride, and bicarbonate. The first three are involved in maintaining water balance in the body, one of the kidney's jobs. Bicarbonate is involved in regulating the acidity of the blood, a job performed by both the kidneys and the lungs. Electrolytes are measured whenever kidney disease or damage is suspected, or when dehydration or excessive fluid loss from the body is apparent. Diarrhea in infants may lead to a depletion of electrolytes if not quickly treated. Use of diuretics may also cause an electrolyte imbalance. (Some adolescent girls who believe they are overweight take over-the-counter [OTC] diuretics. If used excessively, too much potassium is lost from the body, resulting in fatigue and lethargy.)

HOW ARE RESULTS RECORDED, EVALUATED, INTERPRETED, AND COMPARED?

Results are reported as being within or not within the normal range established by that laboratory or physician's office.

HOW RELIABLE IS THE TEST?

Electrolytes are not "static," meaning that the body is always adjusting fluid levels. Therefore, retesting is common.

Galactosemia Screening

WHOSE RECOMMENDATION AND/OR PERMISSION IS NEEDED?

Generally performed on a newborn infant, this blood screening is required by some states as part of a neonatal screen.

WHAT DOES THE TEST TEST?

This screening establishes the presence of galactose transferase, an enzyme needed to break down galactose, a sugar in milk. Therefore, the test establishes that the enzyme is present. If it is not, the infant is given a milk substitute, because ingesting foods with galactose, without the needed enzyme present, leads to tissue damage, abnormal liver and kidney function, and cataracts.

HOW ARE RESULTS RECORDED, EVALUATED, INTERPRETED, AND COMPARED?

A normal (positive) result means that galactose transferase is present.

HOW RELIABLE IS THE TEST?

False negatives occur about 10 percent of the time.

WHAT FURTHER TESTS MIGHT BE RECOMMENDED?

The test could be repeated if an infant shows the early symptoms of galactosemia because the first test could have been one of the 10 percent false negatives.

Glucose Tests: Random Blood Sugar (RBS), Fasting Blood Sugar (FBS), 2-Hour Postprandial Blood Sugar (2-Hour PP), or Glucose Tolerance Test (GTT)

WHAT DOES THE TEST TEST?

Glucose is the main source of energy for all of the tissues of the body, and we commonly refer to it as blood sugar. Glucose levels in the blood that are either too low or too high suggest a number of health problems, the most well known of which are hypoglycemia (when levels are too low) and diabetes (when glucose levels are too high).

WHAT, IF ANY, PREPARATION IS NECESSARY?

There is no preparation for an RBS, and it is usually done as part of a larger blood study. For an FBS, a 12- to 14-hour fast is required *before* the blood is drawn. When a 2-hour PP is done, your child will have the blood drawn two hours *after* eating a normal meal.

The GTT is a more complex test. The test is generally done in a clinic or hospital setting, and a fast of several hours is required. A blood sample (as well as a urine sample) is taken prior to the beginning of the test. Your child will then be asked to drink a concentrated sugar drink. Blood is then drawn at intervals for the next 3 to 5 hours.

HOW IS THE TEST PERFORMED, AND WHAT SHOULD BE EXPECTED?

The health professional monitoring your child should be looking for symptoms—weakness, sweating, mental confusion, and so on—that may be severe enough to stop the test. (These symptoms generally occur when glucose levels fall quite low.)

HOW ARE RESULTS RECORDED, EVALUATED, INTERPRETED, AND COMPARED?

With the GTT, the rise and fall of glucose levels are charted on a graph and compared to patterns associated with diabetes or hypoglycemia. The results of the other glucose tests would be expressed as falling within or outside normal values.

HOW RELIABLE IS THE TEST?

Physicians differ in their current use of the GTT. In children, the other blood glucose tests would most likely be used first if actual symptoms are present. (A family history of diabetes is a factor that is considered.) A GTT might follow an FBS if the result is marginal. Physicians also differ in their opinions about hypoglycemia. Low blood sugar levels in children would likely be linked to other conditions before a diagnosis of hypoglycemia is considered.

Human Growth Hormone (HGH)

Human growth hormone is also called somatotropin.

WHAT DOES THE TEST TEST?

Human growth hormone (HGH) regulates normal growth. Abnormal production of HGH can result in dwarfism or giantism: that is, abnormally short or tall stature. This test is sometimes given to children who are on drugs for hyperactivity, because such medications may slow production of HGH.

WHAT, IF ANY, PREPARATION IS NECESSARY?

An 8- to 10-hour fast is necessary for this test. In addition, the child may be asked to rest in a quiet room for a period of time before the blood is drawn.

HOW ARE RESULTS RECORDED, EVALUATED, INTERPRETED, AND COMPARED?

Blood levels of HGH are compared with those established as normal.

HOW RELIABLE IS THE TEST?

Because medications, time of day, and other factors can affect the result, a child would generally be retested if the test result indicated a problem.

WHAT DOES THE TEST NOT TEST?

This test may suggest the presence of other conditions, such as diabetes, but does not diagnose them.

WHAT FURTHER TESTS MIGHT BE RECOMMENDED?

HGH may be measured periodically to monitor treatment progress or to follow those children with other conditions that affect growth.

Lead Screening

WHAT DOES THE TEST TEST?

A lead screening measures the lead level in the blood. In that the test is more common now than in the past, many localities encourage lead screening for all children in the hopes of catching a problem before the symptoms of toxicity—lethargy, mental slowness, loss of appetite, convulsions—appear.

HOW ARE RESULTS RECORDED, EVALUATED, INTERPRETED, AND COMPARED?

The blood's lead content is compared with a given laboratory's "normal" values, which are often based on legally established limits in a locale. (Blood levels considered within the normal range vary widely from one locale to another.)

HOW RELIABLE IS THE TEST?

The test is considered reliable in that lead is either detected or it is not; levels are then determined.

WHAT DOES THE TEST *NOT* TEST?

The lead screen does not determine damage done by elevated lead levels.

WHAT FURTHER TESTS MIGHT BE RECOMMENDED?

After the sources of lead in the environment have been discovered and eliminated, further testing is done to see if lead levels have fallen.

Mononucleosis Tests (Monospot, Heterophile)

WHOSE RECOMMENDATION AND/OR PERMISSION IS NEEDED?

Physicians recommend the tests for mononucleosis and technicians or nurses may draw the blood.

WHAT DOES THE TEST TEST?

These tests are done when symptoms indicate that a person might have mononucleosis (commonly referred to as "mono"), an infection caused by the Epstein-Barr virus. The symptoms are associated with other infections, however, and the test may be ordered to rule out the illness.

HOW IS THE TEST PERFORMED, AND WHAT SHOULD BE EXPECTED?

The monospot is a screening test that can be performed in a physician's office or emergency room. (The stick method can be used to draw the blood.) The heterophile is used to confirm a positive result of a monospot, and the blood sample is generally sent to a laboratory for analysis.

HOW ARE RESULTS RECORDED, EVALUATED, INTERPRETED, AND COMPARED?

When results of the tests are negative (normal), the person does not have mononucleosis. However, a positive result on the monospot can occasionally be caused by a condition other than mononucleosis, so a heterophile is done to confirm an initial diagnosis.

HOW RELIABLE IS THE TEST?

A normal result may later be determined as a false negative because a mononucleosis infection may not be evident in the blood for several weeks. Therefore, if symptoms persist, retesting is often recommended.

Phenylketonuria (PKU) Screening

WHOSE RECOMMENDATION AND/OR PERMISSION IS NEEDED?

This test is generally done as part of a neonatal screening, required by most states.

WHAT DOES THE TEST TEST?

Phenylketonuria (PKU) is an inherited inability to metabolize the amino acid phenylalanine; if not discovered and treated early, this results in mental retardation. This test measures the amount of phenylalanine in the blood.

WHAT, IF ANY, PREPARATION IS NECESSARY?

The test must be done 24 hours after the newborn has taken his or her first milk. (Treatment for the problem consists of changing the formula. Breast-fed babies may need to change to a special formula to keep phenylalanine within normal limits.)

HOW ARE RESULTS RECORDED, EVALUATED, INTERPRETED, AND COMPARED?

PKU blood values greater than normal would generally lead to immediate retesting.

WHAT FURTHER TESTS MIGHT BE RECOMMENDED?

Some physicians recommend that breast-fed infants be screened again about one month after birth because the problem sometimes does not appear at the time of the initial screening.

Sickle Cell (Hemoglobin S) Test

WHAT DOES THE TEST TEST?

The sickle cell test detects sickle cell anemia or sickle cell trait, both of which are inherited abnormalities. The disease is an abnormality of the hemoglobin molecule, which produces "sickling" in red blood cells containing abnormal hemoglobin (hemoglobin S); the disease results when a person has inherited two genes for hemoglobin S. Sickle cell trait does not produce disease in the carrier, but the sickle cell gene can be passed on. Some states require a sickle cell test as part of a newborn screening. Both the disease and the trait are found almost exclusively in black populations.

HOW ARE RESULTS RECORDED, EVALUATED, INTERPRETED, AND COMPARED?

The presence of sickle cells is considered a positive test result.

HOW RELIABLE IS THE TEST?

A false negative result can occur if a child has had a blood transfusion in the three months prior to the test.

WHAT DOES THE TEST *NOT* TEST?

The sickle cell test does not predict onset of symptoms or the course of the disease.

WHAT FURTHER TESTS MIGHT BE RECOMMENDED?

If a positive result is obtained, a more sophisticated test, the hemoglobin electrophoresis, is needed to make a definitive diagnosis.

Thyroid Function T4 (thyroxin), and TSH (thyroid stimulating hormone) for newborns. These and FSH (follicle stimulating hormone), T3 uptake, LH (luetinizing hormone), and ACTH (adrenocorticotrophic hormone) may be measured in older children.

WHOSE RECOMMENDATION AND/OR PERMISSION IS NEEDED?

Thyroid screening is often part of a neonatal screen, required by most states. It is a common test in diagnosing malfunction of the thyroid gland.

WHAT DOES THE TEST TEST?

In newborns, the test detects an inherent defect in the thyroid gland, which, if left untreated, would result in delayed growth and development (cretinism). In older children, thyroid hormones are tested for a variety of reasons, including growth lags, obesity, menstrual irregularity, and delayed menarche (first menstruation).

HOW ARE RESULTS RECORDED, EVALUATED, INTERPRETED, AND COMPARED?

Results are compared to normal values established for the general population. Age and gender are factors in these hormone studies.

HOW RELIABLE IS THE TEST?

Numerous things can affect thyroid tests. If your child is taking medications, for example, this should be noted. Girls who have begun to menstruate will have widely varying levels of some thyroid hormones, depending on the phase of the menstrual cycle an individual is in at the time of testing.

WHAT FURTHER TESTS MIGHT BE RECOMMENDED?

Thyroid tests are repeated periodically as part of the process of monitoring treatment.

Other Common Blood Tests

Antistreptolysin-Titer (ASO Titer)

ASO is an antibody that appears in the blood a week to a month after some strep infections. ASO levels (titers) are measured to diagnose streptococcal disease—rheumatic fever, for example.

Hepatitis Virus Tests

Hepatitis, an inflammation of the liver, can be caused by various types of virus infections to which the body responds by producing specific antibodies. Blood tests can differentiate hepatitis A, which is normally spread by contaminated water or food, from hepatitis B, which is most often acquired by contact with virus-infected blood (i.e., blood transfusions, contaminated needles, sexual contact). Individuals can have hepatitis B for 4 to 5 months before symptoms develop. Therefore, they may spread the disease before they know they have it. A test for hepatitis B is now performed on all blood donated at a blood bank.

Toxoplasmosis Tests

Toxoplasmosis is caused by a parasite carried by many animals, including house cats. (Pregnant women can pass the disease to a fetus, with serious birth defects or stillbirth a possible result.) The test is performed on infants and young children when the symptoms of toxoplasmosis (swollen lymph nodes, eye infections, and so on) are present. The body produces antibodies to the toxoplasmosis parasite. These antibodies can be detected in the blood.

Tay-Sachs Screening

Tay-Sachs disease is a fatal, degenerative disease of the central nervous system. Nowadays, this test is often done before pregnancy to screen those considered to be at high risk. (Anyone can be a carrier, but Ashkenazi Jews are at highest risk of being carriers.) However, when prenatal screening has not occurred, an infant suspected of having the disease may undergo this test. Unfortunately, a newborn may appear normal for as long as six months before the progressive deteriorating symptoms appear.

Glucose 6-Phosphate Dehydrogenase (G6PD)

G6PD is an enzyme found in red blood cells. An inherited deficiency of this enzyme can lead to anemia. Blacks, Asians, and people whose ethnic roots are in the Mediterranean countries are the groups most frequently affected by a deficiency of this enzyme. More males than females are affected. The blood test can be used to screen for the presence of the enzyme; the actual quantity of it can also be measured. A test of G6PD is done in neonatal screens in many hospitals.

CULTURES

WHOSE RECOMMENDATION AND/OR PERMISSION IS NEEDED?

Cultures are recommended by physicians; samples may be collected by nurses or medical technicians.

WHAT DOES THE TEST TEST?

The majority of cultures are done to test the sample for bacteria linked to infections. Cultures are commonly done on blood, urine, stools, fluids from wounds and sores, and sputum. Less often, cultures are done to test for fungi or viruses.

HOW IS THE TEST PERFORMED, AND WHAT SHOULD BE EXPECTED?

The sample is placed under conditions in which the suspected organism will grow. Normally occurring bacteria must be distinguished from the organism suspected in the disease. If the colonies of the suspect bacteria grow in the culture, they are identified by size and shape. A culture can take 2 to 10 days to show a result, sometimes longer.

HOW ARE RESULTS RECORDED, EVALUATED, INTERPRETED, AND COMPARED?

The test result is reported as positive if the suspected bacteria is present. If no colonies have formed, the test result is reported as negative. An infection resulting from a virus will produce a negative result.

HOW RELIABLE IS THE TEST?

The use of cultures is quite common and is a valuable tool for differentiating various types of infection. However, many factors can affect the outcome of a culture, including mishandling of the specimen or obtaining an inadequate sample. Culture samples collected after antibiotics have been started may also alter results.

WHAT DOES THE TEST *NOT* TEST?

A culture only rarely reveals information about viruses or fungal infections, nor does a culture explain why an illness was contracted. Cultures for viruses generally require specialized equipment, usually found in public facilities rather than private. In addition, viral cultures take weeks or even months to grow. It is unlikely that your child will need such a procedure.

WHAT FURTHER TESTS MIGHT BE RECOMMENDED?

Antibiotic sensitivity testing is sometimes performed to determine which antibiotic will be most effective against the particular bacteria that is causing the illness. This is done on the culture sample and does not involve the patient. In general, further patient testing depends on the condition being treated, its severity, or its persistence.

Blood Culture

WHAT DOES THE TEST TEST?

A blood culture detects bacteria in the blood, which is generally a sign of decreased immunity. This condition is always considered serious because blood-borne bacteria can quickly spread to any part of the body.

WHAT, IF ANY, PREPARATION IS NECESSARY?

Blood is taken from a vein after the skin area has been thoroughly cleansed with iodine and alcohol to avoid contaminating the blood sample with bacteria from the skin. More than one sample may be taken and the procedure may be repeated the following day.

HOW ARE RESULTS RECORDED, EVALUATED, INTERPRETED, AND COMPARED?

Results may be reported in 1 to 2 days, although some organisms take 7 to 10 days to appear on a culture, and there is no way to hasten the process of growing a culture of bacteria.

HOW RELIABLE IS THE TEST?

In the early stages, bacteria causing infections in other parts of the body can enter the bloodstream; thus, a positive finding does not always indicate the more serious blood-borne infections. Generally speaking, however, no bacteria is found in the blood and therefore its presence must be investigated. In addition, contamination of the sample must be ruled out.

WHAT DOES THE TEST *NOT* TEST?

A blood culture does not reveal the presence of bacteria in other parts of the body; that is, there may be infection even if the blood culture is clear.

Skin/Wound Culture

WHAT DOES THE TEST TEST?

A wound, sore, burn, or surgical incision may be cultured to identify an infection that could spread or cause scarring. Specimens may also be taken from the eye or the ear canal, or from the vagina if a girl has persistent vaginitis.

WHAT, IF ANY, PREPARATION IS NECESSARY?

Depending on the age of the child, the reason for the culture, and the area of the body where the sample is taken, it is best to explain what will take place. Young children may need to be held still to avoid unnecessary pain or trauma to the area from which a culture is taken.

HOW IS THE TEST PERFORMED, AND WHAT SHOULD BE EXPECTED?

A sterile cotton swab will be used to collect the sample from the area. The person taking the sample may need to squeeze the sore or wound to extract pus or other fluid. If the area is inflamed or tender, this could cause pain.

HOW ARE RESULTS RECORDED, EVALUATED, INTERPRETED, AND COMPARED?

Bacteria commonly found in skin or wound cultures are reported both in terms of their presence and amount.

Sputum Culture

WHAT DOES THE TEST TEST?

Sputum is the thick and cloudy material produced in the lungs and bronchial tubes. A sputum culture identifies the bacteria causing an infection in the bronchial tubes or lungs.

WHAT, IF ANY, PREPARATION IS NECESSARY?

The child should be given fluids prior to the test, and the physician should be told if antibiotics have been taken recently.

HOW IS THE TEST PERFORMED, AND
WHAT SHOULD BE EXPECTED?

The child will be asked to cough deeply and expectorate; the sputum is collected in a sterile cup. A parent or a health care provider may tap on the child's chest or back to loosen the sputum.

HOW ARE RESULTS RECORDED, EVALUATED,
INTERPRETED, AND COMPARED?

The results of a sputum culture are generally available in 2 to 5 days. The particular bacteria present will be differentiated from bacteria normally present in the mouth, in that normal bacteria can contaminate the sputum sample. The test could be repeated if the sample is contaminated and symptoms persist.

Stool Culture

WHAT DOES THE TEST TEST?

A stool culture is done to detect intestinal infections, or the presence of an intestinal parasite.

WHAT, IF ANY, PREPARATION IS NECESSARY?

Various medications can affect the results of a stool culture, so discuss the scheduling of the test with your physician. If you are collecting the sample at home, as opposed to a hospital, you will be given a stool collection kit. The parent assisting the child should be careful to avoid contact with the stool, in that doing so could result in exposure to infectious bacteria.

HOW IS THE TEST PERFORMED, AND
WHAT SHOULD BE EXPECTED?

The child should empty his bladder before the stool sample is collected. The child passes the stool into a dry cup. You then take an applicator stick and place a lump of the stool into each of two vials. (Both items are provided in the kit.) The vials contain different preservatives and the stool sample is mixed with the contents of the vial. Each vial is then labeled with your child's name and the date. (Samples may be collected on successive days.) The sample is then delivered to the doctor's office or mailed to the lab.

HOW ARE RESULTS RECORDED, EVALUATED,
INTERPRETED, AND COMPARED?

The bacteria likely to be causing symptoms is differentiated from normal bacteria in the intestine. (Do note, though, that an overabundance of some normal bacteria can cause problems, too.) Certain bacteria are associated with particular diseases. The presence or absence of parasites and their eggs (ova) is also noted.

HOW RELIABLE IS THE TEST?

Stool cultures tend to be less reliable in evaluating the significance of the presence of too much of the normal bacteria type. Mishandled samples may also skew results.

Throat Culture

WHAT DOES THE TEST TEST?

Most throat cultures performed on children are for the purpose of identifying the type of bacteria causing sore throat, swollen glands, or enlarged tonsils with white spots (pus). It is important to diagnose or rule out group A strep (commonly called strep throat) because these bacteria can spread to the kidneys or the heart valves and cause serious illness. Strep infection is usually accompanied by swollen glands, pus on the tonsils, and a fever. Your physician will most likely begin treating a suspected strep infection with antibiotics before the results of a throat culture are available. A sore throat may be a symptom of a common cold or a minor inflammation of the tonsils. In these cases, a culture would not be performed.

WHAT, IF ANY, PREPARATION IS NECESSARY?

A throat culture is most often done in a physician's office. Most parents and physicians agree that it is best to explain what is about to occur and get the child to cooperate. Babies and toddlers will need to be held during the procedure.

HOW IS THE TEST PERFORMED, AND WHAT SHOULD BE EXPECTED?

The child should open his or her mouth as wide as possible; a young child may need coaxing. The physician usually presses the tongue down with a tongue depressor and uses a long cotton-tipped swab to collect the sample. This causes a normal gagging response—one reason children may be resistant if they are familiar with the procedure. Sometimes more than one sample is needed.

HOW ARE RESULTS RECORDED, EVALUATED, INTERPRETED, AND COMPARED?

The results of a throat culture are usually available in 1 to 2 days. Infection can be caused by the overabundance of certain bacteria normally present in the throat. Foreign bacteria will be detected in the culture as well.

Urine Culture

WHAT DOES THE TEST TEST?

A urine culture is done to determine the type of bacteria present in an infection occurring in any of the organs of the urinary tract. It is also done when an abnormal number of white cells are found in the urine during a routine urinalysis, suggesting that an infection is present even if there are no symptoms.

WHAT, IF ANY, PREPARATION IS NECESSARY?

See Urinalysis (pages 82–88).

HOW IS THE TEST PERFORMED, AND WHAT SHOULD BE EXPECTED?

The sample must be collected in a sterile container and should be cultured immediately or refrigerated.

HOW ARE RESULTS RECORDED, EVALUATED, INTERPRETED, AND COMPARED?

Bacteria normally found in the urethra are distinguished from those causing a bladder infection. This is expressed in terms of the number of bacteria in a given amount of urine (the colony count). You will be told that an infection is either present or absent.

HOW RELIABLE IS THE TEST?

The test does not detect the presence of bacteria that do not grow in routine urine cultures. Contamination is often a problem, requiring a second culture.

Electroencephalogram (EEG)

WHOSE RECOMMENDATION AND/OR
PERMISSION IS NEEDED?

Physicians, generally neurologists, order this test.

WHAT DOES THE TEST TEST?

An EEG measures electrical impulses produced by brain waves, and records them on paper so that they can be analyzed for diagnostic purposes. In children, the test is generally ordered to diagnose epilepsy or other seizure or convulsive disorders. It can be used to evaluate the location and extent of a head injury that has caused a variety of adverse symptoms. It is also used in the diagnosis of meningitis.

WHAT, IF ANY, PREPARATION IS NECESSARY?

A child should eat prior to taking the test, but foods containing caffeine, such as chocolate, soft drinks, or coffee, should be avoided. There is no advantage to not eating, and results could be skewed if a child's blood sugar levels are low. You will usually be told to wash the child's hair the night before the test so that the electrodes attached to the head will stick better. In some cases it is important that the child be asleep while a portion of the tracing is made. If this is the case, a sedative will be given. If a child is already taking certain medications for a neurological problem, they may be discontinued a week or so before the test.

HOW IS THE TEST PERFORMED, AND
WHAT SHOULD BE EXPECTED?

The child lies on a table or, in some cases, sits in a reclining chair. Up to thirty small electrode pads are attached to the scalp with adhesive agents that conduct electrical impulses. Sometimes tiny needles are used. It is important that the child lie very still as the brain wave tracings are made—another reason why a sedative may be given. A portion of the tracings may be made while the child is stimulated by flashing lights (which can be annoying) or when instructed to take short, fast breaths. The test takes from 30 to 60 minutes. It is generally a painless procedure. However, if needles are used to attach the electrodes, a pin prick sensation may be frightening or annoying to a small child.

HOW ARE THE RESULTS RECORDED, EVALUATED, INTERPRETED, AND COMPARED?

When necessary, the results can be interpreted immediately. However, most often the tracings are sent to a neurologist and the results reported up to several days later.

HOW RELIABLE IS THE TEST?

Because they cause altered patterns in the brain waves, certain illnesses can be diagnosed with a degree of precision. At other times, the report will state that specific abnormalities have been ruled out. The results should be discussed with you in some detail.

WHAT DOES THE TEST *NOT* TEST?

This test does not offer any information about intelligence or abilities, nor can it diagnose emotional disorders.

WHAT FURTHER TESTS MIGHT BE RECOMMENDED?

When epilepsy is diagnosed, and medication is begun, follow-up EEGs may be ordered to see if the medication is working. When organic illness is ruled out, other causes of symptoms might be investigated, including psychological assessments and physiological tests and studies.

Fungus Infection (Fungal Scraping)

Fungi can cause numerous types of infections in the body, including athlete's foot, ringworm, thrush, and those that affect the genitals (i.e., "jock itch" and vaginal yeast infections). These are often treated without testing. If, however, there is a question about a diagnosis, a sample, called a scraping, can be taken and placed on a slide and viewed under a microscope. The particular fungus can then be identified. Sometimes blood tests are used to diagnose fungal infections.

Lumbar Puncture (Spinal Tap, Spinal Puncture)

WHOSE RECOMMENDATION AND/OR PERMISSION IS NEEDED?

A physician always recommends, performs, and interprets the results of a lumbar puncture.

WHAT DOES THE TEST TEST?

A lumbar puncture, a procedure in which a sample of spinal fluid is removed for examination, is done for numerous reasons. However, in childhood, one of the common reasons is to diagnose meningitis (bacterial or viral). It may also be performed following a head or back injury.

HOW IS THE TEST PERFORMED, AND WHAT SHOULD BE EXPECTED?

A local anesthetic will numb the area of the back where the needle used to draw the fluid is inserted. The child may be on his or her side in a fetal-like position or may be sitting up and bending slightly forward. You will probably be allowed to stay with your child while the procedure is done. In all likelihood your child will have already been admitted to the hospital because of severe symptoms or an injury. The child may experience a headache after the test.

HOW ARE RESULTS RECORDED, EVALUATED, INTERPRETED, AND COMPARED?

The presence of white cells in the spinal fluid is considered a sign of infection. The fluid is also examined for color and transparency.

HOW RELIABLE IS THE TEST?

The lumbar puncture may rule out meningitis or identify the less serious viral meningitis. It does not, however, explain the presence of symptoms that are caused by other problems. For example, if a severe headache is not explained by the lumbar puncture, a CAT scan or an MRI could be ordered to determine the presence and extent of a brain injury. In the case of a head injury, both a spinal tap and an imaging test such as MRI could be ordered.

Magnetic Resonance Imaging (MRI)

WHOSE RECOMMENDATION AND/OR PERMISSION IS NEEDED?

Physicians recommend this test and a radiologist generally performs it and interprets the results. You may be asked to sign a consent form.

WHAT DOES THE TEST TEST?

An MRI is most frequently ordered for children to investigate head and spinal cord diseases, or injuries. The applications, however, for this relatively new technology are becoming increasingly numerous and an MRI could be suggested whenever it is considered advantageous to have a distinct "picture" of an area of the body.

WHAT, IF ANY, PREPARATION IS NECESSARY?

Because MRI uses the principle of magnetism, all metal objects must be removed from the child. In addition, the child *must* lie still for 15 minutes or longer and will be sedated. The machine itself looks forbidding and even adults complain of the claustrophobic environment necessary to perform the test. The sound of the machinery may also be frightening. It is not, however, a painful procedure.

It is likely that a parent will be with the child and he or she will also be asked to remove metal objects. Policies vary among MRI facilities, however, and parents should discuss arrangements prior to the test.

HOW IS THE TEST PERFORMED, AND WHAT SHOULD BE EXPECTED?

The child is placed inside a tunnel-like tube in which a magnetic field is generated. This causes certain atoms in the nucleus of the body cells to align or "line up." A radio signal is then directed to the part of the body being examined. This allows the position of the atoms to be recorded and a picture of that part of the body results. This picture is used to diagnose, or rule out (exclude), a variety of conditions.

HOW ARE RESULTS RECORDED, EVALUATED, INTERPRETED, AND COMPARED?

A normal MRI result means that no abnormalities in the position or size of any organ is apparent. An abnormal result would be expressed by describing the abnormalities (lesion, growth, and so on) that appeared on the picture.

HOW RELIABLE IS THE TEST?

Because MRI is relatively new (in use since the early 1980s), professionals vary in their opinions about the value of using MRI, which is very expensive, in cases where a less expensive CAT scan might be as accurate. (The CAT scan exposes the patient to radiation, however, and MRI does not.) MRI is also a tool that requires skill and experience to use. Therefore, more than one physician may be asked to interpret the results. MRI technology is constantly being expanded and improved and most physicians agree that it is a most significant advance in diagnostic medicine.

Orthopedic (Skeletal) Screening

WHOSE RECOMMENDATION AND/OR PERMISSION IS NEEDED?

Physicians, nurse practitioners, chiropractic physicians, and occupational therapists generally screen for skeletal problems throughout childhood.

WHAT DOES THE TEST TEST?

Orthopedic screening detects possible problems of the skeletal system from birth through late adolescence. Screening begins shortly after birth when possible birth injuries are evaluated.

Techniques used in orthopedic screenings include observation, manipulation of the head and the extremities, and directing the child in specific body movements. This is done in order to observe range of motion, the shape or curve of the spine, or postural characteristics. More extensive examinations, including x-ray testing, may then be used to establish a diagnosis and the severity of the problem. Physicians generally plan and monitor treatment, but other health care providers may perform most screening procedures.

The following are the common conditions screened for.

Brachial Palsy. A birth injury to the cervical nerves, which may cause paralysis of the upper arm. This is often first noticed when Moro's reflex, commonly known as the startle reflex, is not fully normal. That is, the affected arm does not move forward in tandem with the other arm. The infant may be neurologically normal in all other ways, however.

Clavicle Fracture. Sometimes occurring during a difficult delivery. The newborn may not move the affected side, and an x-ray confirms that a fracture has occurred.

Torticollis. Meaning twisted neck. This is a deformity of the head and neck, in which the head tilts to one side because of shortened muscles. The chin then rotates toward the opposite shoulder.

Congenital Hip Dislocation (CHD). The examiner may detect CHD during routine manipulations shortly after birth. Obvious limited motion, delayed walking, or certain postural characteristics may signal its presence in an older child.

Metatarsus Adductus. A condition in which the forefoot is turned in. The arch may be higher than normal and the space between the first and second toes may also be unusually wide. (This condition sometimes reverses itself; orthopedic treatment is recommended when it doesn't.)

Flat Feet. Most infants and toddlers appear to have flat feet; only particular types require evaluation.

Toe Walking. Most children do toe walking as part of play and imitation. However, some toe walking is a sign of muscular or neurological abnormality.

Femoral Anteversion. A common cause of in-toeing in young children. When established through screening, it is monitored and sometimes postural corrections are suggested. In its severe form it is considered a deformity, often accompanied by other skeletal problems.

Genu Valgum (Knock Knees). Considered normal in young children, ages 2 to 6, this condition is monitored and referral to an orthopedist is made if it does not correct itself.

Genu Varum (Bowlegs). Considered normal in children ages 2 to 3, this condition is usually self-correcting. However, if it is not outgrown it must be treated. When there is a strong family history, treatment may start early. (The type of bowlegs seen as a result of nutritional deficiency is called pathologic bowlegs. The type most frequently seen in this country is referred to as physiologic bowlegs.)

Internal Tibial Torsion. An abnormal angle in the lower leg at the ankle, often resulting when the child sits or sleeps for long periods in a position that puts pressure on the lower leg. Pediatricians may ask parents about the so-called "TV squat" if the condition is seen developing. It is usually self-correcting when the sitting position is changed. (This same angle is considered normal in early infancy.) Referral to an orthopedist is made when the condition does not correct itself.

Overriding Toes, Pronation, and Toeing In. Conditions of the feet. These tend to run in families. Corrective treatment or postural adjustments may be recommended, depending on the severity of the problem.

Kyphosis. An exaggerated convex curve in the upper spine, this condition may cause backaches. Most common among adolescent girls, kyphosis is considered a developmental condition and may be secondary to a congenital disorder such as scoliosis. Physical therapy, postural "retraining," and participatory sports that improve posture (such as swimming and dancing) may be recommended. An orthopedist or chiropractor may be needed to monitor treatment.

Lordosis. An exaggerated concave curve of the lower spine, which usually accompanies kyphosis. When severe, lordosis is painful and the child may develop a limp.

Scoliosis. An S-shaped curve in the spine. There are many types of scoliosis, and severity varies greatly. It is seen more frequently in girls than in boys, but unlike some other skeletal conditions, its presence may not be obvious to a parent or a casual observer. And, because it is not painful, it must be specifically screened for, preferably at yearly examinations. Until recently, scoliosis was thought to be a condition of adolescence. However, screening is now recommended for children age 5 or 6 and older. The professional doing the screening will look for numerous signs that may indicate that scoliosis is developing: differences in the level of the shoulders, the prominence of one hip, and so on.

Treatment generally consists of wearing a brace designed to correct the curve as the child grows. Surgery may be suggested if the curve progresses despite other less invasive treatments.

Limps. Abnormal walking or running characteristics. A limp may be caused by something as simple as shoes that are too tight. However, a limp may result from numerous orthopedic conditions and diseases. In these cases, the limp is considered secondary to the condition causing the problem.

Parents may first notice a subtle limp when the child complains of knee, leg, or hip pain that persists and can't be attributed to an injury. Limps will often correct themselves when postural conditions are identified and treated.

Tests for Parasites

We generally think of parasites in terms of worm-like organisms that enter the body and reproduce there. However, not all parasitic conditions conform to the stereotype. Scabies, for example, is caused by a tiny mite, and some parasites are single-cell organisms that invade the intestinal tract.

Parasite infection may be diagnosed in numerous ways: stool, skin, or blood smears; various blood tests; urinalysis; and actual biopsies of organs. But there are two parasitic infections common in children in which a method other than these is used.

Scabies: A tiny mite that burrows in the skin and causes itching and red bumps. To confirm scabies, one or more of the bumps is opened and a sample is taken and placed on a slide (a procedure called a smear). The smear is examined under a microscope. The mites or the eggs may be present.

Pinworm infection: A parasitic infection that can be picked up by playing in dirt or through contaminated clothing, pinworm infection is characterized by anal itching, especially at night, often intense enough to disturb normal sleep. The pinworms deposit their eggs on the skin surrounding the anus. (Girls may experience vaginal itching as well.) Because of the location of the eggs, a stool culture is not considered the best way to diagnose pin-worms. Rather, a test known as the cellophane tape test is used. A piece of tape is folded over a standard tongue depressor and placed between the buttocks until it stops at the anus. (It is best to do the test before the child gets out of bed.) The tape and the stick are brought to the doctor's office and examined under the microscope to see if pinworms or eggs are "caught" on the sticky surface of the tape. The test is usually repeated at least three times. There are commercial kits for this test, closely resembling the home-made materials, which appear to work just as well.

Pulmonary Function Tests (PFTS)

WHOSE RECOMMENDATION AND/OR PERMISSION IS NEEDED?

Physicians generally order these tests, which are performed in a clinic, hospital, or a specialist's office.

WHAT DOES THE TEST TEST?

These tests are performed to evaluate a person's ability to in-hale and exhale. They are used to help diagnose many lung disorders, including asthma.

WHAT, IF ANY, PREPARATION IS NECESSARY?

You may be told not to allow your child solid food for several hours before the test. (A full stomach may limit lung expansion.) The child should wear loose clothing; it may be suggested that he or she empty the bladder prior to the test. You should make sure the physician is aware of any medications your child is taking.

HOW IS THE TEST PERFORMED, AND
WHAT SHOULD BE EXPECTED?

The child sits or stands in the testing room and is asked to breathe into a mouthpiece, which is connected to a machine. The technician gives the child instructions about how to breathe (deeply, rapidly, normally, exhaling quickly, and so on). The tests may be repeated after a special medication (bronchodilator) is given, which expands the airways of the lung. The test itself is not painful but the child could become tired or light-headed. If a child's breathing is severely restricted, the apparatus used could be perceived by the child as "suffocating."

HOW ARE RESULTS RECORDED, EVALUATED,
INTERPRETED, AND COMPARED?

The volume of air exhaled during the breathing test is recorded on a piece of paper in the machine used for the measurements. The result is a recorded "picture" called a spirogram. Numerous measurements can be made from the spirogram: the total capacity of the lung, quantity of air exhaled in one second, the rate of air-flow during forced exhalation, and so on.

WHAT DOES THE TEST *NOT* TEST?

These tests do not identify specific allergens.

WHAT FURTHER TESTS MIGHT BE RECOMMENDED?

Allergy tests may be recommended as part of diagnosing or monitoring asthma. Arterial blood gases may also be measured.

Sweat Test

WHOSE RECOMMENDATION AND/OR PERMISSION IS NEEDED?

Physicians recommend this test, and it is usually performed by a medical technician.

WHAT DOES THE TEST TEST?

The sweat test measures concentrations of sodium and chloride in sweat. It is used to diagnose cystic fibrosis, an inherited disease affecting many parts of the body. Children would be given this test if there is a family history of cystic fibrosis, and if they have frequent colds and infections, poor food absorption, recurrent or chronic diarrhea, and are gowing more slowly than normal.

WHAT, IF ANY, PREPARATION IS NECESSARY

The procedure itself is not painful, but it is lengthy and involves a period of waiting. Parents should probably bring books or a toy along to help pass the time.

HOW IS THE TEST PERFORMED, AND WHAT SHOULD BE EXPECTED?

The test is performed on the right thigh of an infant; on the right forearm of a toddler or older child. After the area is washed and dried, two electrodes are attached with straps. Two gauze pads are positioned under the electrodes. One pad is soaked in saltwater; the other is soaked with pilocarpine, a drug that produces sweating. A tiny electric current is then applied, carrying the drug into the skin and causing the sweating to begin. This part of the test takes 5 to 10 minutes. The child should feel only a slight tingling. (It may feel like tickling to the child.)

When the electrodes are removed, the skin is washed and dried and a gauze pad, the exact weight of which is known, is placed on the spot where the drug was applied. The pad, referred to as the sweat patch, is covered with plastic and taped to the child's skin. It is left on for 30 to 45 minutes, after which it is removed and placed in a sealed bottle. The sweat on the pad can then be weighed and the sodium and chloride content analyzed.

If a child seems to be in pain, the electrodes should be inspected. If they are not properly placed, they can produce a burning sensation. The right arm or leg is used to reduce the chance that the electrical current will affect the heart. The risk of electric shock is, however, very low.

HOW ARE RESULTS RECORDED, EVALUATED, INTERPRETED, AND COMPARED?

The levels of sodium and chloride in the sweat are compared to normal values. High levels indicate the presence of cystic fibrosis, particularly if other conditions (e.g., adrenal insufficiency or kidney failure) that cause increased sodium and chloride levels in sweat are ruled out.

HOW RELIABLE IS THE TEST?

Hot weather can deplete the body's supply of sodium, producing a false normal result in children who, when tested at a later time, are found to have cystic fibrosis.

Sexually Transmitted Diseases (STD)

WHOSE RECOMMENDATION AND/OR PERMISSION IS NEEDED?

Physicians or nurses and nurse practitioners generally recommend and administer these tests. State laws vary about parental notification if the tests are performed in publicly funded clinics. Some tests are done in conjunction with routine gynecologic examinations for young women, or because symptoms of an STD have prompted young men to seek medical help. Some schools have health clinics in which these tests can be performed, with the minor's right to privacy as a patient viewed as the same as an adult's. The issue of parental permission and notification will continue to be debated throughout the 1990s. Statutes that are in place today may be replaced tomorrow, only to be challenged in the courts and perhaps changed again.

WHAT DOES THE TEST TEST?

The term STD is a general name given to a group of diseases that are *usually* "caught" from an infected sexual partner. Regardless of one's view of the wisdom or morality of adolescent sexual relationships, the fact is that these diseases are very common, always serious, and highly contagious. When left untreated they may lead to infertility; some of these conditions are life threatening. Although these days acquired immune deficiency syndrome (AIDS) may be uppermost on parents' minds, other STDs are far more common among teenagers.

It should also be noted that the sexual partner(s) should be notified when an STD is diagnosed. (This is mandated by law for some diseases.) If one partner is treated and the other is not, the disease will likely be retransmitted, a phenomenon known as the "ping-pong" effect. Additionally, the untreated person may spread the disease to a new partner, who in turn may pass it on to someone else. This is indeed how epidemics occur.

The information here about STDs should by no means be considered complete. Symptoms, the course of the disease, and the long-term effects on various parts of the body are complex subjects and an entire book could be written about them. Space also does not allow for a complete discussion of *prevention* methods or of all of the ways the diseases may be transmitted. The following is a list of common STDs and the tests used to diagnose them.

AIDS. A syndrome affecting the immune system, caused by the human immunodeficiency virus (HIV). The presence of HIV in the blood is determined through a blood test and the person is told that he or she is HIV positive. This means that he or she can transmit the virus to others through bodily fluids (i.e., semen and blood). The virus can also be transmitted through hypodermic needles used by some drug users and through transfusions of HIV-infected blood. It should be noted that to date there is no vaccine or cure for AIDS, facts that young people should know.

Chlamydia. An extremely common STD, caused by bacteria, that may produce only very mild symptoms in both women and men—so mild in fact that they usually aren't noticed early on. In women, mild vaginal itching may lead to a discharge and chronic pelvic pain. If men become symptomatic, they may have a burning sensation during urination or a discharge from the penis.

Chlamydia is generally diagnosed by culturing the discharge. Results are available in 2 to 3 days. Reculturing may be necessary if initial results were negative and symptoms persist. Chlamydia is often "silent," and when left untreated it can cause pelvic inflammatory disease (PID) in women, which in turn can lead to infertility.

Chlamydia is a very common STD, far more so than gonorrhea. It is treated with antibiotics; sexual partners should be tested and treated, too. Physicians are not required to report chlamydia cases to their local health department, but notifying recent sexual partners is still crucial.

Gonorrhea. A bacterial infection that in the early stages causes mild or even unnoticeable symptoms in women, thereby giving it an opportunity to spread to the fallopian tubes, the ovaries, and into the abdominal cavity. Untreated gonorrhea can result in PID (see Chlamydia). In men, symptoms often appear within two days, although it may take up to a few weeks for a man to be symptomatic. Gonorrhea is characterized by a thick yellow or greenish-yellow discharge from the penis or the vagina (when a woman has early symptoms at all). Men also experience a burning sensation upon urination.

The presence of a gonorrhea infection is confirmed with a culture or by viewing the stained specimen under a microscope (Gram's stain). The sample is taken from the mouth of the cervix (the os) and the vagina, or the urethra in men. The culture can be taken in women even when no unusual discharge is noted. A test for gonorrhea is part of the general protocol in some gynecologic clinics, and is performed during a pelvic exam. The Gram's stain method is often used so that treatment with antibiotics can be started immediately. A culture may take 2 to 5 days.

Unlike with chlamydia, health care professionals are currently required to report gonorrhea to the local health department. The infected person will be asked for the names and addresses of recent sexual partners. This requirement is difficult to enforce, because the person can't be forced to reveal this information. However, the long-term consequences of untreated gonorrhea and the highly contagious nature of the disease make it an ethical imperative to tell sexual partners, who should seek medical advice immediately, even if no symptoms are present.

Gonorrhea infection can occur in other parts of the body: the eye, the back of the throat, the rectum, and so on. Therefore, a sample for testing may be collected in any area with unusual discharge. When test results for gonorrhea are negative, chlamydia is considered the next most likely cause of symptoms.

Herpes. Or herpes simplex virus (HSV), includes Type 1, which causes oral cold sores and fever blisters and Type 2, which causes sores on and around the genital organs. Type 2 is known as genital herpes, the first outbreak of which produces clusters of small blisters that may itch or burn. Some people may also experience fever, rashes, and swollen lymph nodes in the groin.

Herpes is diagnosed in one of two ways. The first is the Tzanck test, in which one of the sores is scraped and the sample spread on a slide and stained. The sample is then examined for the cells associated with herpes. Results are available immediately. However, false negatives are common, and a more accurate diagnosis can be made with a herpes virus culture, best performed when the sores are fresh. Results of a culture are available in a few days.

Herpes outbreaks may recur—frequently or infrequently—over a lifetime because the virus never goes away. Any blister or sore in the genital region should be considered a possible herpes outbreak, and sexual contact should be avoided. The herpes virus is transmitted during this active stage.

Syphilis. A bacterial infection in which stages are denoted to describe the severity of the advancing disease. Initially, syphilis is characterized by a sore on the part of the body that comes in contact with an infected lesion, usually, but not always, in the genital regions. The sore usually appears within three weeks of the exposure. Women may not notice the sore if it is inside the vagina. The sore heals with or without treatment, but the disease is still present.

After the sore heals, a skin rash appears, usually on the palms and the soles of the feet. This rash will also disappear without treatment. Symptoms of the disease may not reappear for 10 to 20 years, when severe heart or brain damage is detected.

When syphilis infection is present, the body produces an antibody-like substance that can be detected in the blood. Screening tests for syphilis rely on detecting this substance. However, false negatives are common and other conditions can produce false positives. Those people with early asymptomatic syphilis can be easily missed.

A test called the FTA-ABS (fluorescent treponemal antibody absorption) is used to confirm a positive result on a screening test. However, its results are not considered reliable until at least three weeks after the body has been infected with the disease. An examination of the fluid from a sore, under a microscope in a process called dark-field examination, is often able to detect the presence of the organism that causes the disease. However, a sore may not be present or noticed.

Many states require screening for syphilis prior to marriage and in early pregnancy. A screening may also be performed when other STDs have been diagnosed. Common sense also dictates testing when a genital sore is present and is not easily attributed to other causes or when exposure to a sexual partner who may have had syphilis is suspected.

Other STDs that are common and diagnosed either by observation or by microscopic examination are:

- **Genital warts**: Caused by a virus. These are easily transmitted, and if sexual partners aren't examined and treated, reinfection is likely.
- **Trichomonas vaginalis**: Caused by a protozoa called trichomonads. Men in particular may be asymptomatic; women often first notice an unusual discharge and vaginal itching.

- **Monilial vaginitis**: Also known as a yeast infection or candidiasis, a common health complaint in women that may occur outside a sexual context. Some of these infections are treated because the symptoms are present and no tests are needed. These infections may also occur after antibiotics have been taken to cure other infections—urinary tract infection or gonorrhea, for example.
- **Pubic lice** and **scabies**: May also be transmitted through sexual contact.
- **Hepatitis B** (see entry under blood tests, page 48): Is sometimes transmitted during sexual contact and is therefore included in the STD category.

HOW RELIABLE ARE THE TESTS?

The reliability of any of the standard tests for STDs depends on the individual characteristics of the disease. The time of testing may be important as well. For this reason, retesting, sometimes using different tests to confirm results, and follow-up examinations and tests are crucial.

WHAT DOES THE TEST *NOT* TEST?

The tests for STDs can't predict the outcome of the disease, nor can they absolutely establish how the disease was contracted.

WHAT FURTHER TESTS MIGHT BE RECOMMENDED?

It is entirely possible for more than one STD to be present at the same time, and therefore, tests for more than one STD may be necessary. It is also possible that treatment with a particular antibiotic will be ineffective and that another must be used after retesting confirms that the disease is not yet cured. A person with a history of STD is advised to have regular follow-up examinations, sometimes for several years. Young people may be ashamed or embarrassed about having contracted an STD. While this is understandable, the long-term consequences of an untreated STD can be so severe that young people must be helped to overcome this emotional reaction and seek treatment and follow-up care.

Toxicology Screening

A toxicology screening test for legal and illegal drug levels in the blood.

WHOSE RECOMMENDATION AND/OR PERMISSION IS NEEDED?

There are situations in which blood testing (usually along with urine testing) is done to detect the presence of illegal substances, alcohol, or steroids in the blood. If your child is involved in an automobile accident, for example, and it is thought that alcohol and/or drugs are involved, a blood test could be mandated by law. Some schools are testing young people in athletic programs for illegal steroid use, use of illegal drugs (marijuana or cocaine), or use of legal drugs (amphetamines or barbiturates, for instance) without a prescription. Although this testing may or may not be done randomly, you as the parent should be notified about the drug screening program and give your permission. (Some drug screening is also allowed in particular jobs where drug-related impairment may endanger others. However, your minor child is not likely to hold such a job.)

This area of testing is extremely controversial and the 1990s will see laws regulating it both passed and challenged. In general, a physician will not perform a drug test simply because the parent requests it, without the child's prior knowledge. This is considered a violation of the privacy guaranteed by the U.S. Constitution. However, such testing *has* happened and case law is being developed. In *routine* toxicology testing, physicians recommend the test.

WHAT DOES THE TEST TEST?

Most toxicology screening is performed to measure levels of drugs given to treat specific illnesses, mainly to aid in adjusting dosage and to prevent the accumulation of excessive levels. If drug levels are allowed to become too high, there may be damage to organs in the body.

HOW ARE RESULTS RECORDED, EVALUATED, INTERPRETED, AND COMPARED?

Results are interpreted according to guidelines established for each drug. For example, if your child is taking Dilantin for epilepsy, a "safe" blood level is determined and monitored regularly. (Obviously, the presence of traces of an illegal drug is noted.)

HOW RELIABLE IS THE TEST?

One reason that testing for illegal drugs is controversial is that opinions about reliability vary widely. If your child is required to have periodic screens, be sure to review the testing procedure and the options for retesting.

WHAT DOES THE TEST *NOT* TEST?

Blood tests do not necessarily report possible damage that excessive levels of drugs (legal and illegal) may have done to the body. Nor can a blood test establish that an illegal or misused drug is being used habitually.

Tuberculosis Skin Test (PPD, Tine Test, TB Test)

WHOSE RECOMMENDATION AND/OR PERMISSION IS NEEDED?

This is a routine test performed by a physician or a nurse; it is required by some school districts for entrance to school. It may be done individually in a physician's office or in a school setting, where groups of children are screened at the same time.

WHAT DOES THE TEST TEST?

The skin test for tuberculosis is a screening test to determine if a child has an active or dormant tuberculosis infection.

WHAT, IF ANY, PREPARATION IS NECESSARY?

Generally, no preparation is needed. There is momentary discomfort when the skin is punctured. The physician should be told if a child has been previously immunized with BCG (cow tuberculosis vaccine commonly used throughout the world, except for the United States and Canada) because a false positive result is likely.

HOW IS THE TEST PERFORMED, AND WHAT SHOULD BE EXPECTED?

In the PPD test, a small quantity of tuberculosis extract is injected under the skin. A small blister results. In the tine test, a small button-like instrument with four tiny needles (tines) is coated with the tuberculosis extract. The needles puncture the skin, usually on the forearm, leaving four tiny holes. The tine test is fast and often used in group screenings. The PPD is considered more accurate.

HOW ARE RESULTS RECORDED, EVALUATED, INTERPRETED AND COMPARED?

Results take 48 to 72 hours. When a child does not have, and has never had, tuberculosis, there is *minimal* redness or swelling (¼ inch or less in diameter), and the test result is said to be negative. Redness or swelling greater than ¼ inch should be investigated. Retesting may be ordered.

HOW RELIABLE IS THE TEST?

False positives are possible, which is why retesting is done in questionable cases.

WHAT DOES THE TEST *NOT* TEST?

The skin test can't distinguish between active and dormant tuberculosis.

WHAT FURTHER TESTS MIGHT BE RECOMMENDED?

In areas where tuberculosis is common, annual screening may be recommended. Chest x-rays, sputum cultures, and occasionally bronchoscopy, a procedure that allows the airways (trachea and bronchi) to be viewed, are performed to determine if the tuberculosis is active or dormant.

Ultrasonography (Ultrasound)

WHOSE RECOMMENDATION AND/OR PERMISSION IS NEEDED?

Any physicians can recommend ultrasound exams, but radiologists and ultrasound technicians generally perform them and interpret the results.

WHAT DOES THE TEST TEST?

Ultrasound is used to examine many parts of the body, using high-frequency sound waves rather than x-rays. Ultrasound is not considered a routine test, and is ordered when a specific problem is suspected or being diagnosed. Ultrasound is most often performed in radiology departments and clinics.

WHAT, IF ANY, PREPARATION IS NECESSARY?

Preparation for most ultrasound procedures is not necessary or is usually minimal. (A special diet or an enema *may* be required under certain circumstances.) Generally, clothing and jewelry around the area being examined will be removed. Whether or not a parent is present will depend on the child's age and the policy at the facility. There is no inherent danger in a parent being in the room because no radiation is involved. Ultrasound is relatively fast, and it is completely painless. However, a child might balk when a water-soluble gel is applied to the area being examined. This gel will feel cold (adults often complain about it), so it is to be expected that a child will voice an objection.

You can reassure your child that there is only a slight feeling of pressure involved during the procedure, but no pain is caused by the test itself. (If an internal injury is being investigated, the child might already be in pain, of course.)

HOW IS THE TEST PERFORMED, AND WHAT SHOULD BE EXPECTED?

An instrument called a transducer, which emits high-pitched sounds, is moved back and forth across the area of the body being examined. (The high-frequency sounds are well above the range heard by humans.) The water-soluble gel improves the transmission of the sound waves. The transducer contains a microphone that records and analyzes the sound waves reflected back from inside the body. An image results, which is displayed on a screen similar to a television screen. (Children old enough to understand that an "inside part" is appearing on a television screen are usually transfixed.) The picture produced by an ultrasound test is called a sonogram, a scan, or an echogram.

HOW ARE RESULTS RECORDED, EVALUATED, INTERPRETED, AND COMPARED?

A physician will always "read" the sonogram and interpret the results. Because nondiseased organs appear on a sonogram in specific, well-known ways, an appearance that deviates from that considered normal is noted. An organ may appear enlarged, for example, or it may be darker or lighter than normal. Tumors, cysts, or abscesses will show up in particular ways, depending on the organ being examined.

HOW RELIABLE IS THE TEST?

Ultrasound is generally used because symptoms are present and their cause is being investigated. The technology itself is reliable, in that it shows what it shows. Interpretation of the sonogram may vary among the specialists diagnosing a problem.

WHAT DOES THE TEST NOT TEST?

This technology is not used to examine bones, the lungs, or the brain.

WHAT FURTHER TESTS MIGHT BE RECOMMENDED?

Because ultrasound is considered safe, it may be repeated to monitor a condition. Many tests, including extensive blood studies and urinalysis, as well as a biopsy if indicated, may accompany ultrasound testing because it is generally used to diagnose conditions that will then require treatment or monitoring.

Urine Tests (Urinalysis)

WHOSE RECOMMENDATION AND/OR PERMISSION IS NEEDED?

Physicians or nurses and nurse practitioners recommend and interpret urine tests.

WHAT DOES THE TEST TEST?

Urinalysis is done as part of a routine examination, as well as to aid in diagnosing countless conditions. Urine, like blood, can reveal information about the overall health of numerous body systems and parts, most especially the kidneys and the bladder.

WHAT, IF ANY, PREPARATION IS NECESSARY?

The way in which urine samples are collected varies depending on the reason for the test. When the urinalysis is done for a routine checkup, the child will be asked to urinate in a sterile container upon arising. (A parent may have to monitor this, of course, to make sure that it is indeed the first morning urine that is collected and in a sufficient amount.) Urine collection may also take place at a physician's office if it isn't considered crucial that the first morning urine be collected.

When a kidney or bladder infection, or other condition, is suspected, a "clean catch" sample is usually required. This means that the area around the urinary opening is cleaned with antiseptic swabs before the urination begins. The child is instructed to begin urinating and allow the stream to flow into the toilet bowl for a few seconds before catching a few ounces of urine in a sterile container. This procedure for collecting urine helps prevent bacteria normally found in the genital area from contaminating the urine sample. The amount and type of help a child needs depends on his or her age, but also on how ill the child is. Common sense and the circumstances will dictate how the procedure is handled.

Collecting urine from infants and babies is generally done with a specially constructed plastic bag that is fastened around the genital area. Once the baby has urinated, the bag is removed and whatever amount of urine is in the bag is used for the test. Powders, lotions, and creams can contaminate the urine, so it is best not to use these products until the sample is collected.

When an infant is *very* ill and diagnosis is uncertain, a sterile urine sample may be needed immediately. In these rare cases, a needle is inserted into the bladder through the lower abdominal wall and urine is extracted. There is always a slight risk of infection, bleeding, or of an accidental puncture of the intestines. For this reason, the procedure would be recommended only when it is believed that waiting for the infant to urinate would delay a crucial diagnosis and immediate treatment.

HOW IS THE TEST PERFORMED, AND WHAT SHOULD BE EXPECTED?

A complete urinalysis consists of

- visually examining the urine for color and clarity;
- measuring the density of the urine sample, referred to as specific gravity (SG);
- measuring acidity or alkalinity (Ph);
- detecting the presence and amounts of certain chemicals (glucose, ketones, bilirubin, urobilirubin, protein, and hemoglobin);
- microscopic examination for blood and epithelial cells (cells that cover body surfaces, including organs of the urinary tract), casts (bits of protein, bacteria, pus, or blood cells that may indicate kidney disease), and crystals (formed in urine sediment); and
- testing for bacteria, the presence of which can indicate infection.

In addition, the odor of urine can offer information about infections or diabetes. The volume of urine passed over a given time period sometimes needs to be known, so all of the urine excreted over a 24-hour period is collected. Urinalysis is also used in toxicology screenings, generally to detect the presence of steroids or illegal drugs.

HOW ARE RESULTS RECORDED, EVALUATED, INTERPRETED, AND COMPARED?

Color and Clarity

Normal values for the color of urine cover a wide range, from nearly colorless to a dark yellow amber. Urine collected upon arising tends to be darker and more concentrated than at other times throughout the day. In addition, many substances and conditions can affect the color of urine. For example, urine that is nearly colorless can be the result of a large fluid intake, or it can indicate diabetes or kidney disease. (Other indicators will also be present in the urine if disease is present.)

Various foods and drugs may also cause unusual color changes. Urine that is pink or red-orange has alarmed many a parent until it was remembered that a food tinted with food coloring, or beets, was ingested the previous day. However, blood in the urine can cause this color change, a condition which must be investigated.

Urine that is brown can be caused by, among other things, lead poisoning, high bilirubin levels, some antibiotics, some laxatives, and other drugs. Therefore, any medications your child is taking should be noted at the time of the testing.

Clarity is judged by holding the sample up to the light. Normal urine is clear or slightly hazy.

Specific Gravity

When the kidneys are healthy, they are able to adjust the amount of water excreted in the urine. Fluid intake affects this balance of urine and pure water. Specific gravity is a measure of the density of the urine as compared to the pure water. It is said to fall above or below normal range.

High specific gravity, which means that the urine is very concentrated, is associated with serious conditions such as diabetes, in which case other abnormalities in the urine will also appear. It can also be caused by temporary fluid loss due to vomiting or diarrhea.

Low specific gravity may be caused by excessive fluid intake, use of diuretics, or kidney disease. (Specialized tests, not part of the routine urinalysis, are done when specific gravity measurements are abnormal and after the routine test is repeated, usually more than once. These tests are done when particular kidney, pituitary, or adrenal disorders are suspected.)

pH

Acidity and alkalinity of the urine varies with the individual's diet as well as time of day. Morning urine samples tend to be more acidic but should become less so during the day.

pH is generally measured on a dipstick, with a range of strongly acidic to strongly alkaline (the midpoint is considered neutral). Certain drugs and large doses of vitamin C will affect pH measurements.

Molecules

Glucose (Sugar). Urine generally contains very little glucose. Therefore, if the glucose level is high, retesting is always recommended because glucose in the urine is a symptom of diabetes. (There are easily performed home tests for glucose in urine when regular monitoring is indicated.)

Ketones. By-products of metabolized fat. The test result for ketonesis is negative if none are detected. When ketones are present they are expressed in small, moderate, and large amounts. (Large amounts of ketones accompanied by high blood glucose indicates diabetic ketoacidosis, a dangerous condition requiring immediate attention.) Ketone levels may be high following strenuous exercise or after an illness that has altered food intake. This is not serious in itself. However, excessive dieting, low carbohydrate intake, and vomiting may result in ketone production. An eating disorder may be investigated if retesting reveals the same results. (Ketones exist in urine [ketonuria] when diabetes is present.)

Protein. Not normally present in detectable amounts. Protein in the urine (proteinuria or albuminuria) is an important indicator of kidney disease. However, a small percentage of healthy people have a harmless condition called postural or orthostatic proteinuria, in which a small amount of protein is excreted in the urine after these people have been on their feet for a long period of time. Retesting with a first-urine catch will generally distinguish this condition from serious kidney disorders. Proteinuria may also come and go during prolonged illness or after strenuous exercise.

Hemoglobin. The presence of hemoglobin (blood) is considered an abnormality and is investigated. In many situations—injury to a kidney, for example—other symptoms are generally present. Retesting is done when no particular cause or explanation is apparent.

Bilirubin/Urobilirubin. Bilirubin is not normally found in the urine, and urobilirubin should be present in only trace amounts. Therefore, retesting and investigation of the symptoms are indicated when results are outside the normal range. In hepatitis, for example, a urine test might be a fast way to establish that liver dysfunction is present, even if other symptoms have not developed.

Microscopic Analysis

Cells. Red blood cells (RBCs), white blood cells (WBCs), and epithelial cells are normally found in the urine in very small amounts. When reported as outside the normal range, retesting is called for because the causes range from the harmless to the serious. Urinary tract infections may produce RBCs and WBCs in the urine, but symptoms may or may not be present. Particular drugs, including aspirin and certain antibiotics, may also cause this test result. For this reason, a physician should always be aware of medications the child is taking.

Casts. These are small structures formed from mineral deposits on the walls of the kidneys and other organs. There are numerous types of casts, none of which are normally present in urine. (The exception is the hyaline cast, which *occasionally* appears in small amounts.) The appearance of casts may indicate such things as infection, sickle cell disease, lead poisoning, and kidney disease.

Crystals. Some types of crystal formations can occur in the urine and be considered normal. Other types may indicate metabolic problems or kidney stone formation.

Bacteria. Urine may be cultured when bacteria is present and symptoms of urinary tract infection have prompted the urinalysis.

Odor. Diabetes that is not being controlled will cause the urine to have a sweet, fruity odor.

Toxicology Screening. If your child is in a school or school athletic program that requires screening for steroid use and use of illegal drugs, you should be notified and, most likely, give your consent. (This is not always clear. Consent to be in an athletic program is sometimes viewed as including consent to have your child screened for drugs.) There should also be a protocol, strictly adhered to, that outlines the way the procedure is done, the time allowed for a collected sample to be sent to a laboratory for analysis, and repeat testing. This is a controversial area of testing, the legalities of which are being challenged and debated, particularly when applied to minors.

Urinalysis is allowed for those holding jobs where impairment may endanger others (e.g., in transportation or day care work). However, it is unlikely that your minor child would be hired for such a position.

It is not considered ethical for a physician to perform a drug screening without a young person's consent just because a parent requests it. While this certainly has happened, it is rare. (See also Blood Tests, page 29, and Toxicology Screening, page 76.)

HOW RELIABLE IS THE TEST?

The number of things that can affect the outcome of urinalysis are so numerous it would take a separate volume to discuss them. However, foods and medications are two factors that parents can be aware of and inform the physician or nurse about. Accuracy is also affected by the handling of the sample. If, for example, it is not tested immediately and refrigerated to preserve it, the chemical composition may change and the results become essentially meaningless. Retesting is common because of the many factors that can interfere with accurate results.

Toxicology screening is especially controversial because accuracy rates reported by laboratories vary widely. False positives are quite common, adding to the difficulty in relying on this testing.

WHAT DOES THE TEST *NOT* TEST?

Urinalysis gives many important clues to overall health and functioning of organ systems. It may help narrow the field of possible diagnoses, leading the way for other testing. It may not, however, in and of itself, result in a specific diagnosis. Other testing may be needed to confirm the physician's "hunch" about the ultimate source of a difficulty.

WHAT FURTHER TESTS MIGHT BE RECOMMENDED?

Routine urinalysis is often done in combination with routine blood tests performed because of suspected illness or following an injury; a wide range of tests could be ordered.

X-RAYS

WHOSE RECOMMENDATION AND/OR PERMISSION IS NEEDED?

Any physician can recommend x-ray testing, but radiologists generally interpret the results and report them to the primary-care physician. Some physicians perform x-rays in their offices and do their own evaluation, although this happens less often now than in the past.

WHAT DOES THE TEST TEST?

X-rays are performed when it is considered necessary to view structures inside the body. They are ordered for numerous reasons—from identifying a fracture in a bone to investigating internal growths to locating foreign objects that a child has swallowed. X-rays should always be used with caution. Although they are indispensable in current medical practice, x-rays themselves carry a risk, albeit generally a small one. Exposure to radiation is not taken lightly these days, and children are more sensitive to x-ray damage than adults (with the exception of pregnant women, who are always considered at high risk).

There are times when the need for an x-ray is very clear. Trauma is an example. If your child has possible multiple injuries from a serious accident, you would not hesitate to agree to x-ray testing. On the other hand, you would normally question the need for x-ray testing if your child had injured a wrist or ankle that was most likely to be a sprain.

Sometimes an area being x-rayed needs to be highlighted and a substance is injected to accomplish this. These substances are called contrast materials, contrast media, or dyes.

The x-ray tests included in this section are those *commonly* encountered in childhood. However, this is not intended to be a guide to all possible uses of x-ray testing.

WHAT, IF ANY, PREPARATION IS NECESSARY?

Preparation varies with individual x-ray procedures and the circumstances under which x-rays are ordered. The individual listings discuss preparation where relevant. Common sense dictates that a child may need to be reassured that the x-ray equipment itself will not cause any pain or discomfort. A parent may or may not be present during an x-ray procedure. This depends on the age of the child, the type of test, and the policy of the facility you are dealing with. If a parent is present, protective lead covering may be required in order to avoid unnecessary exposure to radiation.

HOW ARE RESULTS RECORDED, EVALUATED, INTERPRETED, AND COMPARED?

X-ray films are "read" by a radiologist, who provides a written report of the findings. The x-rays themselves are usually turned over to the primary care physician, and may become a permanent part of the child's health history.

HOW RELIABLE IS THE TEST?

X-ray testing is considered extremely valuable for any number of uses. Reliability depends in part on the conditions of the testing, the child's ability to cooperate being one factor. Also, x-rays vary in their accuracy, and retesting is not uncommon.

WHAT DOES THE TEST *NOT* TEST?

X-ray technology is not a substitute for observation, and evaluation of symptoms, blood tests, cultures, and so on. X-ray testing is not generally used to diagnose infections or certain types of organ dysfunction: diabetes, thyroid problems, and so on. X-rays can detect a "mass" or abnormality, but they do not distinguish between benign and malignant cells.

WHAT FURTHER TESTS MIGHT BE RECOMMENDED?

Recommendations for further testing depend entirely on the reason for the testing in the first place.

Abdominal X-Ray

WHAT DOES THE TEST TEST

The abdominal x-ray is done when abdominal and urinary tract organs need to be viewed.

WHAT, IF ANY, PREPARATION IS NECESSARY?

All clothing and jewelry must be removed.

HOW IS THE TEST PERFORMED, AND WHAT SHOULD BE EXPECTED?

The x-ray machine is positioned over the child's abdomen, and the technician will tell the child to hold his or her breath while each x-ray is taken. The number of x-rays depends on the purpose of the testing. The child might have one x-ray while standing, one taken lying on his or her side, and one taken while lying on his or her back.

HOW RELIABLE IS THE TEST?

If the child moved during the test, repeat films may be needed.

WHAT FURTHER TESTS MIGHT BE RECOMMENDED?

Other, more extensive x-ray tests may be recommended. For example, a barium enema may be done if ulcerative colitis is suspected, or an upper GI series may be performed if a stomach or duodenal ulcer is suspected.

Bone X-Ray (Extremities)

WHOSE RECOMMENDATION AND/OR PERMISSION IS NEEDED?

A physician will order this test, often in an emergency room setting. Radiologists generally interpret it.

WHAT DOES THE TEST TEST?

In young people, bone x-rays are usually ordered to confirm a preliminary diagnosis of a bone fracture. Detecting the presence of a tumor or an infection in the bone are two less frequent reasons children receive this test. A bone x-ray is generally able to reveal the location and severity of a fracture; the treatment plan is devised based on what the test reveals.

WHAT, IF ANY, PREPARATION IS NECESSARY?

A child should be told that the test itself is not painful.

HOW IS THE TEST PERFORMED, AND
WHAT SHOULD BE EXPECTED?

Standard bone x-rays include three views: front, side, and angled. A fracture, particularly those smaller fractures referred to as hairline, are easily missed unless multiple projections or pictures are obtained. Although this is a painless procedure, the x-rayed area must be held very still. Movement will blur the picture, which may mean that the x-rays must be repeated. When necessary, lead vests or covers are used to protect other areas of the body from exposure to radiation, particularly the reproductive organs.

HOW ARE RESULTS RECORDED, EVALUATED,
INTERPRETED, AND COMPARED?

The results are fairly straightforward when diagnosing trauma to a bone. Fractures show up on x-rays as lines across the bone. More severe injuries reveal bone fragments. When only the outer layer of the bone is injured, the bone will appear to have a slight thickening, but with no actual break evident. This is often associated with sports injuries. Infection or tumors appear on x-rays as irregular holes, but early stages of bone disease often do not appear on standard x-rays.

HOW RELIABLE IS THE TEST?

In most cases, bone x-rays, especially when taken from multiple angles, are considered highly reliable diagnostic tests. However, breaks in the wrist, elbow, or ribs may not immediately appear as an injury on an x-ray. In these cases, follow-up x-rays are generally ordered a few days after the injury occurred if symptoms still suggest a fracture.

Because of the development of other, more precise imaging procedures, an x-ray would not be considered a reliable diagnostic test for diseases of the bone. However, it is an excellent and inexpensive screening test if a bone disease is suspected.

WHAT FURTHER TESTS MIGHT BE RECOMMENDED?

For trauma to the bone, x-rays are generally sufficient. When bone disease is suspected, a nuclear bone scan is generally considered the most sensitive diagnostic test. CAT scans or MRI scans may also be necessary.

Chest X-Ray

WHAT DOES THE TEST TEST?

In children, a chest x-ray would commonly be ordered to diagnose suspected pneumonia and, occasionally, bronchitis. It may also be done to see if pneumonia is accompanying asthma.

WHAT, IF ANY, PREPARATION IS NECESSARY?

The child's jewelry and above-the-waist clothing must be removed.

HOW IS THE TEST PERFORMED, AND WHAT SHOULD BE EXPECTED?

The child stands with his or her chest positioned against the x-ray machine. Two x-rays are usually done, one taken from back to front (posterior-anterior) and one from the side (lateral). The child will be asked to take a deep breath and hold it while the film is being taken.

HOW RELIABLE IS THE TEST?

Chest x-rays are normally developed and interpreted quickly, and in most cases the results are straightforward.

WHAT DOES THE TEST *NOT* TEST?

A chest x-ray does not diagnose conditions that cause wheezing or difficulty in breathing, such as asthma or allergies.

Computerized Axial Tomography (CAT Scan or CT Scan), Head and Body

WHOSE RECOMMENDATION AND/OR PERMISSION IS NEEDED?

A CAT scan is usually performed and interpreted by a radiologist with the assistance of a specially trained technician. You may be asked to sign a consent form.

WHAT DOES THE TEST TEST?

A CAT scan is a way of viewing tissues inside the body from many angles. It produces cross-sectional images of the part of the body selected for viewing. It is one of the high-tech procedures now used to diagnose myriad health problems, from unexplained headaches and neurological abnormalities to injuries and disease in internal organs and the spine. Note: A CAT scan could be ordered for your child to *rule out* serious problems.

WHAT, IF ANY, PREPARATION IS NECESSARY?

If a contrast material is used, your child *may* need to fast for about four hours before the test and not drink water for about one hour prior to testing. However, this is not standard in all facilities. As the contrast material is injected through a needle placed into a vein, the child may experience a flushed or warm sensation. (A few people do have allergic responses to the contrast materials and this will be monitored.) If oral contrast material is used, the child will be asked to drink a "milkshake" type of liquid. This may cause diarrhea. A hospital gown will be worn for CT scan of the head. No garments are worn when a scan is done of the body. Because it is essential for the child to lie perfectly still, he or she will generally be sedated about thirty minutes prior to the test. For this reason, it is important that the physician ordering the test be knowledgeable about your child's health history and prior adverse reactions to various drugs. Parents may or may not be allowed in the x-ray room. Hospital and clinic policy varies greatly on this.

HOW IS THE TEST PERFORMED, AND WHAT SHOULD BE EXPECTED?

The CT scan is one example of a test in which the equipment and environment may be frightening to the child. However, the test itself is painless.

Head: The child lies on a table and the head is placed in a headrest that is in the middle of a doughnut-shaped ring called the scanner ring. (The ring contains the x-ray tube.) A computer operates the scanner, and the picture taken (a slice) is limited to the exact area chosen. The table moves to reposition the head for each picture ordered. A computer processes, displays, and stores the information picked up by the x-ray beam. Information from many slices are combined to create the desired view. Although the procedure is painless, the child must lie very still during the procedure, which takes about thirty minutes. The machine itself makes buzzing or clicking sounds.

Body: The child will be positioned on the table so that the area being examined is in the middle of the scanner ring. The table will move every few seconds.

HOW ARE RESULTS RECORDED, EVALUATED, INTERPRETED, AND COMPARED?

A structure or organ that is diseased or injured will appear lighter or darker than normal tissue. Tissues and structures may also appear displaced.

HOW RELIABLE IS THE TEST?

Reliability varies with the purpose of the testing and the quality of the pictures obtained. This technology is enormously valuable, but it is not foolproof, and retesting is sometimes needed.

Skull X-Ray

WHOSE RECOMMENDATION AND/OR PERMISSION IS NEEDED?

Physicians generally recommend skull x-rays. They may be performed by an x-ray technician, but a radiologist generally interprets them.

WHAT DOES THE TEST TEST?

A skull x-ray is usually ordered because of a suspected head injury. (Nowadays, depending on the circumstances and the perceived severity of the injury, a CT scan may be the preferred test. See page 94.) X-rays of the sinuses may be ordered to investigate head or facial pain or obstructions. If an infant or young child's skull is unusually shaped, a skull x-ray may be ordered to aid in evaluation.

WHAT, IF ANY, PREPARATION IS NECESSARY?

Parents may be asked to help hold a young child still during the procedure, which in itself is painless. However, the room and the equipment could be intimidating. Pads or bands may be needed to hold the head in various positions.

HOW IS THE TEST PERFORMED, AND WHAT SHOULD BE EXPECTED?

Front, back, and side views are generally taken, and other angles may be needed, depending on the location of the suspected injury. The child will either lie on a table or sit in a chair.

HOW ARE RESULTS RECORDED, EVALUATED, INTERPRETED, AND COMPARED?

Three groups of bones are viewed in a skull x-ray: the vault (calvaria), the jaw (mandible), and the bones in the face. A skull fracture usually appears as a thin, translucent line. Films of the sinuses may reveal signs of infection or obstruction.

DEVELOPMENTAL TESTING

L ong before there was a field of study or scientific discipline known as child development or developmental psychology, mothers and fathers were observing their infants and noting what appeared to be, by their definition, normal or abnormal growth and mastery of certain basic skills. Most parents do not need to be told that during the first year babies should do such things as roll over, sit up alone, make babbling noises, smile, reach and grasp, crawl, and pull themselves up and try to walk. Indeed, they usually show great pleasure over these "milestones," which encourages their babies to proceed in the hard work of development. Parents intuitively know that a baby who cannot, or has no interest in, reaching for a rattle, or responding to familiar voices, or moving from one place to another, may have some type of growth or developmental problem. Most parents also know that if a baby is born prematurely, the developmental timetable assumed to be "normal" or "average" may need to be adjusted.

The field of child development encompasses far more than watching for the appearance of certain basic skills. It is in the developmental arena that many of the theories about heredity versus environment have been debated. The field also gives rise to theorizing about human emotional and social needs and the meaning of maturity.

In the context of testing and observation, child development specialists and psychologists have attempted to alert us to the need for early intervention when a child appears to have growth-related difficulties. The tools these specialists use range from relatively simple screening tests to more sophisticated diagnostic tests. Thus, if a screening tool detects difficulty in language development, a clinician might attempt to determine if the problem is related to receptive rather than expressive language. He might also ask if the child is able to adequately discriminate between sounds. Particular tests have been developed to both qualify and quantify the problem. Is it a minor developmental lag, likely to "work itself out" in time? Or is the difficulty perhaps neurological, one that will improve only with special help?

Developmental testing is also done when there is a known difficulty, one that parents and pediatricians can identify early. Severe retardation, physical handicaps, and visual and hearing impairments may be detected early in infancy. The specialist's role is to quantify the problem, advise, and often implement the course of action considered appropriate for that individual child. A blind child, for example, may need help with motor development because his motivation to move about through an environment may be compromised by the disability.

Developmental testing tends to be less controversial when an obvious impairment exists or special conditions are present, as in the case of prematurity, or a known birth-related brain injury.

Controversies appear when children are labeled, kept out of school, or put in special programs based on the results of certain types of testing. It's important to remember that there are wide differences in the manner and rate individual children develop specific skills—a fact acknowledged by all reputable child development specialists. We also know that numerous factors affect development: nutrition, stimulation, parental attitudes, and the social environment all play a role in the way young children develop various attributes and skills.

We have grouped developmental tests with many speech and language, auditory, and visual perception tests because when a young child is having difficulties, the tests used to diagnose, qualify, and quantify the problem often fall into these categories; similar tests, given to older children, often in a school setting, can be found in the educational testing category.

Developmental testing is also done when young children have behavioral or emotional difficulties. Children who are extremely hard to manage, who are very withdrawn and quiet, who can't tolerate even slight frustration, or who show no desire for social interaction are often evaluated by specialists. Nowadays, the setting for this type of evaluation might be a hospital or university-based clinic; private practitioners also perform evaluations and then make recommendations for treatment. In recent years, there has been an increasing realization that specialists should work as a team. Thus, pediatricians, pediatric nurses, child psychologists, speech/language clinicians, occupational therapists, and audiologists might all be involved in evaluating a young child, each gathering and interpreting information and recommending appropriate help.

Like educational testing, developmental testing is inseparable from public policy and the allocation of funds. Indeed, the debate over continuing Head Start funding is enmeshed with the concepts of "early intervention" and identifying children considered "at risk." Hospital- and university-based clinics also operate on the principle that early developmental delays should be investigated and treated as early as possible to allow each child to develop his or her potential fully, however great or limited it might be. And there is no question that parents who have documented information about their child's special needs have an easier time securing the best possible educational environment when the time comes, whether the child is considered gifted or has identified disabilities.

As with all testing, it is important to remember that no developmental test is perfect and that no one test can reveal all of the information necessary to make diagnostic or treatment decisions. Child development is by no means an exact science. Scores may be less important than the overall impressions of the examiner. For this reason, you are well within your parental rights to question the professionals involved in the testing about their experience and philosophies.

You also have the right to know what a given procedure involves so that you can choose the best time of day for the testing as well as the amount of time involved. A tired, cranky child will not "perform" well on any test. When a problem may be quite subtle, the environment in which the testing is done can be important. The child's rapport with the examiner is also crucial. A rigid or inflexible examiner may not be the best person to work with your child.

In many cases we say that no special preparation is needed for a test. However, your own common sense will dictate what you tell your child about the test activities and how you will schedule them. In most test profiles you will notice that we do not indicate that specific permission is required. However, when testing is administered with preschool-age children, your permission is *always* required. If your child is being regularly evaluated in a hospital-based clinic, you may give general permission for screenings and evaluations on a periodic basis; therefore, your permission would not be required for each procedure every time it is performed. In school settings your permission for periodic testing may be granted when you enroll your child. Therefore, if you object to a test, you must speak up in order to prevent testing from taking place.

Assessment of Children's Language Comprehension (ACLC)

WHOSE RECOMMENDATION AND/OR PERMISSION IS NEEDED?

The test is usually given by a speech/language clinician in a school or clinical setting.

WHAT DOES THE TEST TEST?

The ACLC tests the receptive language skills. (Ages 3 to 7.)

WHAT, IF ANY, PREPARATION IS NECESSARY?

No special preparation is necessary.

HOW IS THE TEST PERFORMED, AND
WHAT SHOULD BE EXPECTED?

The test is given individually and is not timed. It usually takes 15 to 20 minutes to complete. The test is divided into four sections. In part A the child is given a spiral-bound book of drawings. The examiner pronounces a word and the child points to the correct drawing from a group of five pictures. Parts B, C, and D test the child's ability to identify vocabulary words within phrases. The examiner pronounces the phrase and the student points to the correct drawing.

HOW ARE RESULTS RECORDED, EVALUATED,
INTERPRETED, AND COMPARED?

The number of correct responses is totaled and converted to a percentage score.

HOW RELIABLE IS THE TEST?

Interpretation of the test results is easiest in children with significant or obvious language problems. Therefore, it is not considered reliable as a general screening test.

WHAT DOES THE TEST *NOT* TEST?

The test does not test intelligence or motor skills; nor does it make any academic predictions.

WHAT FURTHER TESTS MIGHT BE RECOMMENDED?

Depending on the purpose of the testing, further developmental or mental abilities tests could be recommended.

Auditory Discrimination Test (ADT)

WHOSE RECOMMENDATION AND/OR PERMISSION IS NEEDED?

The ADT is usually given by a special-education teacher or a speech/language clinician.

WHAT DOES THE TEST TEST?

The ADT tests auditory discrimination ability. (Ages 5 to 8.)

WHAT, IF ANY, PREPARATION IS NECESSARY?

No special preparation is necessary.

HOW IS THE TEST PERFORMED, AND WHAT SHOULD BE EXPECTED?

The test is administered individually and is not timed. The examiner pronounces forty pairs of words, one pair at a time. The word pairs differ by only one sound. The child must determine whether the words are the same or different. When the examiner pronounces the words, he or she covers his or her mouth so that the child cannot use visual skills to differentiate word sounds.

HOW ARE RESULTS RECORDED, EVALUATED, INTERPRETED, AND COMPARED?

A rating scale is used to evaluate performance. The scale provides descriptions ranging from "very good development" to "below adequate development" for the child's age.

HOW RELIABLE IS THE TEST?

The ADT is considered quite reliable as long as it is clear that the child understands the directions and the concept of same versus different.

WHAT DOES THE TEST *NOT* TEST?

The test does not measure a child's mental abilities, nor does it predict academic performance.

WHAT FURTHER TESTS MIGHT BE RECOMMENDED?

If a child does poorly, further hearing tests may be suggested. The Auditory Memory Span and Auditory Sequential Memory Span are two possible follow-up tests.

Bayley Scales of Infant Development (The Bayley)

WHOSE RECOMMENDATION AND/OR PERMISSION IS NEEDED?

Pediatricians, psychologists, occupational therapists, and pediatric nurses are among those who might give the Bayley. Parents' permission is needed, and a parent is usually present.

WHAT DOES THE TEST TEST?

The Bayley is designed to assess development of children from 2 months to 2½ years of age. It tests a wide range of components, ranging from gross and fine motor development to verbal communication and memory. The Bayley is used to identify developmental problems and can help identify children who need special services or intervention.

WHAT, IF ANY, PREPARATION IS NECESSARY?

No special preparation is needed.

HOW IS THE TEST PERFORMED, AND
WHAT SHOULD BE EXPECTED?

The test consists of interaction and observation. A parent will most likely hold a baby or sit close to a toddler as the activities are observed. The examiner scores items separately. They include such things as attention span, social responsiveness, sitting alone, reaching and grasping (infants), and problem solving and naming objects (toddlers).

HOW ARE RESULTS RECORDED, EVALUATED,
INTERPRETED, AND COMPARED?

Scores are standardized for fourteen age groups in two areas: mental and psychomotor development.

HOW RELIABLE IS THE TEST?

The test scales were developed by gathering data in a wide variety of settings: hospitals, pediatricians' offices, well-baby clinics, and so on. (Premature infants and babies with known developmental difficulties were not included in the standardizing process.) Reliability is somewhat dependent on what the examiner is looking for and whether the test is being used as a screening tool or is being used to measure progress. The Bayley is useful in providing developmental information about an individual as compared to other babies of the same age. However, it can't be used to predict future development.

WHAT DOES THE TEST NOT TEST?

The Bayley does not diagnose specific medical problems, nor does it predict future abilities or aptitudes.

WHAT FURTHER TESTS MIGHT BE RECOMMENDED?

The Bayley is often given at intervals to track developmental progress. An infant whose development is being tracked may require diagnostic testing in areas where problems are suspected: neurological development, vision, hearing, and so on.

Beery-Buktenica Developmental Test of Visual-Motor Integration (VMI)

WHOSE RECOMMENDATION AND/OR PERMISSION IS NEEDED?

The VMI is usually given by a classroom teacher, special-education teacher, occupational therapist, or psychologist.

WHAT DOES THE TEST TEST?

The VMI tests the visual-motor integration skills. (Ages 2 to 15.)

WHAT, IF ANY, PREPARATION IS NECESSARY?

No special preparation is necessary.

HOW IS THE TEST PERFORMED, AND WHAT SHOULD BE EXPECTED?

The VMI is a pencil-and-paper test; most often administered individually, it may also be given to groups. The child is given a booklet containing twenty-four geometric forms and is instructed to copy the forms. The child is not allowed to erase any drawing or rotate the booklet. While the test is not timed, it usually takes 10 to 15 minutes. Testing continues until three consecutive errors are made.

HOW ARE RESULTS RECORDED, EVALUATED, INTERPRETED, AND COMPARED?

The total number of correct copies are added to determine a raw score. The test can then be assigned age, standard, and percentile scores.

HOW RELIABLE IS THE TEST?

The VMI is considered a reliable screening tool if the child is able to concentrate and handle the test. It is sometimes difficult to determine whether the child's mistakes are due to visual problems or poor motor skills.

WHAT DOES THE TEST *NOT* TEST?

The VMI does not measure intelligence, nor does it predict academic performance.

WHAT FURTHER TESTS MIGHT BE RECOMMENDED?

Other tests of visual-motor perception might be used if a VMI score is low. Tests that diagnose visual or motor skills individually might also be used.

Brigance Inventory of Early Development, Revised

WHOSE RECOMMENDATION AND/OR PERMISSION IS NEEDED?

Pediatricians, nurses, occupational therapists, special-education teachers, and early childhood specialists are the professionals most likely to recommend and administer this test.

WHAT DOES THE TEST TEST?

This inventory measures developmental skills of children from birth through age 7, including gross and fine motor development, speech and language, social interaction, general readiness for school, and basic knowledge.

WHAT, IF ANY, PREPARATION IS NECESSARY?

No special preparation is required.

HOW IS THE TEST PERFORMED, AND WHAT SHOULD BE EXPECTED?

The child is examined individually; some of the assessment is done by observing the child. The inventory may take from 30 to 60 minutes, depending on how many of the eleven sections are used. Verbal or written responses are required for some tasks and the child is asked to point to correct pictorial answers to some questions. Parents are also interviewed to provide information about the child's skills.

HOW ARE RESULTS RECORDED, EVALUATED, INTERPRETED, AND COMPARED?

The child's developmental age is calculated by placing achievement on a developmental scale in each tested area. However, the score is meant to be for individual use only, in that weak areas can be noted and, if necessary, explored further.

HOW RELIABLE IS THE TEST?

Because the Brigance Inventory of Early Development is considered an informal, criterion-referenced test, reliability depends on the skill of the examiner and the quality of overall impressions. The inventory is often used for the purpose of measuring progress in particular areas with children known to be low-functioning. It should not be used by itself to place children in special programs or keep them out of school. It can help identify children who may be "at risk," but is not a diagnostic tool.

WHAT DOES THE TEST *NOT* TEST?

This test does not measure intelligence, nor does it diagnose specific developmental or learning disabilities.

WHAT FURTHER TESTS MIGHT BE RECOMMENDED?

The test can be repeated at intervals to measure progress, or other, more specific developmental tests may be given. For example, a comprehensive language abilities test could be suggested if scores on the Brigance inventory are low.

Bruininks-Oseretsky Test of Motor Proficiency (Bruininks-Oseretsky Test), Complete Battery, Short Form

WHOSE RECOMMENDATION AND/OR PERMISSION IS NEEDED?

The test is usually given by physical- or special-education teachers, or physical or occupational therapists.

WHAT DOES THE TEST TEST?

The Bruininks-Oseretsky tests both gross and fine motor development. (Ages 4 to 14.)

WHAT, IF ANY, PREPARATION IS NECESSARY?

The child must wear athletic or crepe-soled shoes.

HOW IS THE TEST PERFORMED, AND
WHAT SHOULD BE EXPECTED?

The test is given individually and some of the activities are timed. In general, the test takes 45 to 60 minutes and can be done in two sessions. The tasks include—among others—running, balance exercises, sit-ups, push-ups, cutting shapes, and stringing beads. A shorter version of the test, called the short form, takes 15 to 20 minutes and is considered a screening test.

HOW ARE RESULTS RECORDED, EVALUATED,
INTERPRETED, AND COMPARED?

Scores on each item are totaled to obtain subtest composite scores. These can be converted to a percentile, which in turn can be converted to an age equivalent.

HOW RELIABLE IS THE TEST?

Overall, the test is considered reliable. However, scores on individual items may vary between testing and retesting.

WHAT DOES THE TEST *NOT* TEST?

The test measures only motor abilities. It is not an intelligence test, nor does it measure other developmental areas.

WHAT FURTHER TESTS MIGHT BE RECOMMENDED?

Further testing depends on the purpose of the testing. When the short form is used for screening, the complete test can be used to diagnose motor difficulties. Results may be used to plan a therapeutic program.

Clinical Evaluation of Language Functions (CELF)

WHOSE RECOMMENDATION AND/OR PERMISSION IS NEEDED?

The test is usually given by a speech-language clinician, special-education teacher, or psychologist.

WHAT DOES THE TEST TEST?

The test is given to school-age children to test for language disabilities.

WHAT, IF ANY, PREPARATION IS NECESSARY?

No special preparation is necessary.

HOW IS THE TEST PERFORMED, AND WHAT SHOULD BE EXPECTED?

The CELF is a paper-and-pencil test. Some sections are timed; the entire test usually takes about an hour. The child is given a variety of exercises designed to measure language functions such as phonology, syntax, semantics, memory, word finding, and word retrieval.

HOW ARE RESULTS RECORDED, EVALUATED, INTERPRETED, AND COMPARED?

The test is scored on a point system: two points if correct, one point if correct after a second reading of the question or cue, and a score of 0 if answered incorrectly. The total number of points is tabulated and turned into a percentile score. It can also be converted into an age norm and a grade level if desired. Failure on three or more subtests may indicate a potential language disorder, but failure of one subtest is not uncommon among normal children.

HOW RELIABLE IS THE TEST?

The CELF is considered reliable when used as part of a screening process. Individual subtests may be evaluated for a pattern of errors.

WHAT DOES THE TEST *NOT* TEST?

The CELF does not measure intelligence, and the child's scores should be considered along with a variety of other tests.

WHAT FURTHER TESTS MIGHT BE RECOMMENDED?

Other language/speech tests would be included in a comprehensive assessment of a discovered language deficit.

Denver Developmental Screening Test (DDST)

WHOSE RECOMMENDATION AND/OR PERMISSION IS NEEDED?

The test is usually given by special-education teachers, occupational therapists, psychologists, speech/language clinicians, or physicians and nurses.

WHAT DOES THE TEST TEST?

The test measures the social, fine and gross motor, and language skills of children. (Ages 0 to 6.)

WHAT, IF ANY, PREPARATION IS NECESSARY?

No special preparation is necessary.

HOW IS THE TEST PERFORMED, AND WHAT SHOULD BE EXPECTED?

The test is individually administered and is not timed. The child should be relaxed and comfortable during the test, with a parent or a familiar caregiver present. The child performs exercises such as walking, jumping, responding to commands, drawing, and picking up objects. The activities vary, based on the age of the child and the developmental expectations. A parent-completed report is part of the test.

HOW ARE RESULTS RECORDED, EVALUATED, INTERPRETED, AND COMPARED?

The items on the test are scored "pass," "fail," "refusal," and "no opportunity." All items are allowed three trials before being marked as failed. If the child's results are determined to be abnormal, he or she should be retested in three weeks. If the results are still abnormal at that time, the child should be referred to a specialist.

HOW RELIABLE IS THE TEST?

The test has been proven reliable in detecting *potential* problems, but as with all testing of this type, the child's mood or discomfort can affect results. Retesting is very important when results are suspect.

WHAT DOES THE TEST *NOT* TEST?

The test does not measure mental abilities.

WHAT FURTHER TESTS MIGHT BE RECOMMENDED?

If the child does poorly in a retest, a physician should determine what type of further testing is necessary.

Developmental Indicators for the Assessment of Learning, Revised (DIAL-R), AGS Edition

WHOSE RECOMMENDATION AND/OR PERMISSION IS NEEDED?

Because DIAL-R is a screening test, it is generally administered to groups of children, such as those entering kindergarten. A Parent Information Card informs the parents about the test and asks for background information about the child. It also gives parents an opportunity to report any concerns they may have about the child. Parents are encouraged to be present during testing, but this is not required. Teachers and other trained people can give the test.

WHAT DOES THE TEST TEST?

DIAL-R is designed to identify young children (ages 2½ to 5½) in need of further diagnostic assessment. It measures motor, conceptual, and language skills considered important in the early years of school. DIAL-R also includes a checklist with which the examiner can describe social and emotional behavior observed during testing.

WHAT, IF ANY, PREPARATION IS NECESSARY?

Parents should complete the Parent Information Card before or during testing. The examiner should also be told about any special factors—known disabilities, illnesses, or medications the child is taking—prior to the testing.

HOW IS THE TEST PERFORMED, AND WHAT SHOULD BE EXPECTED?

DIAL-R consists of game-like activities that use a variety of materials—blocks, shapes, beanbags, and pictures. The child responds to questions (1) orally, (2) by pointing, and (3) by manipulating materials. The test is administered by a screening team, which individually screens three children at a time. There is a separate "station" for each of the three areas (motor, conceptual, and language), and each child moves from one station to the next until completing the entire battery. Screening for all three areas takes about 20 to 30 minutes.

HOW ARE RESULTS RECORDED, EVALUATED, INTERPRETED, AND COMPARED?

The examiner at each station records the child's responses and scores each one on a scale from 0 to 4. A raw score is determined for each area, and the three scores are added to yield a total score. The individual area scores and the total score can be expressed as percentiles or placed into classifications: "potentially advanced," "okay," or "potential problem." Children who score in the "potential problem" range may be referred for a more thorough, diagnostic evaluation.

If parents are present, they may help interpret or clarify the child's behavior, which may add to the understanding of the child's performance.

HOW RELIABLE IS THE TEST?

DIAL-R is considered reliable for screening purposes only. Placement decisions should not be made on the basis of results.

WHAT DOES THE TEST *NOT* TEST?

DIAL-R does not screen for vision or hearing problems, nor does it measure intelligence.

WHAT FURTHER TESTS MIGHT BE RECOMMENDED?

If a child scores in the "potential problem" range, he or she might be referred for a more thorough evaluation of intelligence, language and motor skills, vision, and hearing.

Developmental Sentence Scoring (DSS)

WHOSE RECOMMENDATION AND/OR PERMISSION IS NEEDED?

The DSS is usually given by a speech/language clinician.

WHAT DOES THE TEST TEST?

The DSS tests a child's grammatical structure ability and can give an estimate of the child's grammatical skills in conversation. (Ages 2 to 7.)

WHAT, IF ANY, PREPARATION IS NECESSARY?

No special preparation is necessary.

HOW IS THE TEST PERFORMED, AND WHAT SHOULD BE EXPECTED?

The clinician provides toys or pictures that he or she thinks will help initiate conversation. The child's conversational skills are then evaluated by the clinician during and after their conversation. (The conversation is generally recorded.)

HOW ARE RESULTS RECORDED, EVALUATED, INTERPRETED, AND COMPARED?

The conversation is evaluated using eight grammatical features considered early components of language. The examiner gives points for correct syntax and semantics used in sentences, as well as points for attempts. The examiner compares the child's scores to the norms for his or her age. The score can also be expressed as a percentile.

HOW RELIABLE IS THE TEST?

When the examiner is skilled and familiar with the complex scoring system, the DSS is a reliable measure of a child's ability to acquire grammar skills over time. It can be given before speech therapy is started; it can also be used to test a child's progress. The score itself might be less meaningful than the particular errors or patterns revealed. The test was designed for use with children who are exposed to standard American English. Dialects can't be measured. The DSS would not be particularly useful with children just learning English. In addition, rapport with the examiner is important, and a shy or frightened child may not be engaged in sufficient conversation to reveal his or her true language abilities.

WHAT DOES THE TEST *NOT* TEST?

The test does not measure intelligence or academic ability, nor does it measure other areas of language development.

WHAT FURTHER TESTS MIGHT BE RECOMMENDED?

Other tests might be used to diagnose specific language deficits. The DSS can also be given multiple times. (A screening test of Spanish grammar, which is similar to the DSS, is available.)

Environmental Language Inventory (ELI)

WHOSE RECOMMENDATION AND/OR PERMISSION IS NEEDED?

The ELI is usually given by a speech/language clinician.

WHAT DOES THE TEST TEST?

The ELI assesses the language skills of children already known to have severe delays in expressive language. The results are often used to design a treatment program. (Ages 2 and up.)

WHAT, IF ANY, PREPARATION IS NECESSARY?

No special preparation is necessary.

HOW IS THE TEST PERFORMED, AND WHAT SHOULD BE EXPECTED?

The test is administered individually. Although it is not timed, it generally takes 30 minutes. The child may be seated on the floor or at a table, with an assortment of objects to play with. The examiner encourages the child to talk while playing and records the child's responses as "intelligible" or "unintelligible." The examiner gives the child pantomime, conversational, and imitation cues to initiate responses. Sometimes parents or teachers bring familiar toys or objects from home or school to use during the test.

HOW ARE RESULTS RECORDED, EVALUATED, INTERPRETED, AND COMPARED?

The examiner records all of the child's responses and calculates the child's ability to use semantic and grammatical rules in speech. The frequencies of unintelligible and intelligible responses are also recorded. The information is then used to plan speech or language therapy. The results can be interpreted informally; that is, no grade or age score is given. Norms have been established for language-delayed and mentally retarded populations.

HOW RELIABLE IS THE TEST?

The test is considered a good way to assess current language skills.

WHAT DOES THE TEST *NOT* TEST?

The ELI does not measure other developmental areas, or other aspects of language development, such as receptive language skills. It does not predict future language skills.

WHAT FURTHER TESTS MIGHT BE RECOMMENDED?

No further tests are recommended, although a child given this test may have numerous developmental problems and may be frequently tested in many areas.

Expressive One-Word Picture Vocabulary Test (EOWPVT)

A spanish edition is available.

WHOSE RECOMMENDATION AND/OR PERMISSION IS NEEDED?

The test is usually given by a speech/language clinician, a special-education teacher, or a psychologist.

WHAT DOES THE TEST TEST?

The EOWPVT tests expressive vocabulary skills. (Ages 2 to 12.)

WHAT, IF ANY, PREPARATION IS NECESSARY?

No special preparation is necessary.

HOW IS THE TEST PERFORMED, AND
WHAT SHOULD BE EXPECTED?

The EOWPVT is individually administered. The child is shown a series of black-and-white drawings and asked to identify the objects. The items are revealed in order of difficulty.

HOW ARE RESULTS RECORDED, EVALUATED,
INTERPRETED, AND COMPARED?

The raw score is determined by the number of pictures the student can name correctly. Raw scores can be changed to mental ages, intelligence quotients, stanines, and percentiles.

HOW RELIABLE IS THE TEST?

The EOWPVT is useful in measuring expressive vocabulary skills. However, cultural backgrounds can affect the score because of the context of the drawings shown. The norms were developed for the English-speaking population. Clinicians may find it useful to analyze the incorrect answers to determine why a child chose a particular answer.

WHAT DOES THE TEST NOT TEST?

The EOWPVT tests only expressive vocabulary; it should not be relied upon for accurate measurement of intellectual functioning.

WHAT FURTHER TESTS MIGHT BE RECOMMENDED?

If scores are low, further language development testing could be recommended; tests that more accurately measure mental abilities could also be suggested.

Marianne Frostig Developmental Test of Visual Perception: "The Frostig" (DTVP)

WHOSE RECOMMENDATION AND/OR PERMISSION IS NEEDED?

Special-education teachers, occupational therapists, or psychologists generally recommend the test.

WHAT DOES THE TEST TEST?

The DTVP evaluates both visual perception and hand-eye coordination in young children. It can also be used for diagnosing learning disabilities in older children. (Ages 3 to 8.)

WHAT, IF ANY, PREPARATION IS NECESSARY?

No special preparation is necessary.

HOW IS THE TEST PERFORMED, AND WHAT SHOULD BE EXPECTED?

The DTVP is a paper-and-pencil test, with tasks given in increasing order of difficulty in five areas of visual perception: eye-motor coordination (drawing continuous straight, curved, or angular shapes), figure-ground (distinguishing embedded figures), constancy of shape (discriminating among common geometric shapes), position in space (distinguishing reversed positions), and spatial relations (joining dots to duplicate forms and patterns).

The test may be given individually or in groups. Instructions for the test are verbal, but adaptations have been developed for the hearing impaired and for non-English-speaking children.

Young children may need more than one testing session to complete the test.

HOW ARE RESULTS RECORDED, EVALUATED, INTERPRETED, AND COMPARED?

Raw scores for each subtest are converted to age scores and scaled scores. The scaled scores on the five subtests are added to obtain a total test score, which is divided by a student's age to arrive at a perceptual quotient. Guidelines are also given for scores considered necessary to enter first grade. Low scores may indicate a need for special help or retesting.

HOW RELIABLE IS THE TEST?

While generally considered a reliable test, the DTVP should not be the only test given to establish visual perception or eye-motor coordination problems, or to retain a child in kindergarten. Other tests should be given for purposes of comparison.

WHAT DOES THE TEST *NOT* TEST?

The DTVP does not definitively establish learning disabilities, nor does a high score rule out problems with language, math, and other subjects. It is not an intelligence or aptitude test.

WHAT FURTHER TESTS MIGHT BE RECOMMENDED?

Depending on the results and the reason for the testing, other visual-motor perception tests could be used. Other developmental tests may be included in a comprehensive assessment.

Goldman-Fristoe Test of Articulation (GFTA)

WHOSE RECOMMENDATION AND/OR PERMISSION IS NEEDED?

Psychologists, pediatricians, early childhood specialists, nurses, classroom or special-education teachers, education diagnosticians, or speech/language clinicians may recommend the test.

WHAT DOES THE TEST TEST?

The GFTA measures articulation of consonant sounds. It is a diagnostic tool used to identify specific speech sounds difficult for the child to produce. (Ages 2 to 16.)

WHAT, IF ANY, PREPARATION IS NECESSARY?

No preparation is needed.

HOW IS THE TEST PERFORMED, AND WHAT SHOULD BE EXPECTED?

The GFTA is given individually and can usually be completed in less than an hour. There are three subtests. The first requires the child to name common objects shown in pictures. The second uses a series of pictures and storytelling techniques to measure spontaneous speech sounds while the child retells a story. The third measures the child's ability to correctly produce a sound that he or she has previously misarticulated. The child is asked to watch, listen, and then mimic the sound the examiner makes

HOW ARE RESULTS RECORDED, EVALUATED, INTERPRETED, AND COMPARED?

The examiner scores the child's response to each item, and records the mispronounced sounds for later analysis. The results can be scored using norms. More important, the test yields diagnostic information by identifying specific speech problems. Test results can then be evaluated in greater detail by using an associated tool, the Khan-Lewis Phonological Analysis, which provides guidelines for planning a treatment program.

HOW RELIABLE IS THE TEST?

This test is considered very accurate in identifying specific errors in forming speech sounds.

WHAT DOES THE TEST *NOT* TEST?

This test does not measure hearing ability, intelligence, or achievement.

WHAT FURTHER TESTS MIGHT BE RECOMMENDED?

When a speech problem has been identified, auditory testing is often recommended.

Goldman-Fristoe-Woodcock Test of Auditory Discrimination (GFW)

WHOSE RECOMMENDATION AND/OR PERMISSION IS NEEDED?

The test is usually recommended and given by a reading specialist, educational diagnostician, psychologist, speech/language clinician, or an audiologist.

WHAT DOES THE TEST TEST?

The GFW tests speech-sound discrimination.

WHAT, IF ANY, PREPARATION IS NECESSARY?

No special preparation is necessary.

HOW IS THE TEST PERFORMED, AND WHAT SHOULD BE EXPECTED?

The test is administered individually, and although it is not timed, it generally takes 20 to 30 minutes to complete. The test is divided into two parts: one with, and one without, background noise. During the first part of the test, the examiner plays a tape of words without background noise and the child points to pictures that represent the words on test charts. During the second part, the child listens to a tape with background noise and points to pictures denoting specific words on the tape.

HOW ARE RESULTS RECORDED, EVALUATED, INTERPRETED, AND COMPARED?

The examiner totals the right answers to determine a raw score. A standard score, based on the child's age, is then derived.

HOW RELIABLE IS THE TEST?

The test is reliable as long as the examiner pays close attention to the details of the answers. The pattern of mistakes may be significant in planning follow-up tests or therapy.

WHAT DOES THE TEST *NOT* TEST?

The GFW does not test intelligence or language comprehension.

WHAT FURTHER TESTS MIGHT BE RECOMMENDED?

Depending on the purpose of the testing, other auditory discrimination tests might be used.

Illinois Test of Psycholinguistic Abilities (ITPA)

WHOSE RECOMMENDATION AND/OR PERMISSION IS NEEDED?

Child development specialists, special education teachers, psychologists, and speech/language clinicians generally recommend this test.

WHAT DOES THE TEST TEST?

ITPA is a diagnostic test that measures a young (ages 4 to 8) child's ability to receive, interpret, and express language. It measures separate functions, such as visual perception and expression, and auditory reception and expression.

WHAT, IF ANY, PREPARATION IS NECESSARY?

No special preparation needed.

HOW IS THE TEST PERFORMED, AND WHAT SHOULD BE EXPECTED?

The child is alone with the examiner and is asked to complete a variety of tasks in the subtests. Each subtest examines one area of development. Some activities involve answering questions with a simple yes or no; others require remembering items in sequence or giving a longer answer. Children with known speech disorders can be given the ITPA because it measures the ability to acquire and use language, but does not measure speech as such. The test takes about an hour.

HOW ARE RESULTS RECORDED, EVALUATED, INTERPRETED, AND COMPARED?

Raw scores are converted to scaled scores, which can then be expressed as psycholinguistic ages (PLAS) for each subtest and the test as a whole. A psycholinguistic quotient (PLQ) may also be computed. A percentile rank can be derived, although this may not be a useful way to report results. Various norms are available, but clinicians often choose to report the results of the test in ways they consider most useful.

HOW RELIABLE IS THE TEST?

The ITPA is helpful in diagnosing problems in many areas; it is valuable because it can be used to assess both normal and severely handicapped children. Individual practitioners vary widely in their opinions of the usefulness of the ITPA, and it would appear wise to question test results very carefully. Some clinicians choose particular subtests that they find valuable; it is not considered necessary to use all of the subtests.

Placement decisions should not be made on the basis of the test, nor should children whose primary language is not English be scored using the norms (developed among English-speaking children only). A child should not be labeled learning disabled on the basis of ITPA scores.

WHAT DOES THE TEST NOT TEST?

The ITPA does not measure speech or hearing, intelligence, or achievement.

WHAT FURTHER TESTS MIGHT BE RECOMMENDED?

Raw scores on particular subtests may indicate a need for further evaluation. In some cases learning disabilities may be *suggested*, but other diagnostic tests are needed to explore the specific areas in question.

Lindamood Auditory Conceptualization Test (LAC)

WHOSE RECOMMENDATION AND/OR PERMISSION IS NEEDED?

The test is usually given by a special-education teacher, speech and language clinician, or a remedial reading teacher. Others, such as teachers' aides, can be trained to give the test.

WHAT DOES THE TEST TEST?

The LAC tests auditory discrimination and perception skills. (Preschool to adult.)

WHAT, IF ANY, PREPARATION IS NECESSARY?

No special preparation is necessary, but the testing room must be free of intrusive sounds.

HOW IS THE TEST PERFORMED, AND WHAT SHOULD BE EXPECTED?

The test is administered individually; it usually takes 10 to 15 minutes, but is not timed. The test is divided into four sections and begins with sample items, to make sure that the child can understand the concepts used in the test (same/different, numbers up to four, left/right, and first/last). The child is then asked to perform a variety of tasks: identifying sounds, determining whether sounds are the same or different, sound order, and the number of sounds in a syllable. The child uses colored blocks to demonstrate his or her understanding of the sounds and patterns.

HOW ARE RESULTS RECORDED, EVALUATED, INTERPRETED, AND COMPARED?

A raw score based on points given for correct identification can be converted to grade level if desired.

HOW RELIABLE IS THE TEST?

The test is considered a good device to evaluate auditory perception skills and to identify possible difficulties. However, the test requires precise verbal explanations and scoring, and the interpretation is complex. The grade-level score is not considered particularly useful. The specific errors should be analyzed if the score is low.

WHAT DOES THE TEST NOT TEST?

The LAC does not test intelligence, nor does it predict academic achievement.

WHAT FURTHER TESTS MIGHT BE RECOMMENDED?

Other auditory discrimination tests may be recommended to confirm results. A parallel form of the LAC can be used to measure progress.

McCarthy Scales of Children's Abilities (McCarthy Scales)

WHOSE RECOMMENDATION AND/OR PERMISSION IS NEEDED?

The McCarthy scales are generally recommended and given by psychologists and special-education teachers.

WHAT DOES THE TEST TEST?

The McCarthy scales are designed to assess intellectual functioning of young children. Some of the eighteen subtests are particularly useful in assessing children with suspected learning disabilities. A gross motor skills scale is also included. (Ages 2½ to 8½.)

WHAT, IF ANY, PREPARATION IS NECESSARY?

No special preparation is needed.

HOW IS THE TEST PERFORMED, AND WHAT SHOULD BE EXPECTED?

If the entire test is given, the child is alone with the examiner for about one hour. The activities are varied and include manipulation of objects, copying designs, recalling numbers in sequence, defining words, using quantitative concepts, and hopping and walking, among others. The exercises are arranged to keep a child interested in the activities, which will resemble a series of short games to the preschooler. In some subtests, a child is given more than one opportunity to complete a task.

HOW ARE RESULTS RECORDED, EVALUATED, INTERPRETED, AND COMPARED?

The raw scores on the subtests are converted to a cognitive index (IQ). This can also be expressed as a mental age score.

HOW RELIABLE IS THE TEST?

The McCarthy scales are widely used in a variety of settings and are considered valuable in assessing young children and certifying the need for special instruction. Some professionals consider this tool more useful for assessing preschoolers than older children. The examiner's impressions may be as important as the score in determining which developmental areas need further evaluation or what type of intervention is needed. Placement decisions should not be made solely on the results of this test.

WHAT DOES THE TEST *NOT* TEST?

The McCarthy scales do not measure social skills or abstract problem-solving skills.

WHAT FURTHER TESTS MIGHT BE RECOMMENDED?

Depending on the purpose of the testing, other measures of mental abilities could be recommended. Tests that measure language skills might also follow.

Merrill-Palmer Scale of Mental Tests

WHOSE RECOMMENDATION AND/OR PERMISSION IS NEEDED?

Pediatricians, psychologists, and others involved in early childhood development may recommend this test.

WHAT DOES THE TEST TEST?

The Merrill-Palmer scale evaluates fine motor coordination, spatial discrimination, the ability to manipulate materials, and memory for words and word groups. (Ages 2 to 6.)

WHAT, IF ANY, PREPARATION IS NECESSARY?

No preparation is needed.

HOW IS THE TEST PERFORMED, AND WHAT SHOULD BE EXPECTED?

The Merrill-Palmer Scale of Mental Tests includes thirty-eight separate tests. The scale is a nonverbal test and can be adapted for use with deaf children and those with other disabilities. Many items require no verbal response, and whereas some items are timed, administration is flexible enough so that when needed the test can be given with breaks and without strict time limits.

HOW ARE RESULTS RECORDED, EVALUATED, INTERPRETED, AND COMPARED?

Some subtests are graded on a pass-fail basis, some on a partial credit basis. Scores are reported in mental age (MA) or as a percentile rank.

HOW RELIABLE IS THE TEST?

As with any developmental test, the scored result of the Merrill-Palmer must be weighed against what is already known about the child. Suspected or known disabilities can be confirmed and evaluated with the Merrill-Palmer scale.

WHAT DOES THE TEST NOT TEST?

The test does not measure intelligence or aptitude, nor can it diagnose emotional problems.

WHAT FURTHER TESTS MIGHT BE RECOMMENDED?

The Merrill-Palmer scale might be repeated at intervals to track progress. Depending on test results, tests to diagnose specific problems could be recommended.

Miller Assessment for Preschoolers (MAP)

WHOSE RECOMMENDATION AND/OR PERMISSION IS NEEDED?

The MAP is usually given by classroom teachers, speech/language clinicians, or mental health professionals.

WHAT DOES THE TEST TEST?

The test is used to screen preschool children for any problems that may affect early learning. The MAP can pinpoint the weaknesses and the strengths of a child's development.

WHAT, IF ANY, PREPARATION IS NECESSARY?

No special preparation is needed.

HOW IS THE TEST PERFORMED, AND WHAT SHOULD BE EXPECTED?

The MAP is given individually. The test features twenty-seven items, falling into five scoring groups and three classifications: sensory and motor abilities, cognitive abilities, and combined abilities. The child is asked to draw pictures, and to perform memory and writing exercises. Parts of the test are verbal.

HOW ARE RESULTS RECORDED, EVALUATED, INTERPRETED, AND COMPARED?

The MAP has three scoring procedures. The child's performance is recorded on the item score sheet chosen for his or her age. Once the raw score on each item is recorded, the child's performance is compared with established norms. A percentile score is derived for the total test. The examiner also rates nine behavioral areas. Although the examiner's observations don't affect the child's score, they can be used to determine areas in which the child may have difficulty.

HOW RELIABLE IS THE TEST?

The MAP is a useful screening tool, but it is a relatively new test and overall statistical reliability has not yet been established. Therefore, placement and other educational decisions should not be made on the basis of MAP scores.

WHAT DOES THE TEST *NOT* TEST?

Although the MAP may be used to report mental age and IQ, it is not a comprehensive test and results can't be considered conclusive. It is basically a screening tool.

WHAT FURTHER TESTS MIGHT BE RECOMMENDED?

Depending on the setting, other tests could be done to explore areas that showed weakness.

Minnesota Infant Development Inventory (MIDI)

WHOSE RECOMMENDATION AND/OR PERMISSION IS NEEDED?

Pediatricians, occupational therapists, or other professionals working in a pediatric setting generally recommend and interpret the MIDI. It is a parent-report questionnaire, although another caregiver can complete it.

WHAT DOES THE TEST TEST?

The MIDI measures gross and fine motor skills, language comprehension, and social development during the first fifteen months.

WHAT, IF ANY, PREPARATION IS NECESSARY?

A seventh-grade reading level is required to complete the MIDI. If needed, the test questions can be read to the parent and an examiner can record the answers.

HOW IS THE TEST PERFORMED, AND WHAT SHOULD BE EXPECTED?

Items relating to developmental milestones are presented in a booklet. A parent responds with yes or no answers to each item. The parent is also asked to describe any problems or concerns.

HOW ARE RESULTS RECORDED, EVALUATED, INTERPRETED, AND COMPARED?

A developmental profile is provided based on age norms. Because the MIDI is a screening tool, apparent developmental delays would be further investigated.

HOW RELIABLE IS THE TEST?

The MIDI is useful in establishing that an infant is developing normally; results can alert parents and pediatricians that a problem might exist. The test should not be used to diagnose specific developmental lags.

WHAT DOES THE TEST *NOT* TEST?

The MIDI does not predict future development, nor does it measure mental abilities.

WHAT FURTHER TESTS MIGHT BE RECOMMENDED?

Pediatricians might recommend a more thorough developmental assessment if a problem is suspected. The same test developer has a similar inventory for young children ages 15 months to 3 years, the Early Child Development Inventory (ECDI).

Motor-Free Visual Perception Test (MVPT)

WHOSE RECOMMENDATION AND/OR PERMISSION IS NEEDED?

The MVPT is usually given by a teacher or occupational therapist. Parents' permission may or may not be required, depending on the setting.

WHAT DOES THE TEST TEST?

The MVPT tests a child's visual perception and processing ability. (Ages 4 to 9.)

WHAT, IF ANY, PREPARATION IS NECESSARY?

No special preparation is needed.

HOW IS THE TEST PERFORMED, AND WHAT SHOULD BE EXPECTED?

The test is divided into five sections. The child will be asked to do such things as identify and compare shapes, and to choose from memory a drawing previously shown in a group of sample drawings. A number of exercises having to do with shape/drawing identification and memory are included. The test is not timed, but it generally takes 10 to 15 minutes.

HOW ARE RESULTS RECORDED, EVALUATED, INTERPRETED, AND COMPARED?

The examiner adds the number of correct responses on the test to determine a raw score, which is then translated into an age equivalent, perceptual quotient, and then a standard score. One score for all of the categories is calculated; however, the individual scores should be investigated to obtain more in-depth information, which may prove more meaningful than the other derived scores.

HOW RELIABLE IS THE TEST?

The MVPT has proven to be a useful diagnostic tool when used as part of a group of tests that measure other aspects of co-ordination. The test tends to be more reliable in the higher end of the age range. Children with language difficulties or a limited command of English may have difficulty understanding directions, making the results difficult to interpret.

WHAT DOES THE TEST NOT TEST?

The MVPT does not test intelligence or the child's learning potential.

WHAT FURTHER TESTS MIGHT BE RECOMMENDED?

Whether further testing is recommended depends on the reason for the testing in the first place. Other developmental tests could be used to confirm results of the MVPT.

Multilevel Informal Language Inventory (MILI)

WHOSE RECOMMENDATION AND/OR PERMISSION IS NEEDED?

The MILI is usually given by a speech/language clinician.

WHAT DOES THE TEST TEST?

The MILI tests the student's expressive language skills. It is designed to measure syntactic development. (Preschool to grade 7.)

WHAT, IF ANY, PREPARATION IS NECESSARY?

No special preparation is needed.

HOW IS THE TEST PERFORMED, AND
WHAT SHOULD BE EXPECTED?

The test is divided into three sections: Survey Scenes, Survey Stories, and Specific Probes. The child is asked to describe pictures and set up situations and scenes, and from memory to repeat stories that the examiner has told.

HOW ARE RESULTS RECORDED, EVALUATED,
INTERPRETED, AND COMPARED?

The student's semantic and syntactic competence is viewed along a continuum, with categories labeled "absent," "emerging," and "mastered."

HOW RELIABLE IS THE TEST?

The MILI is a valuable tool to measure progress in speech therapy. It can also be used to help design a therapy program. However, children with multiple impairments may find portions of the MILI overwhelming.

WHAT DOES THE TEST NOT TEST?

The MILI does not measure any other mental abilities. It is valuable only as a language measurement tool.

WHAT FURTHER TESTS MIGHT BE RECOMMENDED?

Other language tests might be given, and, depending on the purpose of the testing, specific developmental difficulties examined.

Peabody Picture Vocabulary Test, Revised (PPVT-R)

A Spanish edition is available.

WHOSE RECOMMENDATION AND/OR PERMISSION IS NEEDED?

The test is usually given by a psychologist, special-education teacher, or a speech/language clinician. Parents' permission is generally required.

WHAT DOES THE TEST TEST?

The PPVT-R tests a child's receptive single-word vocabulary. Various forms of the test are suitable for children ages 2½ and up.

WHAT, IF ANY, PREPARATION IS NECESSARY?

No special preparation is necessary.

HOW IS THE TEST PERFORMED, AND WHAT SHOULD BE EXPECTED?

The child will be given a book of drawings. The examiner will pronounce a word appropriate for the child's age group and the child will point to the picture corresponding to the word. No writing or reading is required. The test usually takes 10 to 20 minutes, but is not timed. The child can also give the number of the picture as the answer; therefore, physically handicapped children can be given the test.

HOW ARE RESULTS RECORDED, EVALUATED, INTERPRETED, AND COMPARED?

Items are scored as correct or incorrect, and the total score can be converted to age equivalents, standard scores, percentiles, and stanines.

HOW RELIABLE IS THE TEST?

The test is considered a good measure of a child's general vocabulary; analysis of the student's errors can reveal information about the specific nature of a vocabulary deficit. The child's attention span is important when taking the test, and a low score may be caused by the inability to scan the visual material. The cultural background of a child may affect the test in that incorrect responses to questions may result from inexperience with the test items, rather than a developmental language deficit.

WHAT DOES THE TEST *NOT* TEST?

The PPVT-R is not an intelligence test, nor does it predict a child's ability to learn. It can only pinpoint certain problems a child may be having.

WHAT FURTHER TESTS MIGHT BE RECOMMENDED?

Other language tests could be used, or, depending on the reason for the testing, tests designed to measure general mental abilities or specific developmental areas. The PPVT-R could be given at intervals to assess progress.

Preschool Development Inventory (PDI)

WHOSE RECOMMENDATION AND/OR
PERMISSION IS NEEDED?

Pediatricians or early childhood education specialists generally recommend and interpret the PDI. It is a parent-report questionnaire, although another caregiver could complete it.

WHAT DOES THE TEST TEST?

The PDI is a screening tool that assesses four developmental areas: motor, language, self-help, and social behaviors. (Ages 3 to 5.)

WHAT, IF ANY, PREPARATION IS NECESSARY?

A seventh-grade reading level is required to complete the PDI. If necessary, the test questions can be read to the parent, with the examiner recording responses.

HOW IS THE TEST PERFORMED, AND WHAT SHOULD BE EXPECTED?

Various behaviors and skills are listed in a booklet, and the parent responds with a yes or no answer to each item. The items deal with basic skills and abilities usually acquired in this age group, such as getting dressed alone, conversational speech, and sharing humor. There is also space provided for a parent to express concerns or ask questions.

HOW ARE RESULTS RECORDED, EVALUATED, INTERPRETED, AND COMPARED?

Scores are based on age norms. However, the results are expressed in terms of "no apparent problem," "possible problem," and "possible major problem," the latter indicating that a serious developmental or behavioral difficulty may be present.

HOW RELIABLE IS THE TEST?

The PDI is considered a reliable screening tool. Generally speaking, an area in which a low score is obtained should be investigated. However, placement decisions should not be made based upon the results of the PDI.

WHAT DOES THE TEST *NOT* TEST?

The PDI does not measure intelligence, nor does it predict future development or school performance.

WHAT FURTHER TESTS MIGHT BE RECOMMENDED?

Depending on the purpose and the setting of the testing, screening tools for vision and hearing could also be given.

Sequenced Inventory of Communication Development (SICD)

WHOSE RECOMMENDATION AND/OR PERMISSION IS NEEDED?

The test is usually given by a speech/language clinician or a special-education teacher.

WHAT DOES THE TEST TEST?

The SICD tests the receptive and expressive communication skills in very young children. (Ages 4 months to 4 years.)

WHAT, IF ANY, PREPARATION IS NECESSARY?

No special preparation is necessary.

HOW IS THE TEST PERFORMED, AND WHAT SHOULD BE EXPECTED?

The test is given individually, and although it is not timed, it usually takes 30 to 75 minutes. Awareness, discrimination, and understanding skills are evaluated. The child's responses to sounds, words, and commands are recorded. Age-based, the exercises have a wide range in difficulty. For example, a three-year-old will most likely be able to name and point to objects, whereas the eight-month-old will be watched for response to a stimulus, such as a shaking rattle. A variety of responses are evaluated, including those involving motor skills.

HOW ARE RESULTS RECORDED, EVALUATED, INTERPRETED, AND COMPARED?

The examiner documents the child's responses to motor or sound clues and compares them with age scales.

HOW RELIABLE IS THE TEST?

A good performance on the SICD is a sign that the child is progressing normally, but a poor performance doesn't mean that the child is not progressing. Lower scores are less reliable.

WHAT DOES THE TEST *NOT* TEST?

The test does not measure the intelligence or the exact motor age of a child. It is a way to obtain a basic idea of a child's functioning, not a measure of exact skill.

WHAT FURTHER TESTS MIGHT BE RECOMMENDED?

If test results are poor, the test can be taken again to determine if a poor performance is a result of, say, the child's mood on a particular day, or of a particular problem.

Slosson Articulation Language Test with Phonology (SALT-P)

WHOSE RECOMMENDATION AND/OR PERMISSION IS NEEDED?

Speech/language clinicians and special-education teachers generally recommend this test.

WHAT DOES THE TEST TEST?

The SALT-P tests articulation, phonology, and language. (Ages 3 to 5 years 11 months.)

WHAT, IF ANY, PREPARATION IS NECESSARY?

No preparation is needed.

HOW IS THE TEST PERFORMED, AND WHAT SHOULD BE EXPECTED?

The child is asked to respond to stimulus pictures, thereby giving the examiner the "raw material" on which to score him or her in a number of areas having to do with oral language development. (There is a quick prescreen segment to establish a general range before the longer screening continues.)

HOW ARE RESULTS RECORDED, EVALUATED, INTERPRETED, AND COMPARED?

Areas screened for are given a pass or fail score. The score is normed by age.

HOW RELIABLE IS THE TEST?

The test is a quick way to determine if a child has deficiencies in particular language areas; for example, the ability to make certain speech sounds correctly or use proper word endings. It does not give a diagnostic label to a problem.

WHAT DOES THE TEST *NOT* TEST?

The SALT-P does not measure vocabulary, nor does it predict future language acquisition.

WHAT FURTHER TESTS MIGHT BE RECOMMENDED?

Diagnostic tests in specific language areas might be recommended if the screening indicates developmental lags.

Southern California Sensory Integration Tests (SCSIT)

WHOSE RECOMMENDATION AND/OR PERMISSION IS NEEDED?

The test is usually given by an occupational or physical therapist.

WHAT DOES THE TEST TEST?

The SCSIT tests the sensory integrative functioning of children 4 to 9 years old, including visual, tactile, and kinesthetic skills; right/left discrimination; motor planning; and coordination of gross and fine motor skills, among others.

WHAT, IF ANY, PREPARATION IS NECESSARY?

No special preparation is necessary.

HOW IS THE TEST PERFORMED, AND
WHAT SHOULD BE EXPECTED?

The child will be asked to perform a variety of tasks designed to provide information on various aspects of motor functioning. The SCSIT is administered individually. Parts of the test are timed; it usually takes 1½ hours to complete. Some clinicians recommend two 45-minute sessions.

HOW ARE RESULTS RECORDED, EVALUATED,
INTERPRETED, AND COMPARED?

The child is given points for performing each exercise correctly. The point totals are compared to age, gender, and physical-size groups and then standardized.

HOW RELIABLE IS THE TEST?

The SCSIT is complex to administer and requires a highly trained examiner. The results are also considered difficult to interpret correctly. Therefore, poor scores should be confirmed with another test of this type.

WHAT DOES THE TEST *NOT* TEST?

The SCSIT does not measure any aspect of intellectual capability.

WHAT FURTHER TESTS MIGHT BE RECOMMENDED?

Sensory integration therapy may be recommended after additional motor skill testing is done.

System to Plan Early Childhood Services (SPECS)

WHOSE RECOMMENDATION AND/OR PERMISSION IS NEEDED?

SPECS is used when a young child is referred to an early childhood program for appraisal. Such a referral can be done by a preschool teacher, pediatrician, or other school or health professional. The appraisal itself is typically done by a team of professionals, which could include a teacher, speech/language therapist, psychologist, social worker, pediatrician, and others. The parents are part of the team.

WHAT DOES THE TEST TEST?

The SPECS system is not a test in the traditional sense. Rather, it is a system that early childhood teams use to make decisions about a child's level of functioning and his or her need for services. SPECS is typically used with children ages 2 to 6 who may require early intervention or special-education services.

WHAT, IF ANY, PREPARATION IS NECESSARY?

No specific preparation is required. The parent may be asked to attend evaluation team meetings and participate in rating the child's functioning and making decisions about the child's needs.

HOW IS THE TEST PERFORMED, AND WHAT SHOULD BE EXPECTED?

The team uses the first SPECS component (called Developmental Specs) to rate the child's development individually. Then, working as a group, the team uses the second SPECS component (called Team Specs) to reach a consensus about the child's functioning and needs. Finally, the team uses the third SPECS component (called Program Specs) to identify the necessary components of a plan to address the child's specific needs.

HOW ARE RESULTS RECORDED, EVALUATED, INTERPRETED, AND COMPARED?

Each team member (including the parent) uses the Developmental Specs to rate the child's functioning in nineteen different areas on a 5-point scale (1 = severe problem, 5 = typical functioning). The nineteen areas range from hearing and vision to attention, self-control, self-esteem, and motivation.

For the other two SPECS components, all results are the product of discussion and negotiation of differences that reach a consensus.

HOW RELIABLE IS THE TEST?

SPECS is a decision-making system, not a test. However, the rating scales used in the Developmental Specs are a form of assessment. The team approach also helps establish a plan in which mistakes in testing can be caught early.

WHAT DOES THE TEST *NOT* TEST?

SPECS is not designed to measure achievement, nor does it provide norm-referenced scores on mental abilities.

WHAT FURTHER TESTS MIGHT BE RECOMMENDED?

SPECS can be used with a wide variety of tests in the early childhood field; it provides a framework for school and health professionals to discuss their individual findings and make decisions about a child's needs. Typically, before SPECS is used, each professional on the team has appraised the child's functioning using a test or method appropriate to that person's area of expertise. After the SPECS process is completed, the child may also be referred for further diagnostic testing in specific areas, if the team so decides.

Test for Auditory Comprehension of Language (TACL)

A Spanish edition is available.

WHOSE RECOMMENDATION AND/OR PERMISSION IS NEEDED?

The test is usually given by a speech/language clinician.

WHAT DOES THE TEST TEST?

The TACL tests auditory comprehension of syntax grammar and morphology in both English- *and* Spanish-speaking children. (Ages 3 to 7.)

WHAT, IF ANY, PREPARATION IS NECESSARY?

No special preparation is necessary.

HOW IS THE TEST PERFORMED, AND WHAT SHOULD BE EXPECTED?

The child is shown a series of 101 black-and-white drawings (three to a page). The examiner makes a statement about one of the drawings on each page. The child is then asked to point to the drawing representing the statement given. No oral response is necessary. The test is not timed, but usually takes 20 to 30 minutes. A screening version of the TACL is also available; it includes twenty-five items from the longer version. Depending on the score on the screening, the complete test could be given.

HOW ARE RESULTS RECORDED, EVALUATED, INTERPRETED, AND COMPARED?

Responses are recorded on a form that includes information about norms established for each item. Raw scores are converted to age-equivalent scores and percentiles.

HOW RELIABLE IS THE TEST?

The test is considered relatively useful when given to English-speaking students; because norms are not given for the Spanish version, it has little diagnostic value.

WHAT DOES THE TEST NOT TEST?

The test does not test intelligence, nor does it predict a child's academic potential.

WHAT FURTHER TESTS MIGHT BE RECOMMENDED?

Other diagnostic language tests might be given, depending on the results and the reason for the testing.

Test of Language Development, 2 (TOLD-2), Primary and Intermediate Editions

WHOSE RECOMMENDATION AND/OR PERMISSION IS NEEDED?

Special-education and classroom teachers and speech/language clinicians generally recommend this test.

WHAT DOES THE TEST TEST?

The TOLD tests both receptive and expressive language skills. (Ages 4 to 19.)

WHAT, IF ANY, PREPARATION IS NECESSARY?

No special preparation is necessary.

HOW IS THE TEST PERFORMED, AND WHAT SHOULD BE EXPECTED?

The test is individually administered and is not timed. The child is asked to perform a variety of exercises such as defining words, pronunciation, word/picture identification, and sentence imitation.

HOW ARE RESULTS RECORDED, INTERPRETED, EVALUATED, AND COMPARED?

The raw score is converted to a language age score, a percentile, and a standard score.

HOW RELIABLE IS THE TEST?

The TOLD should be viewed as a screening device only, used for quick assessment of basic language skills.

WHAT DOES THE TEST *NOT* TEST?

The test does not measure intelligence or make any academic predictions.

WHAT FURTHER TESTS MIGHT BE RECOMMENDED?

If a child does poorly on the TOLD, further language tests will be necessary to determine more precisely what, if any, language deficiencies exist and to what degree.

Token Test for Children (Token Test)

WHOSE RECOMMENDATION AND/OR
PERMISSION IS NEEDED?

The test is usually given by a speech/language clinician.

WHAT DOES THE TEST TEST?

The Token Test measures receptive language skills and auditory comprehension. Clinicians can also form impressions about a child's ability to listen to directions and carry out a sequence of tasks. (Ages 3 to 12½.)

WHAT, IF ANY, PREPARATION IS NECESSARY?

No special preparation is necessary.

HOW IS THE TEST PERFORMED, AND
WHAT SHOULD BE EXPECTED?

The test is administered individually, and although it is not timed, it usually takes 15 minutes. The examiner spreads twenty tokens out in front of the child. They are in two shapes (circle and square), two sizes (large and small), and five colors (yellow, red, blue, green, and white). The examiner first determines that the child understands the meanings of the words *square, circle, large,* and *small.* (If the child doesn't understand these concepts, the testing is stopped.) The child is given commands involving the tokens; each command is given only once. The child may be asked to point to, arrange, or touch tokens of various shapes and colors. The entire test must be given to obtain a score. The commands become increasingly complex as the test progresses, and the number of items needed for a complete test varies with the age of the child.

HOW ARE RESULTS RECORDED, EVALUATED, INTERPRETED, AND COMPARED?

Correct responses are totaled and the raw score is converted to scores scaled for grade and age. The scores can be divided into "average," "superior," and "inferior." Children with low scores should be tested further.

HOW RELIABLE IS THE TEST?

The test is a quick measure of basic skills, but it should be noted that severely language- or hearing-impaired children may have difficulty understanding the commands, which could lead to a sense of failure before the test is even scored. The test is sensitive enough to pick up *mild* auditory comprehension deficits.

WHAT DOES THE TEST *NOT* TEST?

This test is not an intelligence test and doesn't predict future academic performance.

WHAT FURTHER TESTS MIGHT BE RECOMMENDED?

Further tests might be recommended to examine areas in which scores were low.

SUPPLEMENTAL TESTS

The following are some additional widely used tests you might encounter in numerous settings. The test formats and the domains being tested are similar to those listed previously. However, it should not be considered inclusive, as it is impossible to list all of the hundreds of developmental tests.

Brazelton Neonatal Behavioral Assessment Scale. A detailed assessment procedure for infants up to about one month, to assess early neurological responsiveness and motor control.

Houston Test for Language Development. A test that measures verbal and nonverbal communication skills in children up to 6 years old. (An infant scale is used with children up to age 2.)

Marin Developmental Ability Test for the Blind. A test that evaluates development and general mental abilities of blind children ages 2 to 10. Examiners are generally pediatricians or professionals trained to work with blind children.

Minnesota Child Development Inventory (MCDI). A parent-completed inventory used to assess development of children ages 1 to 6.

Receptive One-Word Picture Vocabulary Test (ROWPVT). A test that assesses vocabulary skills of children ages 2 to 12 through matching an object or concept with its name.

Reynell Developmental Language Scales (RDLS). A test that assesses verbal comprehension and expressive language and the nature and extent of a child's speech and language difficulties. This test can be used with even severely handicapped, distractible children and those who are withdrawn.

Screening Kit of Language Development (SKOLD). A screening test designed to identify language disorders or delays early. It assesses vocabulary, comprehension, story completion, and the like.

Smith-Johnson Nonverbal Performance Scale. A nonverbal developmental assessment of children ages 2 to 4. Often used with children who are known to be hearing impaired or to have developmental problems.

Test of Oral Structures and Functions (TOSF). A test that assesses oral structures and functions, and both verbal and nonverbal oral functioning.

Utah Test of Language Development. A tool that identifies children and teenagers (ages 2 to 14) with language disabilities that may affect academic performance.

Wepman Auditory Memory Span Test (AMST). A test that assesses the ability to retain and recall familiar spoken words. Ages 5 to 8.

Wepman Auditory Sequential Memory Test (ASMT). A test that assesses immediate memory (short-term) ability to determine if a particular type of learning disability will interfere with learning such things as math and spelling. Ages 5 to 8.

Wepman Visual Memory Test (VMT). A test that assesses the ability to recall previously unfamiliar forms. Ages 5 to 8.

EDUCATIONAL TESTING

Educational testing has been a fact of life for centuries, and standardized national achievement tests have been common in many countries for decades. However, the way tests are used has changed considerably in recent years. Today, the results of a school district's tests are often published in newspapers, discussed on television and radio programs, and are even used by real estate agents to sell houses: "The test scores in this community's school are above the national average."

For the individual child, testing has taken on new importance, too. While certainly not a nationwide trend, there are communities in this country where it is common for young children to be given the equivalent of entrance exams to enter private preschools. Results of "readiness" testing may determine if a child may enter kindergarten or is ready for the academic demands of first grade. From that point on, children are regularly tested to measure individual progress, sensory development, school achievement relative to other schools, and to gauge national progress.

Test scores are viewed by many as a way of judging how well teachers and administrators are doing their jobs. Accountability has literally become a "tax-payers' issue." In fact, much of the mandated testing many states have adopted exists because of the demand for accountability. (Many of the tests listed in this section are used for school district, state, and national comparison.)

In the early 1990s, the debate over a national test has become increasingly intense—and loud. In fact, both proponents and critics of testing are using public forums to make their positions clear. Many governmental bodies are involved, from Congress to your local school board. If I had a child in school today, I'd pay close attention to this debate and try to determine how new policies and public mandates would affect my child.

Critics of this extensive testing environment often say that teachers are forced to "teach for the test," rather than attempting more individualized instruction. A fourth-grade teacher recently told me that she is "supposed" to be teaching long division to her students, but she discovered that, as a group, their multiplication skills were weak. She has chosen to concentrate on strengthening that skill, knowing that when the yearly standardized tests are given in the spring, her students will appear to be behind. She threw up her hands and declared, "They'll have an easier time learning long division when the time comes, but for now, *I'll* look bad on *their* tests."

As a parent, you may wonder what happens to individual children in this setting. What about the child who is a real math whiz and is probably way ahead of his or her peers? And what happens to the child who has great difficulty with math and may not yet be ready for multiplication? Depending on the school and its policies, a variety of things could take place—the first being nothing. Some classroom teachers still do the best they can to challenge the quick students and to help the slower ones. In other schools, some students are sent to special labs for accelerated learning or remedial tutoring. In others, the quicker students help the slower in programs called peer tutoring. Many schools provide teacher aides or student teachers to work with special groups.

I use math as only one example. The same options generally apply to reading, but could also describe variations in the teaching of writing skills, the sciences, or social studies. Policies and resources vary widely throughout the country.

Educational testing is also used to measure a child's progress in basic skill areas, without comparing his or her skill level with others (criterion-referenced testing). Individual test scores can be useful when determining if remedial programs or tutoring are helping a child. These scores may also be used when a team of education specialists are deciding if extensive testing is needed to diagnose learning disabilities or psychological difficulties interfering with school functions.

Because of the controversies surrounding educational testing, your child's school may be using, or planning to use, more criterion-referenced testing. This means that your child's grasp of actual material taught will be measured, allowing for an individualized look at strengths and weaknesses. Many districts and states are exploring this approach, which also relies less on a global judgment about what a child should know at a particular age or grade.

Assessment is an important concept in current education practice. It is often in the school setting that actual, suspected, or potential problems are first noticed. Your child's classroom teacher may be the first person to notice difficulties. The suspected or identified problem—academic, behavioral, physical, or other—determines the areas considered in assessment. In some cases a team of professionals is involved, each contributing information from his or her area of expertise. Decisions to place a child in full-time special education, for example, would typically involve extensive assessments by educational diagnostic professionals because a child must be deemed eligible for these more costly services. Indeed, Public Law 94-142, the Education for All Handicapped Children Act, mandates this approach.

States differ in the diagnostic labels used in such cases. *Educationally handicapped* and *learning disabled* are two common terms. Some school districts consider gifted children exceptional and therefore entitled to special services. Others do not provide these programs. Threshold scores on IQ tests used to diagnose mental retardation also vary from one locale to another.

Some tests used in assessments are considered quite easy to give, and teachers' aides may be trained to administer them. Others are more complex and require the skills of educational diagnosticians, reading or math specialists, psychologists, speech/language clinicians, audiologists, and so on. As a parent, you have the right to ask about the examiner's qualifications. This should be among your first questions, especially if a test result does not appear to reflect what you know about your child. Keep in mind, though, that classroom teachers are often the first to notice when test results and actual performance don't seem to match.

As young people move through their school years, various tests are often used to determine what types of high school courses they are encouraged to choose. Critics of educational tests argue that such "tracking" has forced young people to make decisions about careers far too early, that tracks tend to separate students into various high status/low status groups, leaving individuals very little room to explore a variety of subject areas. It is also argued that parents actually determine the track, not the school or the students.

The best way for a parent to find out the process by which tests are chosen and the schedule for testing of students is to call the superintendent of schools in the district. When you ask about testing policies you will learn when your state requires schools to test children. For example, if you live in Alaska, you would be told that children are tested statewide in grades 4, 6, and 8, using the Iowa Basic Skills Tests. In Montana, students are tested annually and the state has a list of approved tests. The state of Georgia requires both criterion- and norm-referenced tests. All of the fifty states have policies and statutes regarding testing, and these are available to the public.

Many school districts institute testing programs that exceed the requirements of the state. In some cases, these tests are approved by a school board; other districts have a special committee or a task force to choose testing programs. I recommend asking questions about the policies concerning testing in your child's school. You may find that some tests are mandated and given routinely in particular grades; you may also discover that your child's school uses other tests in addition to those used statewide. In other words, your child may be tested annually, twice a year, every other year, and so on, with a variety of tools. You may also learn that criterion-referenced testing is being added, with standardized tests remaining as part of the schedule. If your child has a learning disability, particular tests may be chosen because the teachers involved prefer them. However, your child may also be required to take the standardized tests mandated by the state or locality.

Because testing is considered important—and controversial—many states and school districts distribute brochures that give the testing dates and describe the types of tests that will be given. In Chicago, for example, the brochures are available in English and Spanish and contain explanations of the areas being tested and the meaning of the scores. I suggest using such information as a basis on which to form your questions; however, do not consider it all of the information you are entitled to.

Many tests your child will take are given because local policy has mandated these specific tests. There is usually an accompanying time-table for their administration. By enrolling your child in a particular school you are giving your permission for this general testing. Therefore, you will be informed about the testing schedules but not asked to give permission every time a test is given. This also applies to the reading or math tests your child might be given throughout a school year. These may be used to determine which learning group he or she is in during that grade. If, however, your child is referred for extensive assessment, your permission is needed.

You should be actively involved in the assessment process, and you should ask for a list of tests given and the results that are reported and interpreted. This includes actual scores and the impressions or opinions of the professional who administered and/or interpreted each test. This gives you a way to keep a test history—a valuable tool if and when discrepancies in performance and test results occur. (Lest you think that every child is automatically evaluated for all possible difficulties, please remember that it is entirely possible for a youngster to complete a dozen years of school taking only the "regular" tests mandated by the particular district or state. However, it is still a good idea to keep accurate records.)

It is *crucial* to note that important educational decisions should never be made on the basis of *one* test result. Too many factors can affect a test, and entrance to school, advancing from grade to grade, admission into special programs, or overall educational planning can be extremely important decisions—too important to rely on test results alone.

The line between educational, developmental, and psychological tests is sometimes a fine one. The decision to place particular tests in the education section of this book was based on the fact that professionals in the various fields discussed use these tests in a school setting. It is possible to encounter some of these tests in hospital-based child development centers, private academic evaluation companies, and university-based research and evaluation centers. In addition, many clinicians use testing in their private practices. You may also find that some tests your child is given in school are listed in other sections of this book.

As in the other sections, various testing terms are used (norm, grade-equivalent, stanine, percentile, and so on). You will find these terms defined in the glossary. Diagnostic terms (learning disability, language deficiency, and so on) are also defined there.

You will also notice that in most cases no special preparation is needed for this group of tests. However, common sense dictates that a child who is taking an extensive achievement test be well-rested, well-nourished, and as relaxed as possible. Most of us can remember mild pretest jitters, a condition considered normal. However, some young people develop more serious test anxiety. Older children may actually verbalize their fears, but very young children might have picked up the idea that adults are placing a lot of importance on a test result. (This is one reason that many educators frown on preschool or readiness testing. They believe children are being pushed too early to compete and be compared to others.)

In the coming years, you will likely encounter extensive discussions of testing practices in your child's school district. Because ideas about preparing for tests vary widely, you may also receive specific instructions or advice from classroom teachers and others involved in testing your child.

Finally, there are literally thousands of educational tests. We would need several volumes to list them all. We have tried to include many of the most common tests and types of tests. For example, almost all standardized reading and math tests have much in common. You will be able to get a good idea about the types of tasks, scores, and so on included in many tests by reviewing the profiles in this section.

ACT (American College Testing Program) Assessment

WHOSE RECOMMENDATION AND/OR PERMISSION IS NEEDED?

The ACT is recommended by high school administrators and guidance counselors. Preenrollment is required.

WHAT DOES THE TEST TEST?

The well-known ACT is an independently developed, standardized test that is part of a program of testing used by many colleges and universities when considering applicants for admission. It has four major sections: English Usage, Mathematics Usage, Social Studies Reading, and Natural Science Reading. It is considered both an achievement and ability test that helps those involved in college admissions determine a student's chances for success at that particular institution.

WHAT, IF ANY, PREPARATION IS NECESSARY?

The issue of preparation for the ACT is one reason the test is considered controversial. Study guides are widely available in bookstores throughout the country, as are private and commercial tutoring. Because a student must do well on the ACT to get into certain colleges, many families consider such preparation necessary. Critics of this test and others like it have pointed out that coaching puts young people whose families can afford it at a distinct advantage. At issue as well is the concern that "teaching a test" proves only that the specific material has been mastered, and does not accurately measure ability or predict future academic success.

Special arrangements can be made to accommodate handicapped students taking the test. Students receive instructions about the date, place, and time, along with instructions about what they must bring (I.D., pencils, and so on).

HOW IS THE TEST PERFORMED, AND WHAT SHOULD BE EXPECTED?

The ACT takes about 3 hours and 15 minutes, including the explanation time and breaks. A proctor, or supervisor, is always in the room to direct seating, answer questions, and maintain the strict time allotments for each section. A student profile section and an interest inventory is included. All sections of the ACT must be taken at the same time. All questions are multiple choice.

HOW ARE RESULTS RECORDED, EVALUATED, INTERPRETED, AND COMPARED?

A student profile report contains standard and percentile scores. Percentile ranks are calculated for the college-bound students from the state and the entire country, and freshmen are enrolled in the colleges to which the student is applying and to which the student's ACT scores are sent. Scores are presented on a scale of 1 to 36. Each section is given a separate score, and a composite score, the average of the four scores, is also reported.

HOW RELIABLE IS THE TEST?

The reliability of the ACT is constantly debated and opponents and proponents of this type of testing have attempted to prove their contentions. Both groups do agree that many things can affect the outcome—such as basic education background, preparation, and skill as a test taker. For example, guessing at answers is encouraged and some young people are better at test-taking strategies, a skill that may have little to do with future occupational competence. Cultural and gender bias, long considered factors in the test, will continue to be issues raised throughout the 1990s.

WHAT DOES THE TEST *NOT* TEST?

The ACT is not an intelligence test, nor does it accurately measure a wide range of aptitudes and abilities. Practical or "life" skills are not assessed.

WHAT FURTHER TESTS MIGHT BE RECOMMENDED?

Some colleges require that their own entrance exam be taken. The score on this test is used along with ACT scores when admission is being determined.

The American College Testing Program, publisher of the ACT, has developed proficiency exams in specific subject areas that are used for advanced placement or for granting college credits for information that has been mastered outside the classroom setting.

Achievement Identification Measure (AIM)

See Group Achievement Identification Measure, page 185.

Achievement Identification Measure, Teacher Observation (AIM-TO)

See Group Achievement Identification Measure, page 185.

Auditory Screening

WHOSE RECOMMENDATION AND/OR PERMISSION IS NEEDED?

Auditory screening is routinely performed upon entry into school, and some states mandate periodic screening throughout the school years. It may also be requested by parents, teachers or other educational professionals, and a variety of health care providers. Nonprofessionals can be trained to perform routine screening. However, only audiologists and otologists (physicians who specialize in problems of the ear and related disorders) are qualified to diagnose and treat auditory disorders.

WHAT DOES THE TEST TEST?

This screening is designed to identify children with possible hearing impairments.

WHAT, IF ANY, PREPARATION IS NEEDED?

No specific preparation is necessary. However, if a child has a cold or an ear infection, testing should be postponed if possible.

HOW IS THE TEST PERFORMED, AND WHAT SHOULD BE EXPECTED?

Although auditory screening can be done in groups, individual screening is currently more common. Most schools use a pure-tone audiometer, which is designed to test mechanisms of the outer, middle, and inner ear.

The child wears headphones and the examiner introduces tones of various frequencies. Frequency is measured in hertz (Hz), meaning the number of cycles per second of a sound. The child is asked to raise a hand when the sound becomes loud enough to hear. (Preschoolers may be asked to put a block in a box or bucket when the sound is heard.) The audiometer is adjusted to introduce various intensities (decibels, dB) of tone. The tones are routed to one ear at a time, as well as to a bone-conduction vibrator, which stimulates the inner ear while bypassing the outer and middle ear. The screening generally takes no more than 10 to 15 minutes.

HOW ARE RESULTS RECORDED, EVALUATED, INTERPRETED, AND COMPARED?

In hearing assessments, the decibel scale is referenced to an established normal hearing level (HL). The decibel and frequency of the tones introduced are expressed in numbers (e.g., 20 dB at 1000 Hz). To "pass" a screening the child must be able to hear stimuli of 25 dB HL at 500, 1000, 2000, and 6000 Hz, and 30 dB HL at 4000 Hz. Failure to hear any of these tones in one or both ears may indicate impairment.

HOW RELIABLE IS THE TEST?

Children who do not meet the criteria of the test should always be rescreened before extensive testing is scheduled. The second screening is generally done two or three weeks after the first testing. Ideally, auditory screening should be done in a sound-treated environment; that is, background noise should be eliminated. This is difficult to achieve in a school setting, but any noise can affect the accuracy of the testing. Results can be skewed by a host of reasons, from asymptomatic ear infections to misunderstanding the examiner's directions. Children with disabilities that may interfere with carrying out the tasks involved in the testing or make them unable to adequately pay attention during testing may also need to be screened more than once if results are questionable.

WHAT DOES THE TEST NOT TEST?

Auditory screening does not identify a specific impairment, and therefore treatment is never begun as a result of this test alone.

WHAT FURTHER TESTS MIGHT BE RECOMMENDED?

If, after a second screening, more evaluation is needed, the child is referred to an audiologist for specialized tests that attempt to specify the type of hearing impairment or to determine that the screening results were inaccurate. These tests could include the pure-tone threshold test, which attempts to find the level at which a child barely hears a sound; acoustic impedance audiometry, designed to detect possible middle-ear disorders; and physical examinations (performed by a physician) that determine if structural problems are present, such as eustachian tube dysfunction. When hearing impairments are diagnosed, speech and language specialists are sometimes consulted, especially if difficulties with word formation are already evident. (Sometimes it is the speech pathologist who has recommended the hearing evaluation in the first place.)

Ball Aptitude Battery

WHOSE RECOMMENDATION AND/OR PERMISSION IS NEEDED?

Psychologists, guidance counselors, career counselors, and mental health professionals may recommend the test. Parents or students may also initiate testing.

WHAT DOES THE TEST TEST?

The Ball Aptitude Battery assesses a variety of aptitudes: English vocabulary, numerical computation, spatial perception, clerical speed and accuracy, several types of reasoning, idea fluency, two types of memory, finger dexterity, and grip strength, among others. The test is given to high school students, usually in their junior or senior year. It is also used with adults.

WHAT, IF ANY, PREPARATION IS NECESSARY?

No preparation is needed.

HOW IS THE TEST PERFORMED, AND
WHAT SHOULD BE EXPECTED?

One portion of the test is given in groups; the others are given individually. Most of the tests are paper-and-pencil format, and responses are recorded in a test booklet. The questions may be asked on tape and responses written in the test booklet. Tests of finger dexterity, grip, analytical reasoning, and so on must be administered individually. All tests are timed, although the time limits are set so that most test-takers can finish the test. The complete test takes 3 to 4 hours, including periodic breaks.

HOW ARE RESULTS RECORDED, EVALUATED,
INTERPRETED, AND COMPARED?

Scores can be compared to norms established for several groups. However, the primary use of scores is to analyze the tests in order to identify strengths and weaknesses. The profile is then compared to the requirements of potential occupations.

HOW RELIABLE IS THE TEST?

Reliability is considered good for high school seniors or older individuals. Younger children whose aptitudes are still developing may show greater change over time. This test is similar to many other aptitude and ability tests, and educational decisions should not be made solely on the basis of the results.

WHAT DOES THE TEST *NOT* TEST?

The Ball Aptitude Battery does not measure intelligence, achievement, or current skills.

WHAT FURTHER TESTS MIGHT BE RECOMMENDED?

When used in career counseling, personality and interest inventories may also be given.

Basic Achievement Skill Individual Screener (BASIS)

WHOSE RECOMMENDATION AND/OR PERMISSION IS NEEDED?

Teachers, guidance counselors, and education specialists generally recommend this test.

WHAT DOES THE TEST TEST?

BASIS measures (for grades 1 through 8) skills in three basic areas: reading, mathematics, and spelling. The child is tested in grade clusters; that is, with groups of questions that increase in difficulty. BASIS is considered a test that evaluates achievement in order to place students in appropriate classroom groups. It may also influence choice of textbooks and other learning materials. An optional writing exercise is included.

WHAT, IF ANY, PREPARATION IS NECESSARY?

No special preparation is needed.

HOW IS THE TEST PERFORMED, AND WHAT SHOULD BE EXPECTED?

BASIS includes both oral and written elements. For example, mathematical computation items are written, but the examiner dictates the word problems. The test takes about an hour. The optional writing exercise takes an additional 10 minutes.

HOW ARE RESULTS RECORDED, EVALUATED, INTERPRETED, AND COMPARED?

A raw score is calculated and is then converted to standardized scores (grade equivalent, percentile, stanine, and so on). The score can also be criterion-referenced, meaning that the results are interpreted against the learning goals established for the child.

HOW RELIABLE IS THE TEST?

When used to evaluate academic strengths and weaknesses, BASIS can be considered reliable. However, it should not be used to retain a child in a grade or place him or her in a special educational environment.

WHAT DOES THE TEST *NOT* TEST?

BASIS does not measure intelligence, creativity, aptitude, or interest. It is a measure of achievement in three well-defined areas.

WHAT FURTHER TESTS MIGHT BE RECOMMENDED?

In most cases, no specific follow-up tests will be needed. The exception would be where a learning disability is suspected. Tests given will vary depending on the age and ability of the child.

Boehm Test of Basic Concepts (The Boehm)

WHOSE RECOMMENDATION AND/OR PERMISSION IS NEEDED?

The Boehm test is usually recommended and given by a classroom teacher, special-education teacher, or speech/language clinician.

WHAT DOES THE TEST TEST?

The test helps to assess a child's understanding of space, quantity, and time concepts. In practical terms, this means a child's ability to understand such concepts as before/after, half/whole, and so on. (Grades K through 2.)

WHAT, IF ANY, PREPARATION IS NECESSARY?

No preparation is necessary.

HOW IS THE TEST PERFORMED, AND WHAT SHOULD BE EXPECTED?

The Boehm contains twenty-five test items and may be given individually or in groups. The child is asked to mark the picture that correctly identifies the concept presented by the examiner. The test in not timed, but it generally takes 30 to 40 minutes.

HOW ARE RESULTS RECORDED, EVALUATED, INTERPRETED, AND COMPARED?

A raw score is converted into a percentile rank. This can then be reported for the age and grade placement. Information on performance levels among various socioeconomic groups is available, and a child's score can be placed on a socioeconomic scale. The results of a group as a whole can be used to plan instruction for a classroom.

HOW RELIABLE IS THE TEST?

The Boehm can be useful in pinpointing needs of the individual students, especially those needing remedial help with language. The test is recommended for grades K through 2, but is considered most effective with the youngest children in this range.

WHAT DOES THE TEST *NOT* TEST?

The Boehm is not an intelligence test, and it does not predict a child's later academic performance.

WHAT FURTHER TESTS MIGHT BE RECOMMENDED?

If the test is being given individually, other language concept tests could be used. In some cases, developmental testing could be recommended.

Brigance K and I Screen, Revised (Brigance K&I)

WHOSE RECOMMENDATION AND/OR PERMISSION IS NEEDED?

Classroom teachers and other educational specialists may administer this screening.

WHAT DOES THE TEST TEST?

The Brigance K&I is a quick screening tool designed to assess development and school readiness. The areas screened include speech and language (vocabulary, syntax, and so on); motor skills (walking, hopping, drawing shapes, and so on); counting, letter recognition, some general knowledge of parts of the body, colors, and so on. It is used with children entering kindergarten or first grade.

WHAT, IF ANY, PREPARATION IS NECESSARY?

No special preparation is needed.

HOW IS THE TEST PERFORMED, AND WHAT SHOULD BE EXPECTED?

The child may be assessed individually by one examiner; if the screening is used as a readiness tool, the child might have more than one examiner, each giving a part of the test. The entire screening can be done in 10 to 20 minutes. The instructions and the required tasks are designed to be done quickly.

HOW ARE RESULTS RECORDED, EVALUATED, INTERPRETED, AND COMPARED?

A point system is used in each skill area, with a possible score of 100 points. Children are compared with others in the same screening group, and are rated as average, higher than average, or lower than average. The examiner(s) may also record observations.

HOW RELIABLE IS THE TEST?

The purpose of the screening is to plan teaching programs for children entering kindergarten or first grade. It is not meant to label children at risk or to exclude them from school. Individual programs can be explored if scores in particular areas are low. However, a child should not be placed in special groups on the basis of this test alone. If your child has a known disability in an area being assessed, you should, of course, inform the examiners before the screening begins.

WHAT DOES THE TEST *NOT* TEST?

The Brigance K&I is a screening tool and does not diagnose developmental or learning disabilities, nor does it measure intelligence.

WHAT FURTHER TESTS MIGHT BE RECOMMENDED?

If scores are inexplicably low, more in-depth testing could be recommended. However, possible examiner error or some other special circumstance should probably be investigated before embarking on an extensive testing program.

The Career Directions Inventory (CDI)

WHOSE RECOMMENDATION AND/OR
PERMISSION IS NEEDED?

Guidance counselors, career counselors, psychologists, and psychiatrists may recommend this test.

WHAT DOES THE TEST TEST?

The CDI is designed to assist high school and college students in educational and career planning by measuring interests related to career areas. Some of the categories are Mathematics, Business, Social Sciences, and Creative Arts. (The CDI is also used with adults in career counseling.)

WHAT, IF ANY, PREPARATION IS NECESSARY?

No preparation is needed.

HOW IS THE TEST PERFORMED, AND
WHAT SHOULD BE EXPECTED?

The CDI takes approximately 30 to 45 minutes to complete. The student is asked to read three statements and choose which would be the most and least preferred activity among the three. There are 100 sets of statements describing job-related activities. The CDI can be administered in groups or individually.

HOW ARE RESULTS RECORDED, EVALUATED,
INTERPRETED, AND COMPARED?

The results of the CDI are reported in a lengthy interpretation provided by the publisher, with profiles of scores in fifteen basic interest scales and seven occupational themes (Realistic/Practical, Enterprising, and Social/Helping, among others). The report includes a comparison of the student's scores with those of others studying or working in various occupations. Three "cluster areas" are chosen for analysis because a student's scores are highest in these areas.

HOW RELIABLE IS THE TEST?

As with all occupational interest testing, results of the CDI should be used as general guidelines in helping to plan future educational or occupational goals. The CDI does not measure values or personality characteristics that would affect career choices, nor does it indicate if a student has the abilities for various occupations. Reliability also tends to be better with older students than for those age 15 or younger. The CDI should not be used as the only basis for placement in particular educational tracks.

WHAT DOES THE TEST NOT TEST?

The CDI is not an aptitude or intelligence test.

WHAT FURTHER TESTS MIGHT BE RECOMMENDED?

In some settings, the Jackson Vocational Interest Survey (JVIS) will be used, particularly if the student is college bound.

Cognitive Abilities Test, Form 3 (COGAT)

WHOSE RECOMMENDATION AND/OR PERMISSION IS NEEDED?

The COGAT is a scheduled standardized test chosen by individual school districts for group use.

WHAT DOES THE TEST TEST?

The COGAT measures intellectual abilities necessary to learn basic math and verbal skills. It includes scales for vocabulary, sentence completion, verbal analogies, and verbal classifications, as well as number series and quantitative relationships. A nonverbal section using figures and shapes is included. Potential difficulties with standard classroom work are noted. The COGAT is known to help in the diagnosis of learning disabilities. (Grades K through 12.)

WHAT, IF ANY, PREPARATION IS NECESSARY?

No special preparation required.

HOW IS THE TEST PERFORMED, AND WHAT SHOULD BE EXPECTED?

The COGAT is a multiple-choice, paper-and-pencil test. Depending on the grade level of the child taking it, the COGAT is timed at slightly less than one hour to slightly over an hour and a half.

HOW ARE RESULTS RECORDED, EVALUATED, INTERPRETED, AND COMPARED?

Raw scores are converted into the norms of those used in the Iowa Test of Basic Skills. This is done to provide comparisons of potentials with actual achievement.

HOW RELIABLE IS THE TEST?

The test should not be relied upon as an accurate measure of true learning ability, especially for young children. Other tests should be done to verify low or unexpected scores.

WHAT DOES THE TEST NOT TEST?

The COGAT doesn't measure actual academic achievement, nor does it supply a definitive diagnosis of a learning disability.

WHAT FURTHER TESTS MIGHT BE RECOMMENDED?

If a learning disability is detected, a child would be given other tests specifically for the area in which a deficiency is detected (e.g., language comprehension or quantitative reasoning). For cases in which test directions were not understood well, the child could be retested using the same test or one considered its equivalent.

Cultural Literacy Test

WHOSE RECOMMENDATION AND/OR PERMISSION IS NEEDED?

This test is generally used in high schools.

WHAT DOES THE TEST TEST?

The Cultural Literacy test assesses general knowledge of the humanities, social sciences, and sciences. It was developed by the Cultural Literacy Foundation, which has created an index to the information it deems necessary for functional literacy. In a sense, this test exists because of wide-spread concern that young people do not have enough "general" knowledge about literature, history, politics, health, and the sciences to be active, participating citizens. (Grades 11 and 12.)

WHAT, IF ANY, PREPARATION IS NECESSARY?

No special preparation is needed. However, if a school chooses to use this type of test, it should be assumed that the information is taught in various required courses. If not, the test would be given to help plan curricula that include the areas being tested.

HOW IS THE TEST PERFORMED, AND
WHAT SHOULD BE EXPECTED?

The test takes about 50 minutes, and is a basic paper-and-pencil test. The 115 multiple-choice test items cover an enormous range of general information, including such areas as the Bible, mythology, fine arts, world and American history, geography, physical science, and technology.

HOW ARE RESULTS RECORDED, EVALUATED,
INTERPRETED, AND COMPARED?

Scores can be reported in numerous ways, including composite national and local percentile ranks, and a score for each subarea (Humanities, Social Science, Sciences). Average raw scores may also be reported. A student brochure called "Your World Knowledge," which describes the background of the test development and its objectives, is included in the report.

HOW RELIABLE IS THE TEST?

The test is too new to be judged by typical reliability standards. Because the scores are meant to be used to change teaching objectives and increase awareness about the topic of cultural literacy, a young person should not be penalized in any way if scores are considered low. The concept of what cultural literacy is and isn't is still being debated in educational circles, and no single, nationally recognized set of standards exists.

WHAT DOES THE TEST *NOT* TEST?

The Cultural Literacy test is not an intelligence test, nor does it measure aptitudes or abilities.

WHAT FURTHER TESTS MIGHT BE RECOMMENDED?

No specific tests are recommended.

Differential Aptitude Tests (DAT); Fifth Edition; Level I, Grades 7 through 9; Level II, Grades 10 through 12

WHOSE RECOMMENDATION AND/OR PERMISSION IS NEEDED?

Guidance counselors might recommend this test for individuals, and some school systems use it for all students. The DAT is also used with adults in career counseling settings.

WHAT DOES THE TEST TEST?

The DAT measures aptitude in eight areas: verbal reasoning, numerical reasoning, abstract reasoning, perceptual speed and accuracy, mechanical reasoning, space relations, spelling, and language use.

WHAT, IF ANY, PREPARATION IS NECESSARY?

No preparation is needed.

HOW IS THE TEST PERFORMED, AND WHAT SHOULD BE EXPECTED?

Each area tested is presented in separate, timed segments ranging from six to thirty minutes. It takes about two hours to complete the entire set of subtests.

HOW ARE RESULTS RECORDED, EVALUATED, INTERPRETED, AND COMPARED?

The DAT is a standardized test and raw scores are placed in norms established for gender and grade. Scores are reported in stanines, percentiles, and scaled scores.

HOW RELIABLE IS THE TEST?

The DAT is a widely used tool and can be helpful in making educational plans. However, it should not be used as the sole method to determine placement in a vocational or college preparatory track.

WHAT DOES THE TEST *NOT* TEST?

The DAT does not measure academic achievement, creativity, interests, or intelligence.

WHAT FURTHER TESTS MIGHT BE RECOMMENDED?

The DAT is sometimes given with the Career Interest Inventory (CII), which measures a student's interest in various occupations. A report combining the results of the DAT with those of the CII is sometimes provided. The DAT Adaptive is a version of the test available for use with a computer. It is a shorter test in that test items are individually selected to match the needs of the student.

Diagnostic Screening Test: Language (DSTL)

WHOSE RECOMMENDATION AND/OR PERMISSION IS NEEDED?

Classroom or special-education teachers generally give this test.

WHAT DOES THE TEST TEST?

The DSTL is designed to estimate overall achievement level in written language and, more specifically, skill levels in grammar, punctuation, capitalization, sentence structure, and spelling rules. (Grades 1 through 13.)

WHAT, IF ANY, PREPARATION IS NECESSARY?

No preparation is needed.

HOW IS THE TEST PERFORMED, AND WHAT SHOULD BE EXPECTED?

The examiner may read questions while the child listens, or the child may read and complete the test by himself or herself. Sometimes the child may read along and answer questions while the examiner reads the items aloud. The test takes 5 to 10 minutes, and can be given to individuals or to classes in order to help place children in appropriate achievement groups.

HOW ARE RESULTS RECORDED, EVALUATED, INTERPRETED, AND COMPARED?

Raw scores are converted to scaled scores in each area. The results can also be expressed as formal knowledge—that is, the child's knowledge of rules—and applied knowledge—the ability to use the rules.

HOW RELIABLE IS THE TEST?

Because the DSTL is a screening test, it indicates only that a problem may exist.

WHAT DOES THE TEST *NOT* TEST?

The DSTL does not measure reading skill or aptitudes for language skills.

WHAT FURTHER TESTS MIGHT BE RECOMMENDED?

If a child's scores are low, he or she should be further evaluated before a placement decision is made.

Durrell Analysis of Reading Difficulty (DARD)

WHOSE RECOMMENDATION AND/OR
PERMISSION IS NEEDED?

Special-education and classroom teachers and reading specialists most often recommend this test.

WHAT DOES THE TEST TEST?

The DARD evaluates various skills involved in reading: oral and silent reading, word recognition and analysis, and listening comprehension, among others. (Grades 1 through 6.)

WHAT, IF ANY, PREPARATION IS NECESSARY?

No special preparation is needed.

HOW IS THE TEST PERFORMED, AND
WHAT SHOULD BE EXPECTED?

The child is alone with the examiner, who leads the child through various activities, some of which require oral responses. It's important that the child understand the directions and what is required with each section. The examiner will note strengths and weaknesses.

HOW ARE RESULTS RECORDED, EVALUATED,
INTERPRETED, AND COMPARED?

Grade norms are available for each grade, and divided into Low, Middle, and High ranges.

HOW RELIABLE IS THE TEST?

This test is widely used in diagnosing reading problems; the pattern of errors may indicate that a particular reading problem exists, suggesting further investigation and perhaps remedial teaching. The examiner's impressions may be as important as the score itself.

WHAT DOES THE TEST *NOT* TEST?

The DARD does not measure intelligence, nor does it predict a child's future reading ability.

WHAT FURTHER TESTS MIGHT BE RECOMMENDED?

Specific tests that measure auditory discrimination or receptive language skills might be recommended to confirm a diagnosis or further explore areas in which a child's functioning is in question.

AGS Early Screening Profiles (ESP)

WHOSE RECOMMENDATION AND/OR PERMISSION IS NEEDED?

Early childhood specialists most often administer the ESP, in a wide variety of settings.

WHAT DOES THE TEST TEST?

The ESP screens children ages 2 years, 0 months through 6 years, 11 months to measure their development in three broad areas, called profiles: cognitive/language, motor, and self-help/social. The Cognitive/Language Profile measures language abilities, reasoning, and basic skills needed in school. The Motor Profile measures gross and fine motor skills. The Self-Help/Social Profile is a questionnaire completed by parents and/or a teacher, measuring the child's development in communication, daily living skills, socialization, and motor skills.

In addition, ESP contains four surveys. The Articulation Survey measures how well the child produces certain sounds, the

Home Survey asks parents to describe the home environment, the Health History Survey is a checklist of health problems, and the Behavior Survey is used by the examiner to describe the child's behavior during testing.

ESP identifies children who may have one or more problems that could interfere with their development. The ESP may also identify potentially gifted children.

WHAT, IF ANY, PREPARATION IS NECESSARY?

No preparation is needed. The parents' forms may be completed while the child is being tested.

HOW IS THE TEST PERFORMED, AND WHAT SHOULD BE EXPECTED?

The child is tested individually, which takes about 15 to 30 minutes to complete. Depending on the purpose of testing, the examiner may choose to administer individual profiles or surveys rather than the entire test. The Cognitive/Language Profile and the Articulation Survey are given using an easel. Questions are presented orally or through pictures. The child responds to questions orally or by pointing. A separate cognitive score can be obtained for children who are nonverbal, have a speech or hearing problem, or do not speak English. The Motor Profile asks the child to do such things as walk a straight line, draw figures, and follow a maze. The Behavior Survey is completed by the examiner during or immediately after testing.

HOW ARE RESULTS RECORDED, EVALUATED, INTERPRETED, AND COMPARED?

The examiner records the child's answers and performance and scores each response. These scores are added to give total scores for the Cognitive/Language, Motor, and Self-Help/Social profiles. For the Articulation, Home, and Behavior surveys, the scores are reported as above average, average, and below average. The Health History Survey is not scored. The scores are normed in two levels: Level I, in which scores are reported in six categories called screening indexes; and Level II, which provides more detailed scores.

HOW RELIABLE IS THE TEST?

ESP is considered a reliable *screening* tool. However, educational placement decisions should not be made on the basis of this test. It indicates only that a problem may exist.

WHAT DOES THE TEST *NOT* TEST?

ESP does not provide detailed information about specific abilities, nor does it measure intelligence.

WHAT FURTHER TESTS MIGHT BE RECOMMENDED?

Based on the recommendations of the screening team, the child may be referred for further evaluation by a psychologist, speech pathologist, physician, counselor, social worker, or physical therapist. A variety of developmental tests and general ability tests could be recommended.

Group Achievement Identification Measure (GAIM)

WHOSE RECOMMENDATION AND/OR PERMISSION IS NEEDED?

This test is usually used in school settings, and parental permission is needed.

WHAT DOES THE TEST TEST?

GAIM was developed to provide a measure of the characteristics that distinguish underachievers from achieving students. (Grades 5 through 12.)

WHAT, IF ANY, PREPARATION IS NECESSARY?

No special preparation is needed.

HOW IS THE TEST PERFORMED, AND
WHAT SHOULD BE EXPECTED?

The GAIM is a paper-and-pencil test. The child marks the response to statements that best describes his or her present behavior and environment. The GAIM usually takes about 30 minutes.

HOW ARE RESULTS RECORDED, EVALUATED,
INTERPRETED, AND COMPARED?

A raw score is converted to a percentile rank.

HOW RELIABLE IS THE TEST?

Results of the GAIM may be useful in correlating information already known about the child. Similarly, results that indicate a degree of underachievement should be confirmed with other tests—observation, interviews, and so on. A child should not be labeled an underachiever on the basis of this test alone.

WHAT DOES THE TEST *NOT* TEST?

The GAIM does not measure ability or actual academic achievement.

WHAT FURTHER TESTS MIGHT BE RECOMMENDED?

If underachieving is suspected, mental abilities testing would accompany the GAIM if it has not already been done. The Achievement Identification Measure-Teacher Observation (AIM-TO) is a teacher report form sometimes used with the GAIM. Achievement Identification Measure (AIM) is a parents' report form sometimes used with the GAIM.

Group Inventory for Finding Creative Talent (GIFT), Second Edition

Available for grade levels K through 2, 3 and 4, and 5 and 6.

WHOSE RECOMMENDATION AND/OR PERMISSION IS NEEDED?

This test is generally used in schools, although parents can also initiate the testing.

WHAT DOES THE TEST TEST?

The purpose of GIFT is to identify students with attitudes, interests, and values usually associated with creativity. Creative characteristics measured include peer independence, curiosity, perseverance, flexibility, and breadth of interests. The test is sometimes used to screen students for inclusion in a gifted program.

WHAT, IF ANY, PREPARATION IS NECESSARY?

No special preparation is needed.

HOW IS THE TEST PERFORMED AND WHAT SHOULD BE EXPECTED?

GIFT is a pencil-and-paper inventory requiring yes and no answers to 32 to 34 questions. The test is not timed, but generally takes 20 to 45 minutes. It is administered in groups.

HOW ARE RESULTS RECORDED, EVALUATED, INTERPRETED, AND COMPARED?

Raw scores are converted to percentile ranks.

HOW RELIABLE IS THE TEST?

The GIFT is a useful tool to gather information about a child and may confirm the presence of special skills and inclinations. However, no test can definitively measure creativity. Parents might find their child's individual responses more interesting than the actual score.

WHAT DOES THE TEST *NOT* TEST?

The GIFT does *not* test the potential for creativity, but only those characteristics and indicators shown at the time of the testing. It is not a test of overall intelligence or achievement.

WHAT FURTHER TESTS MIGHT BE RECOMMENDED?

Further testing depends on the purpose of the test and the setting. For example, if a child is being tested for inclusion in a "gifted" program, then mental abilities tests would be used. PRIDE (Preschool and Kindergarten Interest Description) is a similar test used with younger children.

Gilmore Oral Reading Test, Forms C and D

WHOSE RECOMMENDATION AND/OR PERMISSION IS NEEDED?

Classroom and special-education teachers and reading specialists generally give this test.

WHAT DOES THE TEST TEST?

The Gilmore Oral Reading Test assesses oral reading accuracy, comprehension, and speed. It provides a way to analyze errors individually. (Grades 1 through 8.)

WHAT, IF ANY, PREPARATION IS NECESSARY?

No preparation is needed.

HOW IS THE TEST PERFORMED, AND WHAT SHOULD BE EXPECTED?

The child is alone with an examiner and is given paragraphs to read out loud. The child is timed, but is not stopped during each paragraph. The examiner notes accuracy errors. Five comprehension questions are asked when the child finishes each paragraph. Testing stops when the child makes ten errors in one paragraph.

HOW ARE RESULTS RECORDED, EVALUATED, INTERPRETED, AND COMPARED?

Raw scores for accuracy, comprehension, and speed are computed separately, and percentiles, stanine, and grade equivalents are given for each category. Errors can be analyzed and individual corrective measures suggested. The speed score can be eliminated without affecting the accuracy of the other scores.

HOW RELIABLE IS THE TEST?

The accuracy, or measure of error, is considered the most reliable score of the Gilmore Oral Reading Test. The comprehension scale requires recall of facts in the written material and does not call for interpretation or abstract reasoning. However, very low comprehension scores may point to a memory problem that should be investigated further A child with speech impairments or with limited English language skills is at a distinct disadvantage.

WHAT DOES THE TEST *NOT* TEST?

The Gilmore Oral Reading Test is not considered a complete achievement test in reading.

WHAT FURTHER TESTS MIGHT BE RECOMMENDED?

Depending on the purpose and the results, a wide range of tests could be recommended. The Gilmore Oral Reading Test can be given again to measure progress.

Gray Oral Reading Tests (Gray Oral), Forms Q, B, C, and D

WHOSE RECOMMENDATION AND/OR PERMISSION IS NEEDED?

Special-education teachers or reading specialists generally give this test.

WHAT DOES THE TEST TEST?

The test measures progress in oral reading and is a diagnostic tool for problems with oral reading. (Grades 1 through college.)

WHAT, IF ANY, PREPARATION IS NECESSARY?

No preparation is needed.

HOW IS THE TEST PERFORMED, AND WHAT SHOULD BE EXPECTED?

The child is alone with an examiner and is asked to read aloud individual paragraphs, each of which is increasingly difficult. The examiner notes errors and observes reading style. The test is timed and the child must stop reading when time is called. A particular number of errors in two successive paragraphs is the designated stopping place in the overall test. The child is then asked questions which reveal comprehension.

HOW ARE RESULTS RECORDED, EVALUATED, INTERPRETED, AND COMPARED?

The number of errors and the time needed to read each passage are combined to form a score. The scores for all passages are combined and the total score is converted to a grade equivalent.

HOW RELIABLE IS THE TEST?

The Gray Oral can be useful in diagnosing specific reading problems—skipping words, mispronunciations, adding words, and so on. However, the grade norms may not be particularly useful in placing a child in an instructional group. A slower reader is penalized; and the value of speed in beginning readers is questioned by many. The test is not valuable for children with known speech impairments or with children who feel especially pressured by time. Children with limited English skills are also at a disadvantage when the norms are used for scoring.

WHAT DOES THE TEST NOT TEST?

The test does not reliably measure reading comprehension. It may point to particular reading problems, but should not be relied upon for placement decisions.

WHAT FURTHER TESTS MIGHT BE RECOMMENDED?

More comprehensive tests of reading ability might be recommended. Parallel forms of the Gray Oral may be given to measure progress.

Hiskey-Nebraska Test of Learning Aptitude (H-NTLA)

WHOSE RECOMMENDATION AND/OR PERMISSION IS NEEDED?

Special-education teachers and psychologists who are trained to work with hearing-impaired children most often recommend this test. Parents' permission is generally required.

WHAT DOES THE TEST TEST?

The H-NTLA was designed to measure the learning potential of hearing-impaired children. There are twelve subtests, but a child will be given a selected number that are suitable within the age range (ages 3 to 17). Because the test is considered a nonverbal way to measure intelligence, it is also used with children who do not speak fluent English or have impairments that make written or oral testing difficult.

WHAT, IF ANY, PREPARATION IS NECESSARY?

No preparation is needed.

HOW IS THE TEST PERFORMED, AND WHAT SHOULD BE EXPECTED?

The child is alone with an examiner, who gives test directions through pantomime. (Note: Proficiency in American sign language is not necessary.) Young children will be asked to reproduce bead patterns, match pictures and colors, and recall visual images shown in sequence. Older children are given subtests consisting of spatial reasoning tasks and picture analogies. The examiner observes the way in which a task is completed, as well as noting correct or incorrect answers.

HOW ARE RESULTS RECORDED, EVALUATED, INTERPRETED, AND COMPARED?

Individual subtests are scored and compared to norms established for hearing populations. A learning age (LA) is determined and then converted to a learning quotient (LQ). The LQ provides a general overview of intellectual capacities.

HOW RELIABLE IS THE TEST?

The H-NTLA is considered a reliable tool and can provide useful information on which to base an IEP (Individual Educational Program) for hearing-impaired children and others who benefit from nonverbal testing. However, its predictive value is not considered foolproof.

WHAT DOES THE TEST *NOT* TEST?

The H-NTLA does not measure academic achievement.

WHAT FURTHER TESTS MIGHT BE RECOMMENDED?

Various achievement, aptitude, and interest tests could be used when a high school or college program is being planned, or when vocational training is being considered.

Iowa Tests of Basic Skills (ITBS): Forms J, G, and H; Primary Battery; Multilevel/Separate Level Editions

WHOSE RECOMMENDATION AND/OR PERMISSION IS NEEDED?

The ITBS is used in schools and is often one of the tests chosen to fulfill mandated testing requirements set by states or school districts. Parents are generally notified as to the dates when testing will take place.

WHAT DOES THE TEST TEST?

One of the most widely used of all of the standardized academic achievement tests, the ITBS measures performance in numerous areas, from early learning skills in the Primary Battery (listening, vocabulary, word analysis, and so on) to social studies and science in the Multilevel Battery (grades 9 through 14). School administrators vary widely in their choices of which "test package" to use at any given time. Therefore, one school district might choose Level 7 of the Basic Battery, which includes fewer tests than Level 7 of the Complete Battery. The Multilevel Battery offers a supplemental writing test. In addition to basic reading, language, and math skills, some levels in ITBS also include tests that assess a child's ability to use reference tools, read maps, and interpret graphs.

WHAT, IF ANY, PREPARATION IS NECESSARY?

No special preparation is needed; however, individual school districts may send a testing schedule home with the child with ideas about preparation for this lengthy test. The publisher also provides a document, "A Message to Parents," which is intended to assist parents in preparing their children for the testing procedures.

HOW IS THE TEST PERFORMED, AND WHAT SHOULD BE EXPECTED?

Generally, the ITBS are given in groups, either in the classroom or in a separate testing setting, such as a library. Practice questions are used for some of the batteries and levels. Testing time varies widely, depending on the level chosen. The ITBS is a paper-and-pencil test, with some questions given orally and others presented in written form. Group testing is not recommended for students with known disabilities, and the form and level of the test chosen should be considered carefully.

HOW ARE RESULTS RECORDED, EVALUATED, INTERPRETED, AND COMPARED?

Numerous derived scores are available, including grade-equivalent, standard scores, and stanines. Local and national normed scores may also be reported, as well as normed scores for Catholic/private schools, cities, and both high and low socioeconomic schools. The scores will be reported to parents along with an explanation of the test and what scores might mean.

HOW RELIABLE IS THE TEST?

The ITBS is considered a useful, reliable measure of academic performance by those who believe large group testing is a valid way to measure achievement. It is the scores on this type of test that are used in the current "accountability" debate. Other groups question the value of this type of testing and argue that a child's actual abilities are not adequately measured in this way. On an individual level, test scores should always be measured against other things known about a child. For example, a low math score may be surprising to a teacher and parent who know that the child actually shows proficiency in math. In this type of case, it is wise to investigate and determine why the low score was obtained. Was it as simple as not understanding the directions? Test anxiety can be a factor as well, a situation that should be explored when results are ambiguous. It is also imperative to investigate any placement decision made on the basis of a test score, especially if you know your child has special needs. And remember, the test assumes that your child has been taught the material being tested.

WHAT DOES THE TEST *NOT* TEST?

The ITBS is not an intelligence test, nor does it measure aptitude or abilities as such.

WHAT FURTHER TESTS MIGHT BE RECOMMENDED?

Individual tests that diagnose learning disabilities could be recommended if test results are low in particular areas, provided that those skills have been taught and no other reason can be found for the low scores.

Kaufman Assessment Battery for Children (K-ABC)

WHOSE RECOMMENDATION AND/OR PERMISSION IS NEEDED?

The K-ABC is given by psychologists, educational and reading diagnosticians, or learning disability specialists. Other professionals can give the test if they are trained to do so. Parents' permission is required.

WHAT DOES THE TEST TEST?

The K-ABC measures both intellectual ability and achievement. The intellectual ability portions of the test measure two ways of processing information—sequential reasoning and simultaneous processing. The former involves the ability to see order and patterns (repeating digits or duplicating a series of hand movements, for instance). The latter involves the ability to see spatially integrated relationships (e.g., arranging shapes to match a model or recalling placement of pictures in a group). The achievement portion of the K-ABC measures such things as word recognition, grasp of concepts, and expressive vocabulary. (Ages 2½ to 12½.)

WHAT, IF ANY, PREPARATION IS NECESSARY?

No special preparation is needed.

HOW IS THE TEST PERFORMED, AND WHAT SHOULD BE EXPECTED?

The child is alone with an examiner and is asked to perform a variety of tasks on each of the ten subtests for mental abilities and on the six achievement subtests. Some of the subtests are timed; depending on the reason for the test and the age of the child, some subtests may not be used. The K-ABC can be administered nonverbally, with instructions given in pantomime, and responses can also be entirely nonverbal.

HOW ARE RESULTS RECORDED, EVALUATED, INTERPRETED, AND COMPARED?

Test results can be reported in grade and age levels and percentiles, as well as standard and scaled scores.

HOW RELIABLE IS THE TEST?

The K-ABC is widely used and considered reliable. However, it is considered a complex test and the examiner must be highly skilled. For a child with known disabilities, age and grade norms are probably not relevant.

WHAT DOES THE TEST *NOT* TEST?

The K-ABC does not measure visual-motor or expressive language skills, nor is it considered a comprehensive intelligence test.

WHAT FURTHER TESTS MIGHT BE RECOMMENDED?

The K-ABC might be part of an assessment that may include developmental screening, vision, speech and language tests, or other achievement tests.

KeyMath Diagnostic Arithmetic Test, Revised (KeyMath-R)

WHOSE RECOMMENDATION AND/OR PERMISSION IS NEEDED?

Math specialists and classroom teachers usually recommend this test. Others, such as teachers' aides, can be trained to give it.

WHAT DOES THE TEST TEST?

KeyMath-R assesses a child's understanding and application of mathematical concepts and skills. It has thirteen subtests in three areas: basic concepts, operations, and applications. It is intended for students in grades K through 9.

WHAT, IF ANY, PREPARATION IS NECESSARY?

No preparation is needed.

HOW IS THE TEST PERFORMED, AND WHAT SHOULD BE EXPECTED?

The test is individually administered, and takes about 35 to 50 minutes to complete. An easel is used to present many of the items, and the child responds orally or by pointing. Other problems are presented on a worksheet and are done using paper and pencil.

HOW ARE RESULTS RECORDED, EVALUATED, INTERPRETED, AND COMPARED?

Items are totaled to give scores for basic concepts, operations, and applications. The scores are compared to national norms. A "Report to Parents" form explains the individual subtests and the examiner can use the results to explain specific needs of the child.

HOW RELIABLE IS THE TEST?

Because KeyMath-R is used to identify strengths and weaknesses in specific areas, and because many items are used in each subtest, it is considered a reliable test.

WHAT DOES THE TEST *NOT* TEST?

KeyMath-R does not measure other academic skills, such as reading or spelling, and it is not an intelligence or aptitude test.

WHAT FURTHER TESTS MIGHT BE RECOMMENDED?

After completing Form A of KeyMath-R, a child might be given Form B (a parallel form) to measure progress. The test is used to plan remedial instruction, and there may be follow-up testing using other paper-and-pencil tests of mathematics achievement. (An instructional program, KeyMath Teach and Practice, is linked to the KeyMath-R content; a school system might use both the program and the test.)

Kraner Preschool Math Inventory (KPMI)

WHOSE RECOMMENDATION AND/OR PERMISSION IS NEEDED?

The test is usually given by a classroom or special-education teacher. Others can be trained to give it.

WHAT DOES THE TEST TEST?

The KPMI tests basic math skills. (Ages 3 to 6½.)

WHAT, IF ANY, PREPARATION IS NECESSARY?

No special preparation is necessary.

HOW IS THE TEST PERFORMED, AND
WHAT SHOULD BE EXPECTED?

The test is untimed and given individually. The child responds orally to the pictures that the examiner presents. The child may be asked to count how many balloons are in a picture, or how many shapes are on the left side and right side of the paper. Sample questions should be given to make sure that the child understands the directions and the material.

HOW ARE RESULTS RECORDED, EVALUATED,
INTERPRETED, AND COMPARED?

The results are recorded and the child is given a mastery age score and a receptive age score, a measure of the level of understanding of the concepts.

HOW RELIABLE IS THE TEST?

The test is useful in certain settings, but language skills are an important component of the test even though it doesn't measure these skills. Children with known language difficulties will not test well.

WHAT DOES THE TEST NOT TEST?

The KPMI does not predict future math ability and performance.

WHAT FURTHER TESTS MIGHT BE RECOMMENDED?

If a child's scores are low, another test of early mathematical ability should be given to confirm the results. Remedial help can then be planned.

Malcomesius Specific Language Disability Test

WHOSE RECOMMENDATION AND/OR PERMISSION IS NEEDED?

The test is usually given by a classroom or special-education teacher.

WHAT DOES THE TEST TEST?

The Malcomesius tests the child's auditory, visual, and kinesthetic skills related to reading, writing, and spelling. (Grades 6 through 8.)

WHAT, IF ANY, PREPARATION IS NECESSARY?

No preparation is necessary.

HOW IS THE TEST PERFORMED, AND WHAT SHOULD BE EXPECTED?

The test is usually given to a group. It is timed, and usually takes 1½ hours to complete. The children are asked to copy paragraphs from a wall chart, discriminate between words that sound alike, match similar words, and write paragraphs from memory.

HOW ARE RESULTS RECORDED, EVALUATED, INTERPRETED, AND COMPARED?

The results are scored individually and evaluated by the examiner, but the scores are not placed on a scale and compared to others' results.

HOW RELIABLE IS THE TEST?

Administering the Malcomesius is considered a good way to assess a child's overall language ability. An individual pattern of errors is useful in determining specific language disabilities and planning a remedial program or other specialized help.

WHAT DOES THE TEST *NOT* TEST?

The Malcomesius does not measure academic performance or other abilities.

WHAT FURTHER TESTS MIGHT BE RECOMMENDED?

Another language test such as the Slingerland may be recommended to explore or confirm low scores.

Norris Educational Achievement Test (NEAT)

WHOSE RECOMMENDATION AND/OR PERMISSION IS NEEDED?

Teachers and child development specialists are most likely to recommend this test. Parents' permission is required.

WHAT DOES THE TEST TEST?

The NEAT is a tool designed to measure basic skills in a variety of areas: math, spelling, word recognition, and oral reading, among others. Readiness testing is also included. (Ages 4 to 17.)

WHAT, IF ANY, PREPARATION IS NECESSARY?

No special preparation is needed.

HOW IS THE TEST PERFORMED, AND WHAT SHOULD BE EXPECTED?

The NEAT is individually administered. The examiner chooses the areas to be tested—readiness for young children, achievement tests for the older group. The oral reading and written portions are optional. The test is basically a quick survey and is completed in about 30 minutes.

HOW ARE RESULTS RECORDED, EVALUATED, INTERPRETED, AND COMPARED?

Raw scores are converted to age and grade norms, as well as an overall score for readiness or achievement. Scores for the optional oral reading and composition portions are graded incrementally from low to high, based on age and grade.

HOW RELIABLE IS THE TEST?

Like all other tests that assess readiness, results of this one test should not be used to make placement decisions. The results for older children may be useful to record progress or to design an IEP. The age and grade norms would not be particularly helpful in reporting the progress of students with known hearing disabilities. Individual progress can, however, be tracked by giving the NEAT periodically.

WHAT DOES THE TEST *NOT* TEST?

The NEAT does not test intelligence. However, it is designed to identify discrepancies between IQ scores and achievement.

WHAT FURTHER TESTS MIGHT BE RECOMMENDED?

Other, more in-depth educational tests could be suggested to further investigate a weak area in a student's progress. Depending on the reason for the test, other diagnostic tools could be given, including an intelligence test or tests that diagnose specific disabilities.

Otis-Lennon School Ability Test (OLSAT), Sixth Edition

WHOSE RECOMMENDATION AND/OR PERMISSION IS NEEDED?

The OLSAT is a test used by some school districts to fulfill testing mandates. It is also widely used in private school settings.

WHAT DOES THE TEST TEST?

The OLSAT is a basic mental abilities test, designed to measure a child's capacity to learn in those areas traditionally taught in school. Some test items are verbal, in that words, word combinations, and word meanings are used to measure verbal reasoning skills. Other test items are nonverbal and assess the ability to evaluate objects and see relationships among various pictorial representations. Numerical and quantitative concepts are also assessed.

WHAT, IF ANY, PREPARATION IS NECESSARY?

No special preparation is needed, although parents may be notified about the date of the testing.

HOW IS THE TEST PERFORMED, AND WHAT SHOULD BE EXPECTED?

The OLSAT takes 1 to 1½ hours, depending on the level used (determined by grade). The test is given in groups, usually to entire classrooms on the same day. The child is timed on each of the subtests. (The number of subtests varies with the level.) The OLSAT is a basic paper-and-pencil test.

HOW ARE RESULTS RECORDED, EVALUATED, INTERPRETED, AND COMPARED?

Raw scores are converted to many derived scores—percentile, stanines, and scaled scores, among others. There is also a school ability index (SAI) for both verbal and nonverbal portions of the test, as well as a combined SAI. Although not called an IQ score, it is considered an equivalent, taking into account that the test was developed to assess a child's ability to learn in a standard school environment. When the OLSAT is used in combination with the Stanford Achievement Test Series, an Achievement Ability Comparisons (AAC) report may be included. This compares a child's achievement with others with the same *measured* ability.

HOW RELIABLE IS THE TEST?

The OLSAT is a widely used test, offering a variety of information that may be used to plan instruction programs for classrooms or individuals. In many cases, scores appear to accurately reflect what you and classroom teachers know about your child. Actual performance seems to "fit" with the score. However, if your child's scores are low and do not match known ability, a number of things could have occurred—misunderstanding directions, test anxiety, and so on. A child with a certain type of learning disability may not do well on this test, nor might a child whose first language is not English.

WHAT DOES THE TEST *NOT* TEST?

The OLSAT does not measure academic achievement.

WHAT FURTHER TESTS MIGHT BE RECOMMENDED?

The OLSAT is often used in combination with the Stanford Achievement Test Series. However, some schools may use the OLSAT with other achievement tests. Questionable scores may lead to retesting, either with the OLSAT or another mental abilities test. This test may be repeated periodically throughout a child's school years.

Peabody Individual Achievement Test, Revised (PIAT-R)

WHOSE RECOMMENDATION AND/OR PERMISSION IS NEEDED?

Classroom and special-education teachers, psychologists, and others who are trained can administer the test.

WHAT DOES THE TEST TEST?

The PIAT-R measures achievement using six subtests: Mathematics, Reading Recognition, Reading Comprehension, Spelling, General Information, and Written Expression. (Grades K through 12.)

WHAT, IF ANY, PREPARATION IS NECESSARY?

No special preparation is needed.

HOW IS THE TEST PERFORMED, AND WHAT SHOULD BE EXPECTED?

The child is alone with the examiner, who asks questions or hands the student items to read. Answers are given orally; writing is required only on the Written Expression subtest. For example, a child will be asked to read a passage and select one of four pictures that best illustrates the meaning of the passage. The PIAT-R is not timed, but it generally takes 30 to 40 minutes. A particular subtest stops when the child answers five out of seven consecutive questions incorrectly. When testing young children, the examiner might start at the beginning of the subtest, but when testing older children, another starting point can be determined based on academic achievement already known. Because writing is not necessarily involved, the PIAT-R is widely used with children who have physical handicaps. However, children with limited English speaking skills would be at a disadvantage.

HOW ARE RESULTS RECORDED, EVALUATED, INTERPRETED, AND COMPARED?

Raw scores on each subtest are converted to grade and age equivalents, percentiles, and standard scores.

HOW RELIABLE IS THE TEST?

The PIAT-R is considered a reliable tool; that is, it can give a good estimate of academic achievement. Scores on individual subtests can point to areas for which further investigation is needed. Because it is an interactive test, the examiner can get an overall impression of thought processes and ways of handling testing situations. Teenagers with experience in taking tests might think out answers more than a first-time test-taker and therefore do better on the test.

WHAT DOES THE TEST NOT TEST?

The test does not measure aptitude, intelligence, creativity, or personality traits. Although it is used to assess such things as giftedness, other tests should be given and results viewed as a whole. The PIAT-R should not be used alone to make placement or special-education decisions, although it is a test commonly used in batteries.

WHAT FURTHER TESTS MIGHT BE RECOMMENDED?

The PIAT-R is most often given as part of an educational battery. Many other tests could be given, including diagnostic tests in specific academic areas—math or reading, for example.

Preschool and Kindergarten Interest Descriptor (PRIDE)

See Group Inventory for Finding Creative Talent, page 187.

Admission Testing Program: Scholastic Aptitude Test (SAT), Preliminary Scholastic Aptitude Test (PSAT), Test of Standard Written English (TSWE)

WHOSE RECOMMENDATION AND/OR PERMISSION IS NEEDED?

The PSAT, SAT, and TSWE are recommended by high school administrators and guidance counselors. Preenrollment is required.

WHAT DOES THE TEST TEST?

The well-known SAT is an independently developed, standardized test of verbal and mathematical abilities and achievement. It is part of the Admission Testing Program (ATP) and is given at designated testing sites throughout the country. The PSAT is a preview of the SAT and also serves as a qualifying exam for the National Merit Scholarship Program and the National Achievement Scholarship Program for Outstanding Negro Students. The TSWE is given with the SAT, but is scored separately. The TSWE score is not included in the final SAT score.

A student's SAT score is considered an important part of the college admissions process. The SAT is considered one measure of a student's ability to do college-level academic work, a type of "readiness" test for college.

WHAT, IF ANY, PREPARATION IS NECESSARY?

The issue of preparation for the SAT is one of the reasons it is a controversial test. Because a high score is often considered important for admission to a "good" college or university, an industry of sorts has developed to help students prepare. Study guides are sold in most bookstores throughout the country, and private tutors and commercial academic organizations sponsor classes and private sessions to help young people prepare. (The "coachability" of the SAT is one reason critics say it is basically unfair. In a sense, the economic status of the student's family determines the type and quality of SAT coaching available.)

Parents may be able to locate a free or low-cost preparation course sponsored by the school district, a trend that may spread because of the growth of commercial courses. The issue is further confused by the philosophical question of whether the tests are achievement tests and therefore coachable, or abilities tests, which would therefore not be as influenced by tutoring.

A student must register to take the SAT and arrangements can be made for handicapped students (extended time, large print edition, braille, and so on). Students receive instructions about the date, place, and time, as well as what they must provide (I.D., pencils, and so on).

HOW IS THE TEST PERFORMED, AND WHAT SHOULD BE EXPECTED?

All three tests are timed: PSAT, 1 hour and 40 minutes; SAT, 2½ hours; TSWE, 30 minutes. The PSAT and sections of the SAT include sentence completion, verbal analogies, antonyms, and reading comprehension. The mathematics sections include reasoning and problem solving, and knowledge of arithmetic, algebra, and geometry. The TSWE measures basic grammar and usage. All three tests are constructed in a multiple choice format.

HOW ARE RESULTS RECORDED, EVALUATED, INTERPRETED, AND COMPARED?

The raw score for the PSAT and the SAT is computed by counting correct answers and deducting a fraction of a point for each wrong answer. The raw score is then converted to a score on a scale from 200 to 800. Separate scores for verbal and mathematics sections are given. The scores are considered meaningful in that they compare a student with vast numbers of same-age students in the country. The TSWE is reported on a scale of 20 to 60+. It does not affect the other two SAT scores. Test scores are reported in five to six weeks.

HOW RELIABLE IS THE TEST?

The reliability of these tests can be discussed only in terms of how valuable they have been in predicting success in college, something which is a complex measurement. Studies exist that both "prove" and "disprove" the predictive value of the SAT. Both proponents and opponents of the test do agree that the student's background in basic skills will affect the score. The way a student is taught to take the test—that is, the advice given to guess at answers or leave them blank—will affect the outcome as well. Students who have shown themselves to be good test-takers usually do better than those who become anxious during testing. The SAT has undergone a recent revision said to have eliminated any cultural and gender bias in previous editions. This contention will be debated throughout the 1990s.

WHAT DOES THE TEST *NOT* TEST?

These tests are not intelligence tests, nor are they wide-range tests of academic achievement. Knowledge in the sciences, social sciences, and the humanities is not assessed. These tests also do not measure practical or "life" skills.

WHAT FURTHER TESTS MIGHT BE RECOMMENDED?

Some colleges require a student to take its own college entrance exam. The score on that test is then used, along with SAT scores, when admission is being determined. The College Board also publishes achievement tests in the sciences, humanities, foreign languages, and the social sciences that may be required for admissions and placement in some colleges and universities.

School Readiness Survey, Second Edition

WHOSE RECOMMENDATION AND/OR PERMISSION IS NEEDED?

The School Readiness Survey is most often used by school systems, rather than by individual professionals. It is given to children due to enter kindergarten. One of the parents is usually the examiner and scorer, although nurses, teachers, pediatricians, and others might administer the test.

WHAT DOES THE TEST TEST?

The test consists of six sections, each of which measures basic skills needed in kindergarten-level activities (e.g., knowledge of colors, shapes, and numbers). General knowledge is evaluated.

WHAT, IF ANY, PREPARATION IS NECESSARY?

The parent chooses the time and place for the test. Each section takes only a few minutes, and one session is usually adequate. However, the test can be given in two sessions if need be. The parent supplies two pencils and a felt-tip marker.

HOW IS THE TEST PERFORMED, AND WHAT SHOULD BE EXPECTED?

The test is interactive, and the child is asked for both oral and written responses. The parent records oral responses on provided sheets.

HOW ARE RESULTS RECORDED, EVALUATED, INTERPRETED, AND COMPARED?

The parent totals the score and compares the number to norms established for gender.

HOW RELIABLE IS THE TEST?

Children score slightly higher when parents give the tests than when other adults are the examiners. (The publisher calls this the "halo effect.") Some school systems use the test to determine a child's readiness for kindergarten. However, testing conditions may not be uniform, or the child could simply be too distractible to test well. The results of this test alone should not be used to deny entry to school. Retesting or further evaluation should be done before placement decisions are made.

WHAT DOES THE TEST *NOT* TEST?

The test is only a basic skills assessment. It neither diagnoses problems nor measures intelligence or achievement.

WHAT FURTHER TESTS MIGHT BE RECOMMENDED?

The publisher includes suggestions for parents to teach basic skills prior to the child beginning school. Very low test scores should be evaluated by a teacher.

Screening Test of Educational Prerequisite Skills (STEPS)

WHOSE RECOMMENDATION AND/OR PERMISSION IS NEEDED?

The STEPS may be required by school systems prior to a child's entering school. Teachers and teachers' aides generally administer the test.

WHAT DOES THE TEST TEST?

The STEPS measures the basic skills 4- to 5-year-olds need for kindergarten. The test is divided into five areas: intellectual skills, verbal information skills, cognitive strategies, motor skills, and attitudes in learning situations. An optional home questionnaire is also included.

WHAT, IF ANY, PREPARATION IS NECESSARY?

No special preparation needed.

HOW IS THE TEST PERFORMED, AND WHAT SHOULD BE EXPECTED?

The child is asked to copy shapes, identify colors, classify objects, and the like. The test takes 10 to 15 minutes.

HOW ARE RESULTS RECORDED, EVALUATED, INTERPRETED, AND COMPARED?

The results are reported in summary form, one for the school and one for the parents. Basically, both reports identify strengths and weaknesses, without comparison to other children. (The STEPS is criterion-referenced.) The reports may also indicate a need for further testing or monitoring.

HOW RELIABLE IS THE TEST?

As with all readiness testing, the STEPS provides information about a child's performance on one test. It may be useful to identify children who need help in particular areas, but it should not be used to deny children entrance to school or to make special placement decisions. Parents should ask for retesting or further evaluation before placement decisions are made.

WHAT DOES THE TEST *NOT* TEST?

The STEPS does not diagnose learning disabilities, nor does it measure intelligence or psychological maturity.

WHAT FURTHER TESTS MIGHT BE RECOMMENDED?

Generally, no specific tests follow. However, very low scores might signal the need for retesting or more in-depth evaluation.

Slingerland Screening Tests for Identifying Children with Specific Language Disability (Slingerland Tests)

WHOSE RECOMMENDATION AND/OR PERMISSION IS NEEDED?

The Slingerland tests are usually given by classroom or special-education teachers, psychologists, and speech/language specialists.

WHAT DOES THE TEST TEST?

The Slingerland tests measure multisensory (visual, auditory, and kinesthetic) skills related to reading and spelling abilities. (Ages 6 to 12.)

WHAT, IF ANY, PREPARATION IS NECESSARY?

No special preparation is necessary.

HOW IS THE TEST PERFORMED, AND WHAT SHOULD BE EXPECTED?

The child is given a series of tests judged appropriate for his or her grade level. The test is divided into four sections; each section has eight subtests. The child is asked to perform a variety of tasks: copy words, match words, retell stories from memory, and choose a mispronounced word in a series, among others. All tasks require written or oral responses. The tests' content is based on material typically found in the classroom.

HOW ARE RESULTS RECORDED, EVALUATED, INTERPRETED, AND COMPARED?

The Slingerland tests are not normed and provide no age or grade-level scores. A child's strengths and weaknesses can be analyzed and specific problems diagnosed.

HOW RELIABLE IS THE TEST?

The Slingerland tests are not viewed as formal tests. Particular subtests can be used for diagnostic purposes and a remedial plan can be devised based on results.

WHAT DOES THE TEST NOT TEST?

The test does not measure intellectual abilities, nor does it predict a child's academic future.

WHAT FURTHER TESTS MIGHT BE RECOMMENDED?

The Slingerland tests could be repeated to measure progress. In some cases, in-depth language testing might be recommended to confirm the presence of a specific language deficit.

Social Skills Rating System (SSRS)

WHOSE RECOMMENDATION AND/OR PERMISSION IS NEEDED?

Teachers, guidance counselors, social workers, or school or clinical psychologists may recommend this test. The SSRS may also be used to screen groups of children. Parents are usually involved in the assessment process.

WHAT DOES THE TEST TEST?

The SSRS measures the behavior of children and adolescents in three areas: social skills (sharing, following rules, and so on), problem behaviors (aggression, hyperactivity, and so on), and academic competence. Teachers rate children in all three of these areas, parents rate social skills and problem behaviors, and the child is asked to describe his or her own social skills.

WHAT, IF ANY, PREPARATION IS NECESSARY?

No preparation is required.

HOW IS THE TEST PERFORMED, AND WHAT SHOULD BE EXPECTED?

The parents, the teacher, and the child each complete a paper-and-pencil questionnaire and report both the frequency and importance of the various behaviors described. The questionnaire takes 10 to 25 minutes to complete. (A third-grade reading level is needed.) The examiner may read the items aloud to a young child.

HOW ARE RESULTS RECORDED, EVALUATED, INTERPRETED, AND COMPARED?

The examiner scores each rater's questionnaire and describes the frequency of the child's behavior in each area as being "more," "average," or "fewer," based on comparison with national norms. The summary scores from all raters are brought together and compared on a composite record form. Interpretation may focus on differences between the raters in their descriptions.

HOW RELIABLE IS THE TEST?

Statistical reliability on the scales varies somewhat, and the importance of the results will vary based on the purpose of the testing in the first place.

WHAT DOES THE TEST *NOT* TEST?

The SSRS does not measure personality, intelligence, or academic achievement.

WHAT FURTHER TESTS MIGHT BE RECOMMENDED?

The SSRS may be used as part of a broad evaluation that also includes measures of ability and achievement. If the SSRS indicates a high degree of problem behaviors, further behavioral ratings or observations may be recommended. Depending on the results, counseling for the child or the family may be recommended.

Stanford Achievement Test Series, Eighth Edition: Stanford Achievement Test (The Stanford), Stanford Early School Achievement Test (SESAT), Stanford Test of Academic Skills (TASK)

WHOSE RECOMMENDATION AND/OR PERMISSION IS NEEDED?

The Stanford tests are used by some school districts to fulfill state or locally mandated testing requirements. They are also widely used in private school settings.

WHAT DOES THE TEST TEST?

The Stanford test series measures many areas of academic achievement: reading, language arts, mathematics, and science, among others. It also includes tests that measure listening skills, and some test items throughout the battery are scored under a category called Thinking Skills. The specific test and level chosen are determined by grade. The TASK, for example, is a high school–level battery.

WHAT, IF ANY, PREPARATION IS NECESSARY?

Parents generally receive notification about the testing schedule in advance. The normal school-day schedule may be changed to accommodate large group testing.

HOW IS THE TEST PERFORMED, AND WHAT SHOULD BE EXPECTED?

The tests are given to groups in the classroom or another location that is set up to accommodate the testing, such as a library. The Stanford is a basic paper-and-pencil test in which test directions are uniform. The Stanford tests are timed; total testing time varies with the level, and ranges from about 1½ to 3½ hours.

HOW ARE RESULTS RECORDED, EVALUATED, INTERPRETED, AND COMPARED?

Raw scores on the test are converted into numerous derived scores: percentiles (local and national), stanines, and grade equivalents, among others. There are also numerous ways the scores can be presented. A student and parent may receive a printout with information about percentiles and grade equivalents, as well as an optional summary report. (The options are chosen by school administrators and, simply put, a "package" is purchased that may or may not include various detailed reports.) Norms for the deaf are also available, as are norms for Catholic and other private schools.

HOW RELIABLE IS THE TEST?

The Stanford tests are widely used and considered statistically reliable. It is assumed that the child has been taught the material tested. If a child has known learning disabilities or is taking longer to learn certain skills, grade norms are not a useful way to express progress or abilities. It is important to find out how the scores will be used. More information should be gathered before a child is held back or placed in remedial classes.

WHAT DOES THE TEST NOT TEST?

The Stanford series tests do not measure intelligence, nor are they designed as career/vocational tests.

WHAT FURTHER TESTS MIGHT BE RECOMMENDED?

School districts that use The Stanford may also use the Otis-Lennon School Ability Test, which is a group-administered mental abilities test. The test is sometimes part of a "package" that is sold to a state or locale. The Stanford Achievement Test, Abbreviated, is a shorter version of the test. Some locales that test every year choose this option.

Strong-Campbell Interest Inventory (The Strong)

A Spanish language version is available.

WHOSE RECOMMENDATION AND/OR PERMISSION IS NEEDED?

The Strong is generally given by school counselors and others involved in career counseling in the late high school years. It is also used with adults.

WHAT DOES THE TEST TEST?

The Strong measures an individual's interests and likes and dislikes for the purpose of suggesting a range of possible appropriate occupations.

WHAT, IF ANY, PREPARATION IS NECESSARY?

No preparation is needed.

HOW IS THE TEST PERFORMED, AND WHAT SHOULD BE EXPECTED?

This is a paper-and-pencil test consisting of 325 items. The choice of answers in the majority of items is Like, Dislike, or Indifferent. The questions describe the type of activities involved in specific occupations, as well as characteristics associated with people working in them: working with people versus working alone, risk-taking versus staying with a sure thing, and so on. The test takes 30 to 40 minutes.

HOW ARE RESULTS RECORDED, EVALUATED, INTERPRETED, AND COMPARED?

Results are reported through three scales: General Occupational Themes, Basic Interest Scales, and Occupational Scales. The scores for the General Occupational Themes Scale are interpreted by using six basic occupational types, all of which have personality characteristics associated with them. The other two scales show how similar or dissimilar the test-taker's interests are to those holding a wide variety of jobs. The test was designed by measuring interests of people already engaged in various occupations. A profile report is provided along with a narrative including a more detailed interpretation.

HOW RELIABLE IS THIS TEST?

The Strong can be used as a tool in a guidance program. It should not be used to make arbitrary placement decisions or necessarily steer students into a specific academic track. Only the most recent versions are valid, because earlier editions had separate test items and scales for men and women.

WHAT DOES THE TEST NOT TEST?

The Strong is not an achievement, intelligence, or aptitude test.

WHAT FURTHER TESTS MIGHT BE RECOMMENDED?

Depending on the reasons for giving the test, aptitude and achievement tools could be recommended.

Test of Achievement and Proficiency (TAP): Forms J, G, and H; Levels 15–18; Basic Battery; Complete Battery

WHOSE RECOMMENDATION AND/OR PERMISSION IS NEEDED?

The TAP is used in schools and may fulfill a particular state or district's mandated testing requirements.

WHAT DOES THE TEST TEST?

The TAP Basic Battery measures four skills: reading, mathematics, written expression, and using sources of information. The Complete Battery includes these four tests, as well as tests in Science and Social Studies. There is also an optional student questionnaire that guidance counselors may use when working with students. There are items in each section that measure skills that could be called "practical"; that is, those skills considered necessary to get along in the world. (Grades 9 through 12.)

WHAT, IF ANY, PREPARATION IS NECESSARY?

No special preparation is needed; however, individual school districts may send a testing schedule home with the child with ideas about preparation for lengthy testing. The publisher also provides a document, "A Message to Parents," which is intended to help parents prepare children for the testing.

HOW IS THE TEST PERFORMED, AND WHAT SHOULD BE EXPECTED?

The TAP is given in groups and takes 2½ to 4 hours, depending on which battery is used. This is a basic paper-and-pencil test and all items are presented in a test booklet.

HOW ARE RESULTS RECORDED, EVALUATED, INTERPRETED, AND COMPARED?

Raw scores can be converted to percentiles, grade equivalents, stanines, and so on. There is also an Applied Proficiency Skills score, which isolates items falling into the "practical skills" category. States that use this test to establish minimum competency in reading and mathematics may use scores to demonstrate that the required competency levels have been reached. In these states, students are given more than one opportunity to pass the test.

HOW RELIABLE IS THE TEST?

The TAP is considered a reliable way to measure basic skills. However, it should not be used alone to place students into particular tracks, nor should a student be held back in any way because of TAP scores. Other evaluation methods should be used if a student's actual classroom performance is not reflected in the test scores. Test anxiety should also be considered, especially if the school administrators use test results to make placement or graduation decisions. It is also assumed that the child has been taught the material the test covers.

WHAT DOES THE TEST *NOT* TEST?

The TAP does not measure intelligence.

WHAT FURTHER TESTS MIGHT BE RECOMMENDED?

Individual tests might be recommended under certain circumstances—a known or suspected learning disability, for example.

Test of Adolescent Language, 2 (TOAL-2)

WHOSE RECOMMENDATION AND/OR PERMISSION IS NEEDED?

The TOAL-2 is usually given by special-education teachers, speech/language clinicians, or any professional who has been trained to give it.

WHAT DOES THE TEST TEST?

The TOAL-2 measures receptive and expressive language, both spoken and written. It provides a fairly complete assessment of a young person's ability to use language skills and acquired vocabulary. (Ages 11 to 18½.)

WHAT, IF ANY, PREPARATION IS NECESSARY?

No special preparation is needed.

HOW IS THE TEST PERFORMED, AND WHAT SHOULD BE EXPECTED?

The child is alone with an examiner, who administers the eight subtests, including a variety of activities: matching words and pictures, identifying like sentence structures, and using words in sentences, among others. The TOAL-2 takes 1½ hours.

HOW ARE RESULTS RECORDED, EVALUATED, INTERPRETED, AND COMPARED?

Raw scores are converted to percentile and stanine scores.

HOW RELIABLE IS THE TEST?

The TOAL-2 is reliable when viewed as a tool to describe an individual's use of language. However, it is a complex test and some students who have language deficiencies might find the directions for some subtests difficult to follow. It can be used to measure progress.

WHAT DOES THE TEST *NOT* TEST?

The TOAL-2 does not measure academic achievement, nor is it an intelligence test.

WHAT FURTHER TESTS MIGHT BE RECOMMENDED?

The TOAL-2 could be repeated at intervals. Other language tests might also be recommended to investigate areas in which scores were low.

Vision Screening

WHOSE RECOMMENDATION AND/OR PERMISSION IS NEEDED?

Physicians, optometrists, nurses, nurse practitioners, teachers, teachers' aides, or trained volunteers perform vision screening in a school setting. Most states mandate basic screening procedures prior to entry into either kindergarten or first grade. Repeat screenings may be mandated at intervals throughout grade school or before entering high school. Some school districts also require screening for students transferring in from other districts. In addition, a child may be referred for screening at any time if he or she exhibits symptoms of visual problems. Parents' permission is generally not required for vision screening. Parents' permission *is* required when referrals are made for more extensive testing, which is generally performed by ophthalmologists or optometrists.

WHAT DOES THE TEST TEST?

The most commonly used screening tests—The Snellen Wall Chart and the Snellen E Test—measure visual acuity (sharpness of vision). Acuity problems are sometimes the cause of a child's inability to distinguish letters or numbers, which results in difficulty with classroom work.

The problems that *may* be revealed in this screening are *hyperopia* (farsightedness); *myopia* (nearsightedness); *astigmatism,* a condition characterized by an irregular curvature of the cornea or lens of the eye; *strabismus,* crossed eyes that result from a muscle imbalance, meaning that the eyes do not work in a coordinated way; *amblyopia,* commonly known as lazy eye, which also results from a difficulty in the eye muscles. Screenings for color blindness are common in later school years or are included in other, more comprehensive vision screenings.

WHAT, IF ANY, PREPARATION IS NECESSARY?

There is no specific preparation needed. However, it is important that a child understand the procedure. A child who already has corrective glasses should always wear them during the screening.

HOW IS THE TEST PERFORMED, AND WHAT SHOULD BE EXPECTED?

With the Snellen Wall Chart, the child is asked to read letters across a printed line. Sometimes a letter is isolated in a line for identification. Children may be grouped in assembly-line fashion for this screening.

The Snellen E Test is often used with preschoolers, who may not be able to name letters. The letter E is presented with the "arms" of the letter pointing in different directions. The child points to or names the direction the arms are facing, or holds a card in the way that matches the presentation of each E.

These screenings generally take less than five minutes to complete. However, a child should not be rushed, and if more time is needed, it should be given. The amount of time taken does not affect the outcome.

HOW ARE RESULTS RECORDED, EVALUATED, INTERPRETED, AND COMPARED?

Test results are expressed in numbers that relate to visual acuity. The scoring system was developed by Herman Snellen, the Dutch ophthalmologist who created the test in 1862. He determined that a line of print of a certain size should be readable at a distance of 20 feet (6 meters). Therefore, normal vision is expressed as 20/20, or 6/6 in the metric system.

Each line on the chart represents a distance a person should be able to read from: 200, 100, 70, 50, 30, and 20 feet. The large E on the Snellen Wall Chart is the 200-foot line. The child's right or wrong answers on each line determine the visual acuity score. If all are answered correctly on the 40-foot line, visual acuity is said to be 20/40. If all are answered correctly on the 30-foot line, visual acuity is 20/30. Visual acuity could be, for example, 20/30 in one eye and 20/40 in the other.

The criterion for referral for further testing is generally 20/40 or less in either eye for children in grades K through 3, and 20/30 or less in either eye for older children.

HOW RELIABLE IS THE TEST?

Because these are screening tests, their reliability is always open to question. A child who is having obvious visual difficulties (e.g., squinting, blinking, frequent rubbing of the eyes, or obvious straining) should not be considered to have normal vision even if the score falls into the range of scores considered normal. Children are often able to be good guessers when identifying the letters; some children even consider this a challenge. Further, problems caused by muscle imbalances may be missed in these screenings. In some cases, the test is repeated in order to establish that referral is necessary.

WHAT DOES THE TEST *NOT* TEST?

Neither screening test results in the diagnosis of any specific visual disorder.

WHAT FURTHER TESTS MIGHT BE RECOMMENDED?

Some school districts are currently using instruments rather than wall charts for vision screening. These instruments, which are generically referred to as stereoscopes, can simulate distance and present different pictures to each eye. In addition, eye coordination and depth perception can be assessed with more accuracy than with a wall chart.

Vision problems should always be considered when a child is having difficulty learning basic skills. If a child complains about fuzziness of letters on a blackboard, this is an obvious sign that something is wrong. However, less obvious signs include a child's complaints about the glare on a printed page or fatigue after only a few minutes of close work.

Wide Range Achievement Test (WRAT)

WHOSE RECOMMENDATION AND/OR PERMISSION IS NEEDED?

Special-education and classroom teachers, and psychologists usually administer the test.

WHAT DOES THE TEST TEST?

The WRAT is a test of reading, written spelling, and arithmetic skills. Two levels of the WRAT are available: one for children ages 5 to 11, and one for ages 11 and up.

WHAT, IF ANY, PREPARATION IS NECESSARY?

No special preparation is needed.

HOW IS THE TEST PERFORMED, AND WHAT SHOULD BE EXPECTED?

The WRAT is usually given individually, although it can be given to groups. It is a paper-and-pencil test, with items presented in order of difficulty. Reading skill is assessed through word recognition, spelling through dictation, and math through basic counting, number recognition, computation, and oral problems. The test takes 20 to 30 minutes and is timed. (A large-print version is available for the visually impaired.)

HOW ARE RESULTS RECORDED, EVALUATED, INTERPRETED, AND COMPARED?

A raw score is calculated for each subtest and is converted to a percentile, a grade score, and a standard score. The results can be presented in numerous ways, however, and the WRAT is often used as a tool to screen for areas that need further teaching or more diagnostic testing.

HOW RELIABLE IS THE TEST?

The WRAT is considered a reliable and quick way to measure a child's achievement in the three areas it addresses. In addition, the results can be helpful in planning remedial teaching or alerting teachers to the special needs of a particular student. For example, the pattern of errors on a subtest may be more important than the actual score. The test should not be considered a complete diagnostic tool, nor should students be included or excluded from special programs based solely on WRAT scores. Some scores, particularly on the arithmetic subtests, may vary depending on the curriculum of individual schools.

WHAT DOES THE TEST *NOT* TEST?

It's important to note that the WRAT does not test reading comprehension or mathematical concepts.

WHAT FURTHER TESTS MIGHT BE RECOMMENDED?

Recommendation for further testing will depend on the purpose the WRAT was given in the first place. If a learning disability is suspected, a wide range of tests could follow. The WRAT is sometimes given as part of a psychological battery that could include projective tests such as the Thematic Apperception Test, the House-Tree-Person test, and an intelligence test.

Woodcock-Johnson Psychoeducational Battery (WJPEB)

WHOSE RECOMMENDATION AND/OR PERMISSION IS NEEDED?

The test is usually given by a psychologist or educational diagnostician.

WHAT DOES THE TEST TEST?

The WJPEB tests a student's cognitive abilities, scholastic aptitude, achievement, and interests. (Ages 3 to adult.)

WHAT, IF ANY, PREPARATION IS NECESSARY

No special preparation is necessary.

HOW IS THE TEST PERFORMED, AND
WHAT SHOULD BE EXPECTED?

The test is long and complex, and some sections are timed, whereas others are not. The cognitive ability test (Part I) has twelve subtests that measure various areas of language, math, memory, and verbal reasoning skills. The achievement test (Part II) is divided into ten subtests that measure a child's knowledge of science, literature, art, problem solving, humanities, and social skills. Part III measures interests and consists of five subtests. The child is asked questions about interest in reading, math, writing, and physical and social activities. The examiner may decide to use only certain sections of the test.

HOW ARE RESULTS RECORDED, EVALUATED,
INTERPRETED, AND COMPARED?

The test is scored in four ways: a subtest profile, which allows quick interpretation of subtest performance; the Percentile Rank Profile, which provides information related to age or grade placement; the Instructional Implication Profile, which relates instructional range to grade placement; and the Achievement Aptitude Profile, in which a comparison is made of the child's expected achievement to actual achievement. There are many ways to interpret scores, which require individual explanation.

HOW RELIABLE IS THE TEST?

The WJPEB can be used as a screening tool or for a larger scale measure of abilities and performance. It is considered reliable for particular uses, such as a way to analyze strengths and weaknesses and plan instruction. It might indicate that a child is behind in certain areas for which special instruction could be planned.

WHAT DOES THE TEST *NOT* TEST?

The WJPEB does not measure a student's overall intelligence or abilities.

WHAT FURTHER TESTS MIGHT BE RECOMMENDED?

Tests in many other areas could be recommended if an extensive assessment is being done.

Woodcock Reading Mastery Tests, Revised

WHOSE RECOMMENDATION AND/OR PERMISSION IS NEEDED?

The test is usually recommended by a classroom teacher and administered by an education diagnostician, reading specialist, or special-education teacher.

WHAT DOES THE TEST TEST?

The test measures several aspects of reading ability through six subtests and a supplementary letter checklist. The subtests are divided into three clusters. The Readiness cluster measures visual-auditory learning and letter identification; the Basic Skills cluster measures the child's word identification and word attack skills; and the Reading Comprehension cluster measures the child's comprehension of words and passages. The test can be used for quick assessment of a child's reading ability, or to obtain more comprehensive diagnostic information. (Grades K through 12.)

WHAT, IF ANY, PREPARATION IS NECESSARY?

No special preparation is needed.

HOW IS THE TEST PERFORMED, AND WHAT SHOULD BE EXPECTED?

The child is alone with the examiner, and gives oral responses to questions. No writing is required, and each subtest has a slightly different format. The child is shown a picture, word, or letter, for example, and the examiner asks the child a question about what is shown. Selected subtests may be used.

HOW ARE RESULTS RECORDED, EVALUATED, INTERPRETED, AND COMPARED?

The examiner converts the raw score to grade or age equivalents, standard scores, or percentile ranks. A profile may also be completed that can be examined to show individual strengths and weaknesses. The examiner can also analyze the child's errors on individual items.

HOW RELIABLE IS THE TEST?

The test is considered a reliable tool to measure specific aspects of reading ability. It can be used to plan reading instruction for an individual child.

WHAT DOES THE TEST NOT TEST?

The test is not an aptitude or intelligence test.

WHAT FURTHER TESTS MIGHT BE RECOMMENDED?

The Woodcock Reading Mastery Tests may be given in conjunction with tests that measure other skills considered necessary to learn to read—auditory abilities, for example.

The Word Test

WHOSE RECOMMENDATION AND/OR PERMISSION IS NEEDED?

The Word Test is usually recommended and given by psychologists, special-education teachers, or speech/language clinicians.

WHAT DOES THE TEST TEST?

The Word Test measures expressive language abilities. (Ages 7 to 12.)

WHAT, IF ANY, PREPARATION IS NECESSARY?

No special preparation is necessary.

HOW IS THE TEST PERFORMED, AND WHAT SHOULD BE EXPECTED?

The Word Test is given orally and the student responds verbally. The test is divided into six subtests: associations, synonyms, semantic absurdities, antonyms, definitions, and multiple definitions. The child is asked to choose synonyms for words, identify sentence problems, give opposites of words, define words, and pick the word that doesn't belong from a group of four.

HOW ARE RESULTS RECORDED, EVALUATED, INTERPRETED, AND COMPARED?

Each correct response is given one point. Raw scores can be converted into age equivalents, percentiles, and standard scores.

HOW RELIABLE IS THE TEST?

The Word Test provides valuable information about a child's ability to use words in their proper context. It can also give the clinician general information about the child's semantic abilities and vocabulary. However, it is not considered a reliable measure of these skills because it was not designed for this purpose.

WHAT DOES THE TEST NOT TEST?

The test is not an intelligence test, nor does it predict future academic performance.

WHAT FURTHER TESTS MIGHT BE RECOMMENDED?

The Word Test is often given along with other tests after a broader language test has shown a need for more specific testing.

SUPPLEMENTAL TESTS

The following are some additional widely used tests you might encounter in numerous settings. The test formats and the domains being tested are similar to those listed previously. However, it should not be considered inclusive; there are hundreds of educational tests.

ADD-H Comprehensive Teacher's Rating Scale. Includes twenty-four scales that describe classroom behavior to aid in the diagnosis of attention deficit disorders. Grades K through 5.

Aprenda: La Prueba de Logros en Español. Similar in format and content to other extensive achievement tests. The test questions are written in Spanish, as opposed to being translated from English to Spanish. Grades K through 8.

California Achievement Tests. One of the most widely used academic achievement tests. Various levels are available to cover grades K through 12.9, the last part of high school. These tests may be used to fulfill state or local testing mandates. Numerous derived scores are reported.

Criterion-Referenced Curriculum, Mathematics (CRC-Mathematics). Teaching plans and tests designed for individual remedial programs and special-education teaching. Grades K through 6.

Criterion-Referenced Curriculum, Reading (CRC-Reading). Teaching plans and tests designed for individual remedial reading programs and special-education teaching. Grades K through 6.

Henmon-Nelson Tests of Mental Ability. A widely used group-administered IQ test. Scores can be reported in both age and grade percentile rank and stanine.

The Kindergarten Readiness Test (KRT). Consolidates various areas of developmental tests into one test that assesses school readiness.

Language Assessment Battery (LAB). Measures language skills in Spanish or English and is used to identify students who are unable to adequately learn in an English-speaking classroom.

La Prueba de Realización. A Spanish language achievement test for grades K through 12. It is similar to other lengthy and extensive academic achievement batteries.

Minnesota Prekindergarten Inventory (MPI). A parent-completed inventory used to assess school readiness.

Nelson-Denny Reading Test. Assesses reading skills of high school and college students that takes about 35 minutes to complete. It includes a reading-rate score.

PRG Interest Inventory. A tool to assess career/vocational interests of the visually impaired. (Large-print format.)

Preschool Language Scale (PLS). A screening test often used in preschool programs that is also used to assess school readiness. It measures receptive and expressive language, along with such things as knowledge of colors and number concepts.

Slosson Oral Reading Test (SORT-R). A quick test that measures reading ability and that is useful in identifying specific difficulties with reading.

Stanford Diagnostic Reading Test (SDRT). Measures skills involved in reading, from first grade through high school, for the purpose of identifying students who need remedial programs and for placement in classroom reading groups.

Test of Early Mathematics Ability, 2 (TEMA-2). Determines strengths and weaknesses in mathematics in children ages 3 to 9.

Test of Early Reading Ability, 2 (TERA-2). Measures reading ability in children ages 3 to 10. Word meanings, use of words, and the like are tested.

Walker Problem Behavior Identification Checklist. Generally used in schools, and usually completed by a teacher, this checklist identifies behavior problems of children, who may be referred for counseling.

PSYCHOLOGICAL TESTING

Perhaps no area of testing is more complex—and more perplexing—than psychological testing. Being told that their child requires psychological testing may trigger two all-too-common reactions in parents—panic and guilt (not necessarily in that order). For this reason, sensitive professionals usually try to reassure parents. Nor is this offering false comfort, because "psychological testing" covers vast ground.

There are numerous reasons psychological testing may be suggested. Psychological testing is used to rule out serious emotional difficulties and organic brain dysfunction. It is also used to determine if a developmental or educational difficulty has some psychological cause. For example, children with persistent speech problems may be given psychological batteries when physical causes have been eliminated. Psychological assessments are also part of diagnosing learning disabilities, as well as hyperactivity and/or attention deficit disorder (ADD)—conditions that may have both psychological and physiological causes and treatments.

Parents may initiate psychological testing, often because they have identified problem behaviors or are concerned about their child's emotional life. One parent took both of her preschool daughters for a psychological evaluation because they seemed more reserved and quieter than their peers. The results of the testing were reassuring; while the girls *were* more reserved and quiet than "average" children, their behavior was normal. In this case, some people would say the testing was unnecessary. However, it was helpful to the parent and not harmful to the child. "Necessary" can be a subjective concept in testing.

Other cases are more pressing, however. A child of six who literally can't concentrate on a task for more than a minute, or who is destructive and aggressive, poses problems both at home and at school. Before testing (or therapy) is begun, the parent and the child's teacher may be asked to complete a type of questionnaire (checklist or inventory) to get a more complete picture of the behavior in question, and a professional may observe a young child in a clinical setting. (An older child may be asked to complete a "self-report" behavior or attitude questionnaire.) Interviews—sometimes informal, in that the examiner asks questions he or she believes will elicit the needed information—are also part of a psychological assessment. Another type of interview, the structured interview, has specific questions and uses a scale to score responses.

Of course, it is also important that the health and family history of the child be discussed. It makes no sense to do extensive—and expensive—psychological testing if a medical problem is a likely cause of the problem. Similarly, when a child experiences a traumatic event—the death of a sibling or parent, or parents' divorce, for example—a period of adjustment is both expected and normal. Grief, after all, is not an illness. Even if the grief is extreme and a therapist becomes involved, psychological testing is probably not necessary.

A child's involvement in court proceedings may necessitate psychological testing. Nowadays, a child may be given a battery of psychological tests when the parents are involved in a serious custody dispute. In fact, two batteries may be done, by two different psychologists, each hired by one of the parents. In some cases, a judge orders the testing, and the court appoints the psychologist. Criminal cases including accusations of physical or sexual abuse of children may also rely on results of psychological testing to use as evidence.

Both sides in such a case may have their own teams of experts to do the testing and evaluations. If parents find themselves in these extraordinary and difficult situations, they should carefully monitor what tests are being performed, under what conditions, and by whom.

In recent years neuropsychological testing has become widely used. A very complex field of study, it can basically be defined as determining the relationship of brain functioning and behavior. This type of testing may become important if it is suggested your child suffers from such things as attention-deficit disorder (ADD), hyperactivity (sometimes included in a diagnosis of ADD), learning disabilities, various types of retardation, brain injury, or developmental delays.

Intelligence tests given individually (one examiner for one child) generally fall into the category of psychological testing, whereas group intelligence tests are generally considered educational testing and are covered in that section of the book. The qualifications of the examiner is very important; many of these tests may be given only by licensed psychologists. Testing conditions and a child's rapport with the examiner are important, too, as is the preparation for psychological testing.

When listing the individual tests, we have usually said that no special preparation is needed. However, common sense dictates that, depending on the child's age, he or she should be told something about what is to take place. For example, a young child should be told that he or she will be alone with an examiner and will be doing a variety of activities. Older children know that individual testing usually means that something about him or her is being explored or evaluated. There is no point in denying this. In fact, being as honest as possible is probably the best policy. However, children should not be made to feel that an "agenda" has been predetermined, or they might attempt to comply with what they know the concerned and powerful adults want to hear. Many young people become quite sophisticated test-takers and begin to view it all as a "game." It is quite natural that a child be concerned about decisions being made on the basis of the test results. For this reason, it should be made clear that the testing is but one part of an assessment process.

It is also important that psychological diagnoses not be made on the basis of one test. For example, tests that require a child to tell a story, complete a sentence, or draw pictures are meant to be used as part of a battery of tests. These tests are projective tools, meaning that the children bring their own attitudes, experiences, and thoughts to the process and that these shape their responses to tasks or questions. Guidelines and norms have been developed for scoring these tests, but no professional would claim that a definitive diagnosis can be made on the basis of one test.

Performing a battery of tests also guards against the "game playing" and attempts to "trick" the test that some young people engage in. Some professionals believe that checklists and interviews completed by others help arrive at a true profile of the child being examined.

You will notice that various testing terms—norms and domains, for example—are used in the test profiles. These terms are defined in the glossary. However, the professionals giving your child a series of tests should be able to help you understand what a descriptive measurement term means in your child's particular case.

As is true in all other areas of testing, the more questions you ask, the more information you will get. And, as in medical testing, second opinions may be helpful and referrals to other specialists can be an expected part of the service you receive. Psychological testing is done in many settings: schools, clinics, hospitals, private practitioner's offices, and, nowadays, in the workplace. Most of the tests listed have numerous applications. Therefore, don't be surprised if you encounter many of these tests more than once.

Advanced Progressive Matrices

See Raven's Progressive Matrices, page 266.

Bender Visual Motor Gestalt Test (The Bender)

WHOSE RECOMMENDATION AND/OR PERMISSION IS NEEDED?

The Bender must be given by a psychologist.

WHAT DOES THE TEST TEST?

The Bender tests visual-motor integration and is sometimes used to detect neurological difficulties or emotional problems.

WHAT, IF ANY, PREPARATION IS NECESSARY?

No special preparation is necessary.

HOW IS THE TEST PERFORMED, AND WHAT SHOULD BE EXPECTED?

The Bender is usually administered individually, but it can be administered to groups. The child is given nine abstract designs to copy. (In a modification of the test, a child may also be asked to draw the designs from memory.) The child may use more than one piece of paper, and erasing and starting over is permitted. (When the Bender is given individually, the examiner pays attention to the child's behavior while taking the test. The examiner notes the child's ability to concentrate, the types of comments he or she makes while drawing, and any signs of frustration. Because this test should not be given alone, the behavioral signs may be helpful when an evaluation is done after the results of all the tests in the battery are in.) When given to a group of children, the de signs are shown on a large screen. The test is not timed, but it usually takes 20 to 25 minutes if given in a group, and 10 minutes if given individually.

HOW ARE RESULTS RECORDED, EVALUATED, INTERPRETED, AND COMPARED?

The child is scored in a number of areas. For example, changing the shape or angle of a line is counted as an error. The child's total score is converted to a developmental age score. The examiner also notes the behavior of the child during the test. The drawings of two children may be similar, but the behavior may be different and that makes the final score different as well. The examiner must be very experienced to score and evaluate the Bender. Reliability studies have shown that the test becomes less meaningful with children older than age 9 or 10. The Bender is generally given to adolescents or adults only when a known deficiency is present.

HOW RELIABLE IS THE TEST?

When used in conjunction with other tests, the Bender is effective for screening and identifying children considered to be at risk for developmental or learning disabilities. Generally speaking, the results are more reliable when applied to visual-motor perception skills only, and less meaningful for evaluating emotional problems.

WHAT DOES THE TEST *NOT* TEST?

The Bender does not test intelligence or achievement and when used alone is not a test for detecting neurological impairment or emotional difficulties.

WHAT FURTHER TESTS MIGHT BE RECOMMENDED?

If a neurological impairment or emotional disorder is suspected, tests in these specific areas would be recommended. If developmental deficiencies are being examined, other developmental tests could be used. The Bender is usually part of a battery of tests.

Bristol Social Adjustment Guides (BSAG)

WHOSE RECOMMENDATION AND/OR PERMISSION IS NEEDED?

The BSAG is generally recommended by school counselors, teachers, and school psychologists. It is completed by a teacher or another adult familiar with the child. Parents' permission is needed.

WHAT DOES THE TEST TEST?

The BSAG is designed to detect and measure the presence of behavioral problems through observation by a teacher or another adult. (Ages 5 to 16.)

WHAT, IF ANY, PREPARATION IS NECESSARY?

No preparation is needed. However, as a parent you will want to participate in the evaluation process.

HOW IS THE TEST PERFORMED, AND WHAT SHOULD BE EXPECTED?

The guides consist of a list of short phrases, descriptive of a child's behavior; the teacher or another adult underlines those behaviors he or she believes apply. An overall assessment of maladjustment may be obtained, as well as subscores in diagnostic categories such as the following: unforthcomingness (lack of confidence, self-assertion, or curiosity), withdrawal, depression, inconsequence (impulsive behavior without regard for the consequences), and hostility.

HOW ARE RESULTS RECORDED, EVALUATED, INTERPRETED, AND COMPARED?

Behaviors indicated are rated on scales that yield scores in the various behavioral categories. (There are separate norms for boys and girls.)

HOW RELIABLE IS THE TEST?

The BSAG is one way to report information about a child's behavior. Its reliability depends on how the information compares with other information known or gathered about a child. Recommendation for special classroom placement or counseling in a school setting should not be made solely on the basis of the BSAG report.

WHAT DOES THE TEST *NOT* TEST?

The BSAG does not measure academic performance, nor does it diagnose specific psychological conditions.

WHAT FURTHER TESTS MIGHT BE RECOMMENDED?

Depending on the results and the reason for the observation, specific areas should be explored. For example, if depression is suspected, other diagnostic methods could be included in an assessment (other observation reports, interviews, and other tests that diagnose depression).

Children's Apperception Test (CAT)

See Thematic Apperception Test, page 275.

Children's Depression Inventory (CDI)

WHOSE RECOMMENDATION AND/OR PERMISSION IS NEEDED?

Psychiatrists and psychologists generally recommend the test. Parents' permission is required.

WHAT DOES THE TEST TEST?

The CDI measures signs of depression in children, including both the presence of symptoms and their severity. Symptoms include such things as sleep disturbance, sadness, and suicidal thoughts. (Ages 8 to 13.)

WHAT, IF ANY, PREPARATION IS NECESSARY?

No special preparation is needed.

HOW IS THE TEST PERFORMED, AND WHAT SHOULD BE EXPECTED?

The CDI consists of twenty-seven items, each of which is read aloud to the child. They are "I" statement sentences, and the child is asked which statement best describes his or her feelings during the previous two weeks. The test is not timed, and it can be given to small groups of children.

HOW ARE RESULTS RECORDED, EVALUATED, INTERPRETED, AND COMPARED?

Each of the items has three possible answers, and each answer is given a numerical score. The scores are added and the total is compared with ranges of scores established for populations considered well-adjusted and not depressed.

HOW RELIABLE IS THE TEST?

The CDI is considered a useful tool to detect the presence of depression. It can confirm what has already been observed or provide clinicians with additional information on which to base further investigation. It is important that the child understand the statements and grasp the idea of the two-week time frame.

WHAT DOES THE TEST *NOT* TEST?

The CDI does not determine the cause of depression, nor does it measure other psychological problems.

WHAT FURTHER TESTS MIGHT BE RECOMMENDED?

The CDI is often given after a psychiatric interview. The Kiddie-SADS (K-SADS) is one of the common interviews used. Both the parents and the child are interviewed, and a teacher's report is also used. If more information is needed, medical tests or other psychological evaluations may be used.

The Child Behavior Checklist

WHOSE RECOMMENDATION AND/OR PERMISSION IS NEEDED?

Special-education teachers and guidance counselors generally suggest the test in the school setting; social workers and psychologists suggest it in a clinical setting (hospitals, community mental heath centers, and so on).

WHAT DOES THE TEST TEST?

The Child Behavior Checklist is not, strictly speaking, a test. Rather, it is a system of questions and responses designed to assess various aspects of a child's behavior from the point of view of those who have consistent contact with him or her. The Checklist assumes that some behavior difficulties are present and seeks to get reports on these behaviors from teachers, parents, and, in the case of teenagers, from the child himself or herself. The Teacher Report Form gathers information on a child's classroom behavior; the Parent Report Form reports on behavior at home. Other observers could report behavior in a clinical setting, with the results compared with the parent, teacher, or "self" reports.

WHAT, IF ANY, PREPARATION IS NECESSARY?

No special preparation is needed.

HOW IS THE TEST PERFORMED, AND WHAT SHOULD BE EXPECTED?

The parent is usually considered the primary informant; it is the parent who will report the presence and frequency of certain behaviors. Some of the times are specific (e.g., bedwetting, suicidal talk, and so on). Some are general (e.g., the child is unhappy, sad, suspicious, and so on). Finally, some items require parental judgment (e.g., the child is "too loud," or "too easily frightened"). If two parents are completing the Checklist, they do so separately. The test is written at about a fifth-grade reading level and generally takes about 20 minutes to complete. The Self Report Form used with older children and adolescents requires the young person to self-report behaviors, feelings, and judgments. Teachers and clinicians report information from their unique point of view.

HOW ARE RESULTS RECORDED, EVALUATED, INTERPRETED, AND COMPARED?

The Checklist is designed to provide an overview of behaviors that are compared to scales developed within normal, or nonproblematic, populations. The results can point to particular difficulties, which can either be diagnosed with other tests or worked on within a clinical setting. It is important to note that results are not assigned a score, nor is a diagnosis made on the basis of the Checklist. Rather, the Checklist identifies patterns of behavior and provides information that may lead to further assessment of emotional difficulties.

HOW RELIABLE IS THE TEST?

The Checklist provides information on which to base decisions about additional testing or treatment. Reliability is an issue only if it is obvious that a parent, clinician, or adolescent didn't understand the directions and therefore skewed results. Because diagnostic labels are not assigned, the Checklist is used more to identify problems than to measure them.

WHAT DOES THE TEST *NOT* TEST?

The Checklist does not measure intelligence or achievement.

WHAT FURTHER TESTS MIGHT BE RECOMMENDED?

Depending on the patterns identified, further psychological or educational tests might be recommended to diagnose a learning disability, or medical testing if organic difficulties are suspected. Problems identified by the Checklist are used to plan appropriate counseling programs.

Coloured Progressive Matrices

See Raven's Progressive Matrices, page 266.

Columbia Mental Maturity Scale (CMMS)

WHOSE RECOMMENDATION AND/OR PERMISSION IS NEEDED?

Psychologists, school counselors, and special-education teachers most often recommend this test. Parents' permission is needed.

WHAT DOES THE TEST TEST?

The CMMS measures mental abilities of children ages 3½ to 10. Usually used with children who have demonstrated motor or speech difficulties, the CMMS is sometimes given to children entering school.

WHAT, IF ANY, PREPARATION IS NECESSARY?

No preparation is needed.

HOW IS THE TEST PERFORMED, AND WHAT SHOULD BE EXPECTED?

The child is alone with the examiner, who presents the test questions on cards. Each item consists of a set of pictures, one of which does not belong in the set. The child can point to the answer or give a verbal response. Severely handicapped children can use eye blinks or head wands to indicate answers. The test is not timed and usually takes 15 to 20 minutes.

HOW ARE RESULTS RECORDED, EVALUATED, INTERPRETED, AND COMPARED?

Raw scores are converted to percentile ranks, stanines, and are also ranked on a maturity index, designed to place the score in a range for each age. For example, a maturity index of 5U means that the child's score was in the same range as children in the norm group age 5 years, 6 months to 5 years, 11 months. A maturity index of 5L places the child in the group that was 5 years, 0 months to 5 years, 5 months.

HOW RELIABLE IS THE TEST?

Presumably, the CMMS is given because disabilities are known to be present and other tests are not appropriate. Therefore, the test can indicate general mental abilities that may not be apparent through testing in other ways. It can be compared to other tests to see if results are consistent.

WHAT DOES THE TEST NOT TEST?

The CMMS does not measure academic achievement or aptitude. It is not a diagnostic test for specific learning disabilities or psychological disorders.

WHAT FURTHER TESTS MIGHT BE RECOMMENDED?

Depending on the reason for the testing, other psychological or educational tests may be given.

Conners Parent Symptom Questionnaire (The Conners)

WHOSE RECOMMENDATION AND/OR PERMISSION IS NEEDED?

Psychologists, psychiatrists, and others involved in clinical evaluation might recommend the Conners. Parents fill out the questionnaire.

WHAT DOES THE TEST TEST?

The Conners is not a test, but rather a checklist-style report designed to assess behavioral problems at home.

WHAT, IF ANY, PREPARATION IS NECESSARY?

No special preparation is needed.

HOW IS THE TEST PERFORMED, AND WHAT SHOULD BE EXPECTED?

The Conners consists of forty-eight items in a paper-and-pencil format. Each item describes a behavior and parents are asked to report to what degree the behavior is present, on a scale of 0 (is not present) to 3 (behavior is present to a great extent).

HOW ARE RESULTS RECORDED, EVALUATED, INTERPRETED, AND COMPARED?

The scores are interpreted and reported in six behavior categories: conduct problems, learning difficulties, psychosomatic problems, impulsivity-hyperactivity, anxiety, and hyperactivity.

HOW RELIABLE IS THE TEST?

The Conners is reliable to the extent that parents' information about a child's behavior can provide the clinician with data from which to proceed with in-depth interviews or further testing. It provides one piece of information, but does not establish a clinical diagnosis.

WHAT DOES THE TEST *NOT* TEST?

The Conners does not measure intelligence or achievement, nor does it diagnose learning disabilities or establish the cause of behavioral problems.

WHAT FURTHER TESTS MIGHT BE RECOMMENDED?

Depending on the results, a wide variety of tests could be recommended. In addition, the Conners can be used to point out the areas that need attention in counseling. The Conners Teachers Rating Scale (TRS) is sometimes used in a similar way as the Conners Parent Symptom Questionnaire.

Goodenough-Harris Drawing Test (Goodenough-Harris)

WHOSE RECOMMENDATION AND/OR PERMISSION IS NEEDED?

This test is usually administered by a psychologist or special-education teacher. However, a psychologist must interpret the score.

WHAT DOES THE TEST TEST?

The Goodenough-Harris tests a child's conceptual and intellectual maturity as well as personality characteristics. It is a *projective* drawing test.

WHAT, IF ANY, PREPARATION IS NECESSARY?

No special preparation is needed.

HOW IS THE TEST PERFORMED, AND WHAT SHOULD BE EXPECTED?

The Goodenough-Harris is a paper-and-pencil test for children ages 3 to 15. The child is asked to draw three pictures: a man, a woman, and then a self-portrait. The instructions are specific and the child is told to draw the entire body, rather than just the head and shoulders. The test is given individually or in groups. It is not timed, and usually takes 15 minutes. The child is free to erase and start over and, when given individually, to talk to the examiner about the drawing.

HOW ARE RESULTS RECORDED, EVALUATED, INTERPRETED, AND COMPARED?

There is a total of seventy-three scorable items, and the examiner looks for and evaluates these items in the student's drawings. The examiner obtains a raw score and converts that to a standard score, although the self-portrait is not standardized. (Note: Drawing *ability* is not scored.)

HOW RELIABLE IS THE TEST?

The skill of the examiner is considered especially important for reliability. Overall, the Goodenough-Harris is thought to be about as reliable as other drawing tests, and there appears to be a wide variation in its applications. It can be used to screen children who may need further diagnostic testing; sometimes, it is used as a projective personality test. Professional opinions about its value appear to vary as well. It should not be used alone to make psychological diagnoses or education placement decisions.

WHAT DOES THE TEST *NOT* TEST?

The Goodenough-Harris does not measure intelligence, achievement, or creativity.

WHAT FURTHER TESTS MIGHT BE RECOMMENDED?

The Goodenough-Harris Drawing Test would be used with other projective tests, such as the Thematic Apperception Test, an intelligence test, such as the Weschler Intelligence Scale for Children (Revised), and, very likely, an academic achievement test appropriate for the child's age and grade level.

The Hand Test

WHOSE RECOMMENDATION AND/OR PERMISSION IS NEEDED?

Psychologists, psychiatrists, and other clinicians may recommend the test as part of a battery. The examiner must be a licensed clinical psychologist.

WHAT DOES THE TEST TEST?

Best described as a *projective* diagnostic test, the Hand Test detects a variety of personality and thought disorders. It is considered a screening tool as well as a diagnostic instrument. Once children can verbalize responses, they are considered old enough for the test, although some clinicians do not consider it particularly useful with children younger than age 5 or 6.

WHAT, IF ANY, PREPARATION IS NECESSARY?

No special preparation is needed.

HOW IS THE TEST PERFORMED, AND WHAT SHOULD BE EXPECTED?

The Hand Test is administered individually and usually takes no longer than 10 minutes. The child is shown nine cards, each of which has simple line drawings of hands in various positions. The child is asked to describe what each hand is doing. A tenth card is blank, and the child is asked to imagine a hand and explain what it is doing.

HOW ARE RESULTS RECORDED, EVALUATED, INTERPRETED, AND COMPARED?

The child's responses are recorded and interpreted within the framework of established norms. Scores are expressed in numbers and in narrative interpretation. The clinician will report scores within diagnostic groupings, such as Conduct Disorder and Anxiety Disorder, among others.

HOW RELIABLE IS THE TEST?

As with any projective test, reliability of the Hand Test depends, at least in part, on the skill of the examiner. The Hand Test has been shown to have predictive value in certain behavioral areas—acting out of aggression, for example. The results or interpretation of the Hand Test should be compared to other tests used in the psychological assessment battery.

WHAT DOES THE TEST *NOT* TEST?

The Hand Test is not a formal measure of such things as intelligence, aptitude, interest, motivation, or creativity, although the clinician may draw *subjective* impressions in these areas.

WHAT FURTHER TESTS MIGHT BE RECOMMENDED?

When used as a screening tool, a battery of psychological and neuropsychological tests could be recommended.

House-Tree-Person Projective Drawing Test (H-T-P Test)

WHOSE RECOMMENDATION AND/OR PERMISSION IS NEEDED?

Psychologists and psychiatrists and others who are involved in diagnosis and treatment in a clinical setting generally recommend this test. The examiner must be a licensed clinical psychologist.

WHAT DOES THE TEST TEST?

The H-T-P is a projective test that evaluates emotional disturbances and is most often used in clinical settings or when the specific nature of internal conflicts is being assessed.

WHAT, IF ANY, PREPARATION IS NECESSARY?

No special preparation is needed.

HOW IS THE TEST PERFORMED, AND WHAT SHOULD BE EXPECTED?

The child is alone with the examiner, preferably the same person who is administering the other tests in the battery. The child will be asked to draw a picture of a house, a tree, and a person. It is believed that these three forms are emotionally "rich," in that how a person depicts them reveals much about experience, conflicts, pathology, and so on.

HOW ARE RESULTS RECORDED, EVALUATED, INTERPRETED, AND COMPARED?

A scoring and interpretation system has been developed whereby the presence or absence of certain features within the drawings are judged to have clinical significance. The drawings are not judged for artistic value, but rather for their content. A person drawn without facial features or hands, for example, would be noted as a scoring factor.

HOW RELIABLE IS THE TEST?

Because the H-T-P is a projective test, it can reveal valuable information that can then be compared with data collected on other tests given in the battery. Diagnosis should not be made solely on the basis of the H-T-P.

WHAT DOES THE TEST *NOT* TEST?

The H-T-P is not an intelligence test, nor does it measure academic achievement.

WHAT FURTHER TESTS MIGHT BE RECOMMENDED?

The H-T-P would be used with other projective tests such as the Rorschach, an intelligence test such as the WISC-R or the WAIS-R, and, depending on the setting, any test that measures academic performance.

Kaufman Brief Intelligence Test (K-BIT)

WHOSE RECOMMENDATION AND/OR PERMISSION IS NEEDED?

School psychologists, clinical psychologists, learning disabilities specialists, reading specialists, social workers, speech/language clinicians, and nurses generally recommend this test. Parental permission is usually required.

WHAT DOES THE TEST TEST?

The K-BIT is used to estimate intellectual ability through two test categories: Vocabulary (verbal) and Matrices (nonverbal). The verbal portion measures school-related skills such as language development, understanding of verbal concepts, general information, and word knowledge. The nonverbal portion measures the ability to solve new problems, to understand relationships among pictures and designs, and to reason by analogy. The K-BIT can provide a *general* idea of a child's intellectual strengths and weaknesses. (Ages 4 to adult.)

WHAT, IF ANY, PREPARATION IS NECESSARY?

No specific preparation is necessary.

HOW IS THE TEST PERFORMED, AND
WHAT SHOULD BE EXPECTED?

In most cases, the entire K-BIT is administered individually, in a single session lasting 20 to 30 minutes. The test items are presented on an easel, positioned so that the child sees the questions and the examiner sees the answers.

The Vocabulary items require the child to respond verbally. For example, the child is shown a picture of a familiar object and is asked to say its name. The Matrices items require the child to point to the correct response or say its letter—for example, to tell which of five pictures goes best with one chosen as the stimulus picture.

HOW ARE RESULTS RECORDED, EVALUATED,
INTERPRETED, AND COMPARED?

A raw score is converted to three standard scores: one for Vocabulary, one for Matrices, and one for the IQ Composite (the two subtests combined). The examiner can interpret each standard score as average, above average, and so on. The standard score can also be converted to a percentile. A parents' report may be included.

HOW RELIABLE IS THE TEST?

The K-BIT is considered a reliable test, but many factors affect test scores. The examiner can calculate a standard score range, rather than thinking of the score as a single, definitive number. The child should not be diagnosed or placed in a special-education program solely on the basis of K-BIT results.

WHAT DOES THE TEST *NOT* TEST?

The K-BIT does not extensively measure intellectual abilities, nor does it predict academic performance.

WHAT FURTHER TESTS MIGHT BE RECOMMENDED?

A comprehensive intelligence test, the Kaufman Assessment Battery for Children (K-ABC) or the Weschler Intelligence Scale for Children, Revised (WISC-R) are two common tests that may be recommended if more in-depth information is needed.

Leiter International Performance Scale, Arthur Adaptation (Leiter Scale)

WHOSE RECOMMENDATION AND/OR PERMISSION IS NEEDED?

The test is usually given by a psychologist.

WHAT DOES THE TEST TEST?

The Leiter Scale assesses the nonverbal intellectual ability of children with difficulties in verbal expression for a variety of causes, e.g. children who do not speak fluent English. (Ages 2 to 12.)

WHAT, IF ANY, PREPARATION IS NECESSARY?

No special preparation is necessary.

HOW IS THE TEST PERFORMED, AND WHAT SHOULD BE EXPECTED?

The Leiter Scale is administered individually; while not timed, it usually takes 30 to 60 minutes. Because the test is designed for language-impaired students, the directions are given in panto-mime. The child is directed to do various exercises that involve using blocks and cards—to match colors and forms and to judge relationships between the pictured items. Special attention must be paid to the child's initial responses in order to be sure that he or she understands the directions.

HOW ARE RESULTS RECORDED, EVALUATED, INTERPRETED, AND COMPARED?

Test items are scored pass or fail. Once the child has completed all of the exercises appropriate for his/her age level, the child goes back and repeats the exercises that he or she got wrong the first time. A specified number of months is credited to each item passed. The months are added to get a mental age, which is then compared to the child's actual age.

HOW RELIABLE IS THE TEST?

While generally considered reliable, the Leiter Scale is not an infallible measure of intelligence. It is not unusual for a hearing- or language-impaired student to have difficulties with it. A child may do poorly because he or she doesn't understand the instructions, not because of low intelligence. Therefore, the pattern of errors, the child's responses, and responsiveness during testing should be noted.

WHAT DOES THE TEST NOT TEST?

The Leiter Scale does not test visual-motor skills, nor does it measure actual academic performance.

WHAT FURTHER TESTS MIGHT BE RECOMMENDED?

If test results are ambiguous, another test of nonverbal intelligence might be suggested. For example, a young child (age 3 to 8) might be given the Pictorial Test of Intelligence (PTI). The Bender Visual Motor Gestalt Test might be recommended if visual motor skills are in question. Language tests may also be suggested if low functioning is known but has not specifically been measured or treated.

Minnesota Multiphasic Personality Inventory (MMPI)

WHOSE RECOMMENDATION AND/OR PERMISSION IS NEEDED?

Psychologists, psychiatrists, and others who are involved in diagnosis and treatment in a clinical setting generally recommend and administer this test. Parents' permission is required.

WHAT DOES THE TEST TEST?

The MMPI is an instrument that measures aspects of personality in order to identify specific syndromes, such as depression, hypochondriasis, hysteria, schizophrenia, and paranoia. (Ages 16 and up.)

WHAT, IF ANY, PREPARATION IS NECESSARY?

No special preparation is needed. However, a sixth-grade reading level is required.

HOW IS THE TEST PERFORMED, AND WHAT SHOULD BE EXPECTED?

The test takes 90 to 120 minutes and is completed in one session, although more than one session is allowed if needed. The test items are presented in a true/false format. (The MMPI is available in a tape-recorded version for use with the visually impaired, or those with limited literacy or other disabilities.)

HOW ARE RESULTS RECORDED, EVALUATED, INTERPRETED, AND COMPARED?

Raw scores are obtained for use on both clinical and validity scales. The MMPI uses scales, developed over many years, designed to detect attempts to "fake" or "trick" the instrument, and it is not considered possible to successfully make a game out of this test. The raw score consists of answers considered deviant responses. Raw scores are entered on profile forms in order to plot individual results. Modern interpretations of the test tend to express results in broader terms and rely less on psychiatric diagnostic labels. The MMPI is considered intricate and complex, and test results are sometimes considered ambiguous. For this reason, the MMPI is not used alone to make diagnoses.

HOW RELIABLE IS THE TEST?

While the MMPI is considered a reliable test overall, numerous factors can skew results—too few questions answered, for example. Results should be correlated with actual observed behaviors. The data gathered from the MMPI can be used in many ways, and may help to confirm a preliminary diagnosis, or to suggest areas to be explored further. An interpretation should be expressed in lay person's terms and include treatment suggestions. Although the MMPI is widely used in many settings, it should never be used alone to establish a diagnosis.

WHAT DOES THE TEST NOT TEST?

The MMPI is not an achievement, aptitude, or intelligence test and should not be used for academic evaluation, although it may be included in a psychological evaluation for young people experiencing difficulty in a school setting.

WHAT FURTHER TESTS MIGHT BE RECOMMENDED?

The MMPI would most often be included in a broader assessment, in which a variety of other tests would be given.

Pictorial Test of Intelligence (PTI)

WHOSE RECOMMENDATION AND/OR PERMISSION IS NEEDED?

Psychologists, pediatricians, and others involved in early childhood assessment are the professionals most likely to recommend the PTI. Parental permission is needed.

WHAT DOES THE TEST TEST?

The PTI is a nonverbal test of intelligence. (Ages 3 to 8.)

WHAT, IF ANY, PREPARATION IS NECESSARY?

No preparation is necessary.

HOW IS THE TEST PERFORMED, AND WHAT SHOULD BE EXPECTED?

The PTI consists of six subtests: picture vocabulary, form discrimination, information and comprehension, similarities, size and number, and immediate recall. The subtests are presented in a multiple-choice format. Answers can be verbal, or the child can point to his or her answer. Guidelines for administering the PTI are flexible and can accommodate children with multiple disabilities or who do not speak English.

HOW ARE RESULTS RECORDED, EVALUATED, INTERPRETED, AND COMPARED?

Raw scores are converted to a score expressed as a mental age (MA) and then to a deviation IQ.

HOW RELIABLE IS THE TEST?

The PTI is a useful tool for evaluating children who have speech or motor disorders and whose intellectual functioning is in question. However, educational decisions should not be made based on the results of this test alone.

WHAT DOES THE TEST *NOT* TEST?

The PTI is not an achievement or aptitude test, nor does it diagnose specific learning disabilities or psychological disorders.

WHAT FURTHER TESTS MIGHT BE RECOMMENDED?

Depending on the reason for the testing, other psychological or educational tests could be recommended.

Quick Neurological Screen Test, Revised (QNST)

WHOSE RECOMMENDATION AND/OR PERMISSION IS NEEDED?

Psychologists, learning disabilities specialists, and speech/language clinicians generally recommend the QNST. Parents' permission is required.

WHAT DOES THE TEST TEST?

The QNST measures neurological integration as it relates to various learning tasks. These include such things as motor development, visual perception, and balance.

WHAT, IF ANY, PREPARATION IS NECESSARY?

No preparation is needed, but because of the variety of items involved, children should be told that they will be asked to do a number of physical tasks in quick succession.

HOW IS THE TEST PERFORMED, AND
WHAT SHOULD BE EXPECTED?

The child is alone with an examiner and is tested in fifteen skills in about 20 minutes. The tasks include such things as eye tracking, standing on one leg, skipping, and recognizing forms.

HOW ARE RESULTS RECORDED, EVALUATED,
INTERPRETED, AND COMPARED?

The examiner assigns a score to each task; the score is then compared to established age norms.

HOW RELIABLE IS THE TEST?

The QNST is an initial screening tool and does not establish a diagnosis. As with all screening tools, it may suggest that a problem requiring further investigation is present. The QNST is considered a valuable tool because it can be administered quickly.

WHAT DOES THE TEST *NOT* TEST?

The QNST does not evaluate any neurological problem in depth.

WHAT FURTHER TESTS MIGHT BE RECOMMENDED?

Test batteries in a variety of areas could be recommended to diagnose such conditions as attention deficit disorder (ADD), vision and hearing impairments, and behavioral problems. The child may also be referred to a neurologist.

Raven's Progressive Matrices, Coloured Progressive Matrices, and Advanced Progressive Matrices (The Raven's)

WHOSE RECOMMENDATION AND/OR PERMISSION IS NEEDED?

Psychologists, psychiatrists, and educational specialists generally recommend the test.

WHAT DOES THE TEST TEST?

The Raven's is an intelligence test involving nonverbal tasks. It is used with children who are age 8 or older, through adulthood. The Coloured Progressive Matrices is used with children ages 5 to 11, and contains both easy and harder tasks. The Advanced Progressive Matrices is used with children who have already demonstrated above-average intelligence.

WHAT, IF ANY, PREPARATION IS NECESSARY?

No preparation is needed.

HOW IS THE TEST PERFORMED, AND WHAT SHOULD BE EXPECTED?

The Raven's is usually given individually. The child is asked to solve problems presented in abstract figures and designs. The test does not require language skills. Hearing- and speech-impaired, as well as non–English-speaking children can be given this test in lieu of a verbally interactive intelligence test. The test isn't timed, but generally takes 15 to 45 minutes.

HOW ARE RESULTS RECORDED, INTERPRETED, EVALUATED, AND COMPARED?

Raw scores are converted to percentile ranks.

HOW RELIABLE IS THE TEST?

Scores have been shown to be more reliable in older children than younger ones; that is, young children will show a greater range of scores when they are retested. The Raven's can reveal valuable information that can be incorporated into a more comprehensive assessment.

WHAT DOES THE TEST *NOT* TEST?

The Raven's does not measure verbal reasoning ability or academic achievement, nor does it test vocational aptitudes and interests.

WHAT FURTHER TESTS MIGHT BE RECOMMENDED?

The Mill Hill Vocabulary Scale is a verbal reasoning test designed to be used with the Raven's where appropriate. The Raven's is generally given as part of a battery of diagnostic tests including other psychological or educational tests, depending on the reason the child is being evaluated in the first place.

Roberts Apperception Test for Children (RATC)

WHOSE RECOMMENDATION AND/OR PERMISSION IS NEEDED?

Psychologists and psychiatrists are most likely to recommend the RATC.

WHAT DOES THE TEST TEST?

The RATC is a projective test designed to assess mental and emotional functioning, thought patterns, and attitudes. The scales measure such things as adaptive behavior, anxiety, resolution of problems, internal conflicts, and depression. (Ages 6 to 15.)

WHAT, IF ANY, PREPARATION IS NECESSARY?

No special preparation is needed.

HOW IS THE TEST PERFORMED, AND WHAT SHOULD BE EXPECTED?

The child is alone with an examiner, who shows the child illustrations of children and adults engaged in a variety of interactions. The child is then asked to describe what he or she sees. The examiner is seeking information about the child's relationship with family members, peers, and so on. The test, which is untimed, takes 20 to 30 minutes. (A set of cards that features black individuals, rather than white, is available.)

HOW ARE RESULTS RECORDED, EVALUATED, INTERPRETED, AND COMPARED?

The examiner notes the presence or absence of various types of responses. The responses are scored in various categories and compared to norms established by testing children judged well-adjusted. A report includes impressions of how key family relationships are structured, which may help determine areas to be dealt with in therapy.

HOW RELIABLE IS THE TEST?

It is important to remember that the RATC is a *projective* test and should not be used alone to diagnose emotional problems. Its reliability is also dependent on the skill of the examiner. The

RATC can be re-administered at a later time to measure progress and development.

WHAT DOES THE TEST *NOT* TEST?

The RATC is not an intelligence or achievement test, nor does it measure creativity or aptitude. It does not, by itself, provide a diagnosis such as depression or psychosis.

WHAT FURTHER TESTS MIGHT BE RECOMMENDED?

Other projective tests, such as House-Tree-Person (H-T-P) or the Kinetic Family Drawing, as well as an individually administered intelligence test and an achievement test might be included in the battery.

Rorschach Psychodiagnostic Test, Second Edition

WHOSE RECOMMENDATION AND/OR PERMISSION IS NEEDED?

Psychologists, psychiatrists, or other mental health professionals usually recommend this test. Parents' permission is required.

WHAT DOES THE TEST TEST?

The test is designed to assess normal or pathological psychological processes and is used to diagnose personality structure and emotional difficulties. It measures the ways a child approaches his or her environment and can detect internal and external pressures and conflicts. It will pick up illogical and psychotic thought patterns. The test can be given to children as young as age 3, and is widely used with adolescents and adults.

WHAT, IF ANY, PREPARATION IS NECESSARY?

No special preparation is needed.

HOW IS THE TEST PERFORMED, AND WHAT SHOULD BE EXPECTED?

The examiner is alone with the child, usually in an office setting. The child is shown ten inkblot cards and asked standard questions about what he or she sees in the cards. Responses are clues to thought processes, perceptions, motivations, and so on. The child's responses are tabulated and put in summary form.

The test must be performed by a trained psychologist; physicians, social workers, teachers, and so on are not considered qualified examiners. In a teaching institution, a graduate student may be the examiner, but a licensed psychologist must supervise the final evaluation. The test is verbally but not physically interactive; the child is not asked to read, draw, mark boxes, or the like.

HOW ARE RESULTS RECORDED, EVALUATED, INTERPRETED, AND COMPARED?

The data is evaluated in two steps. First, the actual content of the response is analyzed. Then the responses are scored on various criteria. The categories have been used—and critiqued—since the test was introduced in the 1920s.

In the mid-1970s, the Exner Standardized Scoring System was developed for the Rorschach when John Exner, Jr., Ph.D. took the best features of prior scoring methods and developed an objective scoring system. Parents should ask if the Exner scoring system is being employed because in addition to being the most widely used, it is considered the most objective and reliable scoring method for the Rorschach.

HOW RELIABLE IS THE TEST?

Since the introduction of the Exner Standardized Scoring System, the Rorschach is viewed as a reliable diagnostic tool when used as one of a battery of tests. While it can be repeated, it should not be administered more than once a year, as more frequent use may skew results.

WHAT DOES THE TEST *NOT* TEST?

The Rorschach is not considered an intelligence or achievement test. And, by itself, it can't diagnose *organic* problems.

WHAT FURTHER TESTS MIGHT BE RECOMMENDED?

The Rorschach should be used as one of a cluster of tests. The Thematic Apperception Test (TAT); the intellectual measures, such as Weschler Scales (WPPSI, WISC-R, and WAIS-R) or Stanford Binet Intelligence Test; Sentence Completion; and Draw-A-Person are examples of tests that are often included in the battery. An evaluation of the results of this group of tests will then lead to further recommendations, investigation, or treatment.

16 Personality Factors (16PF)

WHOSE RECOMMENDATION AND/OR PERMISSION IS NEEDED?

School counselors and psychologists are the most likely persons to recommend and administer the test.

WHAT DOES THE TEST TEST?

Used with persons age 16 and up, 16PF measures elements of personality, including assertiveness, emotional maturity, self-sufficiency, anxiety, and rigidity. The test can be used for such things as determining potential adjustment problems for college-bound adolescents, constructing treatment plans, and aiding vocational or rehabilitation counseling.

WHAT, IF ANY, PREPARATION IS NECESSARY?

The basic form requires about a seventh-grade reading level. Two additional forms are available, requiring a sixth-grade and third-grade reading level respectively.

HOW IS THE TEST PERFORMED, AND WHAT SHOULD BE EXPECTED?

The 16PF may be administered in groups or individually. It is a paper-and-pencil test that takes 45 to 60 minutes.

HOW ARE RESULTS RECORDED, EVALUATED, INTERPRETED, AND COMPARED?

The 16PF is considered a flexible tool in that the profile that results can be interpreted and used in many ways. Scores for particular traits—anxiety or rigidity, for example—can be isolated and further explored. The test doesn't yield a diagnostic label. It can, however, be used to plan counseling programs. The 16PF is sometimes used in career and vocational counseling.

HOW RELIABLE IS THE TEST?

The 16PF is considered a reliable indicator of personality tendencies and can *assist* in diagnosis and treatment of emotional problems, but does not diagnose mental illness. Other tests should be used before treatment decisions are made.

WHAT DOES THE TEST *NOT* TEST?

The 16PF does not test academic achievement, intelligence, aptitude, or creativity.

WHAT FURTHER TESTS MIGHT BE RECOMMENDED?

Depending on the setting, a variety of tests could be included in an assessment. Other psychological tests could be recommended if treatment is considered. An aptitude or interest test could be given in a vocational counseling setting.

Slosson Intelligence Test for Children (SIT)

WHOSE RECOMMENDATION AND/OR PERMISSION IS NEEDED?

Classroom and special-education teachers, psychologists, counselors, pediatricians, nurses, and other trained professionals generally recommend the SIT. Parents' permission would generally be needed.

WHAT DOES THE TEST TEST?

The SIT is a screening test for mental abilities. (Infants to adults.)

WHAT, IF ANY, PREPARATION IS NECESSARY?

No preparation is needed.

HOW IS THE TEST PERFORMED, AND WHAT SHOULD BE EXPECTED?

The SIT is a verbal test; no reading, writing, or performance tasks are required. It generally takes about 30 minutes. Word meanings, memory, and numerical reasoning are assessed.

HOW ARE RESULTS RECORDED, EVALUATED, INTERPRETED, AND COMPARED?

Raw scores are converted to mental age, IQ, percentile, and stanine scores.

HOW RELIABLE IS THE TEST?

Because the SIT is a screening tool, the pattern of errors may be more important than the score. In some cases, more in-depth investigation would be needed to corroborate results. The SIT is not an appropriate tool on which to make *any* educational decision. Some professionals question the test's usefulness with infants and young children, particularly those who have difficulties with verbal expression.

WHAT DOES THE TEST *NOT* TEST?

The SIT is not a comprehensive mental abilities test, nor does it measure achievement. It also does not diagnose learning disabilities or speech/language deficits.

WHAT FURTHER TESTS MIGHT BE RECOMMENDED?

Low scores might indicate a need for further evaluation in a variety of areas. For example, a low score on word meanings might be followed with a more comprehensive verbal abilities test. If the test is being used to assess readiness, other tests should be given to provide more complete information. If it is used to evaluate infants, many other developmental assessment tools are available for use in retesting.

Thematic Apperception Test (TAT)

WHOSE RECOMMENDATION AND/OR PERMISSION IS NEEDED?

Psychologists, psychiatrists, and other mental health professionals may recommend the TAT as part of a psychological battery. Parents' permission is generally required.

WHAT DOES THE TEST TEST?

The test is designed to identify conflicts, attitudes, stressors, and aggressive tendencies, which can then be associated with psychological health and illness. Children as young as age 3 or 4 can be given the test, provided they are able to express themselves verbally. The TAT is often used with adolescents and adults.

WHAT, IF ANY, PREPARATION IS NECESSARY?

No special preparation is needed.

HOW IS THE TEST PERFORMED, AND WHAT SHOULD BE EXPECTED?

The child is alone with the examiner during the test. The TAT consists of a group of twenty pictures displayed on separate cards. Eight to fifteen cards are used in a standard testing situation. The examiner chooses the cards that he or she thinks will elicit responses in the areas he suspected as troublesome or significant to the individual. The cards generate verbal responses, which revolve around a particular theme—conflict, relationships, family, loneliness, or competition, for example. The examiner asks the child to make up a story—a narrative that has a beginning, a middle, and an end—about each picture. The examiner also asks the child to describe how the characters in the story are feeling. The test is not timed, so the child is free to explore each story for as long as he or she wishes.

The test must be performed by a trained psychologist. (Physicians, social workers, teachers, and so on are not considered qualified examiners.) In a teaching institution, a graduate student may be the examiner, but a licensed psychologist must supervise the final evaluation. The test is verbally but not physically interactive; the child is not asked to read, draw, mark boxes, or the like.

HOW ARE RESULTS RECORDED, EVALUATED, INTERPRETED, AND COMPARED?

Each response is examined and interpreted by the examiner on the basis of the theme the card is intended to explore. The examiner then summarizes the attitudes and conflicts the child's story illustrated. There is neither a raw score nor an objective scale.

HOW RELIABLE IS THE TEST?

The expertise of the examiner is very important in evaluating the TAT. It is considered more subjective than other tests typically used in the same battery (Sentence Completion, Stanford Binet Intelligence Test, Rorschach Diagnostic Test, and so on).

WHAT DOES THE TEST *NOT* TEST?

The TAT does not measure achievement, intelligence, or any type of academic ability. It is not useful in diagnosing specific learning disabilities or organic problems.

WHAT FURTHER TESTS MIGHT BE RECOMMENDED?

The TAT should be used as one of a cluster of tests. The Rorschach; the intellectual measures, such as Weschler Scales (WPPSI, WISC-R, and WAIS-R) or Stanford Binet Intelligence Test; Sentence Completion; and Draw-A-Person are examples of tests that are often included in the battery. An evaluation of the group of tests will then lead to further recommendations, investigation, or treatment.

Vineland Adaptive Behavior Scales (The Vineland)

WHOSE RECOMMENDATION AND/OR PERMISSION IS NEEDED?

The Vineland may be recommended by a social worker, school or clinical psychologist, or other qualified professional. The parent may be involved in the assessment process.

WHAT DOES THE TEST TEST?

The Vineland measures personal and social skills in four areas, or, as this test describes them, domains: communication (listening, speaking, and writing); daily living skills (personal, domestic, and community); socialization (interpersonal relationships, play and leisure, and coping skills); and motor skills (fine and gross). An optional Maladaptive Behavior scale is also available.

WHAT, IF ANY, PREPARATION IS NECESSARY?

No preparation is required.

HOW IS THE TEST PERFORMED, AND WHAT SHOULD BE EXPECTED?

There are two versions of the Vineland: an Interview Edition (birth to age 8+) that is completed by an examiner, based on an interview with the parent or other caregiver, and a Classroom Edition (ages 3 to 12) that is completed by a teacher. The Interview Edition has both a relatively brief Survey Form (20 to 60 minutes) and a longer Expanded Form (60 to 90 minutes). (A Spanish-language version of the Survey Form of the Interview Edition is available.)

HOW ARE RESULTS RECORDED, EVALUATED, INTERPRETED, AND COMPARED?

For both the Interview and Classroom editions, the examiner combines the scores from individual items (each of which concerns a particular type of behavior) into scores covering all areas tested and into an overall Adaptive Behavior score. These composite scores are compared to established norms. In addition, composite scores may be compared with those obtained by various groups of handicapped children. Ratings on several subdomains within each domain may be classified into five levels, ranging from "high" through "low." Scores for each edition are summarized in a report to parents, available in English or Spanish.

HOW RELIABLE IS THE TEST?

Overall, the Vineland is considered a reliable test. However, in order for the Classroom Edition scores to be valid, the teacher should have had an opportunity to observe the child's behavior over a period of several months.

WHAT DOES THE TEST *NOT* TEST?

The Vineland does not measure personality, intelligence, or academic achievement.

WHAT FURTHER TESTS MIGHT BE RECOMMENDED?

The Vineland is often administered in conjunction with intelligence tests or academic achievement batteries.

Weschler Adult Intelligence Scale, Revised (WAIS-R)

WHOSE RECOMMENDATION AND/OR PERMISSION IS NEEDED?

School and clinical psychologists, school counselors, or psychiatrists generally recommend the test as part of a battery. The examiner must be a licensed clinical psychologist.

WHAT DOES THE TEST TEST?

The WAIS-R measures the general intelligence of persons age 16 and older, and is used widely with older adolescents. It is commonly used in both school and clinical settings; it contains eleven subtests, scored on either Performance or Verbal scales.

WHAT, IF ANY, PREPARATION IS NECESSARY?

No preparation is needed.

HOW IS THE TEST PERFORMED, AND WHAT SHOULD BE EXPECTED?

The Performance and Verbal subtests are given alternately. Those classified as Verbal include Information, Digit Span, Vocabulary, Arithmetic, Comprehension, and Similarities. Performance subtests include Picture Completion, Picture Arrangement, Block Design, and Object Assembly.

The recording of responses is considered objective, but scoring of some subtests allows the examiner more leeway. In some settings, the examiner makes the judgment to either eliminate one or more subtests or items within the subtests. This is done to shorten examination time. The test is given individually, and involves verbal interaction and completion of tasks. It takes about two hours to complete.

The Verbal subtests are often used alone with the visually impaired. If signing is used with the hearing impaired, a qualified translator should be used. Those with established motor impairments can be tested, but special accommodations should be made.

HOW ARE RESULTS RECORDED, EVALUATED, INTERPRETED, AND COMPARED?

The examiner hand scores the test and raw scores are then converted to scaled scores and IQs.

HOW RELIABLE IS THE TEST?

The WAIS-R is considered a reliable measure of intelligence and correlates well with actual performance. However, there are always exceptions and the WAIS-R should not be used by itself to determine placements, psychological treatment plans, and so on. The test should be considered one piece of information in a general assessment process. The skill of the examiner is also considered of critical importance. Overall reliability of the WAIS-R may be comprised when the client is anxious or tense, heavily medicated, or otherwise impaired. The WAIS-R is not considered a particularly reliable measure of giftedness.

WHAT DOES THE TEST *NOT* TEST?

The WAIS-R cannot be considered a reliable test of personality disorders or brain dysfunction, although it can report what psychologists refer to as "soft" signs of such problems. The test does not adequately measure motivation, creativity, or achievement, nor does it predict in any absolute sense academic or professional success or failure.

WHAT FURTHER TESTS MIGHT BE RECOMMENDED?

Because the WAIS-R is rarely used alone, many other tests are given in an assessment battery. These could include, but are not limited to, the Rorschach, H-T-P Drawing Test, and the WRAT-R. The test may also be part of the Halsted-Reitan Neuropsychological Test Battery.

Weschler Intelligence Scales for Children, Revised (WISC-R)

A Spanish language edition is available.

WHOSE RECOMMENDATION AND/OR PERMISSION IS NEEDED?

School and clinical psychologists, school counselors, or psychiatrists generally recommend the test as part of a battery. The examiner must be a licensed clinical psychologist.

WHAT DOES THE TEST TEST?

The WISC-R is designed to test general mental abilities and can identify those children who are in a learning environment either beyond or below their intellectual capacities. Programs for gifted and/or learning disabled children may also use this test. (Ages 6 to 17.)

WHAT, IF ANY, PREPARATION IS NECESSARY?

No preparation is needed.

HOW IS THE TEST PERFORMED, AND WHAT SHOULD BE EXPECTED?

The child is asked to perform tasks and to respond verbally to questions. The twelve subtests are divided into Verbal and Performance scales. The Verbal scales measure understanding of verbal concepts and the ability to respond orally. Performance scales measure problem-solving skills demonstrated by manipulating objects, following mazes, matching shapes, and the like. The test takes about an hour and is generally done in one session.

HOW ARE RESULTS RECORDED, EVALUATED, INTERPRETED, AND COMPARED?

The examiner hand scores the test and the raw scores are then converted to scaled scores and IQs. Perhaps more important than the final IQ score are the individual scores on the subtests. For example, low scores on certain tests could indicate deficits in certain areas, such as visual-motor perception or language abilities. Particular learning disabilities may also be detected. Large discrepancies between Verbal and Performance scores should also be further investigated. Such discrepancies could indicate difficulty understanding what was required; low scores could be considered diagnostic information to use in a complete assessment.

HOW RELIABLE IS THE TEST?

The WISC-R is widely used because it is considered quite reliable, providing valuable information in evaluating a child's overall mental capabilities. However, the information yielded within each subtest may be more important than the total score.

WHAT DOES THE TEST *NOT* TEST?

The WISC-R does not measure academic achievement or personality characteristics.

WHAT FURTHER TESTS MIGHT BE RECOMMENDED?

Depending on the purpose of the testing, the child could be given achievement batteries or tests that measure developmental areas such as receptive and expressive language and visual-motor perception. The WISC-R is also commonly used as part of a psychological battery that includes projective tests.

Weschler Preschool and Primary Scale of Intelligence, Revised (WPPSI)

WHOSE RECOMMENDATION AND/OR PERMISSION IS NEEDED?

School and clinical psychologists, counselors, or psychiatrists generally recommend the Weschler as part of a battery. The examiner must be a licensed clinical psychologist. Parents' permission is needed before the battery is administered.

WHAT DOES THE TEST TEST?

The WPPSI measures intellectual abilities of young children. (Ages 3 years, 3 months to 7 years.)

WHAT, IF ANY, PREPARATION IS NECESSARY?

No preparation is needed.

HOW IS THE TEST PERFORMED, AND WHAT SHOULD BE EXPECTED?

The child is asked to perform tasks and respond to questions. There are twelve subtests, which fall into two broad categories: Verbal and Performance. Although a specific sequence of subtests is recommended, the examiner is free to change the order to maintain a child's interest. The complete test takes about one hour and 15 minutes. The activities include such things as picture completion, supplying word meanings, expressing similarities, and tracing mazes.

HOW ARE RESULTS RECORDED, EVALUATED, INTERPRETED, AND COMPARED?

A raw score is obtained for each subtest. The scores are then translated to scaled scores. The sum of scaled scores are converted to IQs.

HOW RELIABLE IS THE TEST?

The WPPSI is a widely used test that can yield information in a variety of areas; it is generally considered reliable. However, the test would not be particularly useful if visual, verbal, or motor difficulties are already known, thereby making many tasks difficult. Certain general information is also assumed, so that children not exposed to the information would not score well. For example, recognition of colors and shapes is required, as is the ability to name common animals.

WHAT DOES THE TEST NOT TEST?

The WPPSI does not measure achievement.

WHAT FURTHER TESTS MIGHT BE RECOMMENDED?

Depending on the reason for the testing, an achievement test could be recommended. In other settings, psychological testing could be performed.

SUPPLEMENTAL TESTS

The following are some additional widely used tests you might encounter in numerous settings. The test formats and the domains being tested are similar to those previously discussed. However, it is impossible to list all of the hundreds of psychological tests, and the list should not be considered inclusive.

AAMD Adaptive Behavior Scale (ABS). A tool to assess possible emotional disturbance, retardation, or other disabilities that may affect a child's ability to adapt to a school environment. Used with children ages 3 to 16.

Beck Depression Inventory (BDI). Designed to measure degree of depression through a twenty-one-item inventory. It is used with older adolescents and adults and is a self-report tool.

Burk's Behavior Rating Scales. A parent- or teacher-completed inventory that identifies behavior problems. There is an edition for children in grades 1 through 9, and one for preschoolers and kindergarteners.

Child Anxiety Scale (CAS). Used in clinical evaluations to identify children (ages 6 to 8) with adjustment problems who might benefit from therapy.

Childhood Autism Rating Scale (CARS). A tool that helps to differentiate autistic children from others with developmental difficulties. The child interacts with an examiner, who rates the child in fifteen behaviors.

Coopersmith Self-Esteem Inventories. Measures attitudes toward school, work, and home in terms of personal performance and satisfaction.

DeGangi-Berk Test of Sensory Integration (TSI). A screening procedure to identify young children with sensory, motor, and perceptual skills developmental delays.

Draw-A-Person. A projective drawing test used as one test in a battery. It is suitable for children ages 5 and up, and it must be administered and interpreted by a licensed clinical psychologist.

Elizur Test of Psycho-Organicity. A short test designed to differentiate between organic and nonorganic brain disorders.

Haptic Intelligence Scale. An intelligence test used with blind or visually impaired children and adults.

Kinetic Drawing System for Family and School. A projective test that assesses children's perceptions of important relationships both at home and at school. The child is asked to make one family drawing and one in a school setting, both of which are to depict interactions.

Personal Experience Inventory (PEI). Helps identify teenagers with all forms of substance abuse problems. Related problems, (family conflicts, sexual abuse, self-image, and so on) are also assessed.

Personality Inventory for Children (PIC). Completed by a parent, this lengthy inventory evaluates personality characteristics of children ages 3 to 16 and is often used prior to counseling.

Piers-Harris Children's Self-Concept Scale (PHCSCS). Identifying children who need further testing or treatment, this test is often used in clinical settings to determine typical coping and defense mechanisms and conflicts.

Prescriptive Reading Performance Test (PRPT). Used to measure reading skills and identify strengths and weaknesses in reading and word-attack skills, and to help diagnose dyslexia.

Rotter Incomplete Sentences Blank. Assesses personality based on the subjective choice of material used to complete forty sentences. The test is used with older adolescents and is usually given as part of a battery.

System of Multicultural Pluralistic Assessment (SOMPA). A tool that measures cognitive abilities, sensorimotor skills, and adaptive behavior of children from varied cultural backgrounds. The SOMPA includes both a Parent Interview (available in Spanish and English) and Student Assessment Materials. This is a multifaceted tool that includes the Bender Visual Motor Test and the WISC-R (see individual entries) as part of its protocol. Overall interpretation should be done by a psychologist and other members of an assessment team.

Tell-Me-A-Story (TEMAS). A projective test that measures personality, emotional patterns, and cognitive processes. The cards used as the cues are available depicting Black, Hispanic, or white individuals.

Wide Range Assessment of Memory and Learning (WRAML). Assesses memory functions in children and adolescents and is used to evaluate learning and school-related problems. The test can help clarify the role of memory deficits in learning disabilities and attention disorders.

APPENDIX I
Prenatal Testing

Until very recently, the growing fetus existed in a hidden, almost mysterious, world of its own. However, prenatal testing has changed all that, particularly for mothers and babies considered at high risk.

Not surprisingly, the advent of prenatal testing has brought with it the necessity to make more decisions. The parents and the physician must decide if a test is necessary and safe. Do the risks outweigh the benefits? What do results mean? Interpreting results is often the most difficult part of prenatal testing. Because false positives and false negatives are common, retesting is sometimes recommended or other tests are suggested to confirm or negate previous findings.

Prenatal testing is emotionally stressful because results may not be immediate and treatment for fetal difficulties may or may not be possible. Meanwhile, the parents must endure the waiting, knowing that decisions about continuing the pregnancy or the necessity for early delivery may need to be made quickly once the information is gathered.

The information provided here is no way meant to be a substitute for information from health care providers. Rather, it is meant to help you ask the right questions, thereby aiding you in making informed choices about testing. Just because various relatively low-risk tests are available does not mean that they are necessary for all high-risk pregnancies. Decisions about what type of prenatal testing is done are made after all of the pros and cons are considered for each case. The following are prenatal tests commonly offered in today's high-tech medical settings.

Alpha Fetoprotein (AFP) Screening

AFP is a protein manufactured in the liver of a fetus. Elevated or low levels of AFP point to developmental difficulties, and therefore the screening is done during those pregnancies considered high-risk.

AFP can be measured in two ways: from a sample of the mother's blood or from the amniotic fluid extracted during another prenatal test, amniocentesis. No risk is associated with a blood test, but amniocentesis presents a more complicated risk/benefit problem. Assuming that a blood sample will be used to measure AFP, the test will be performed at about the sixteenth week of pregnancy, a time when a routine blood test is usually done anyway.

Elevated AFP may suggest neural tube defects, meaning that the brain or part of the spinal cord is not developing normally. It can also suggest abnormalities in the abdominal wall. While these problems are often serious, some may be surgically corrected shortly after birth. High AFP levels can also indicate, among other things, an increased risk of low birth weight and premature delivery.

Low AFP levels can indicate chromosomal disorders—Down's syndrome, for example. Amniocentesis is generally recommended, if the risk of miscarriage is not considered too high, to further investigate abnormal AFP levels. Ultrasound (sonogram) is also used to confirm a defect.

Unfortunately, over 90 percent of abnormal readings are false positives, meaning that more tests must be performed, and the waiting period can cause more anxiety. It is recommended that women have two tests and an ultrasound before a definitive result is established. Even then, in about 15 percent of cases, no cause of abnormal AFP levels can be found.

It is unlikely that an AFP screening would be done by itself. Generally, the test is recommended for those who show a family history of neural tube defects and other disorders.

Amniocentesis

Amniocentesis is a method by which a sample of the amniotic fluid is obtained for genetic analysis or to evaluate the well-being of the fetus. The procedure is generally performed between the fifteenth and seventeenth weeks of pregnancy, although it is sometimes done a bit earlier. Amniocentesis may be recommended in late pregnancy to evaluate certain aspects of fetal development and readiness for delivery. However, there is some risk of triggering premature labor.

Ultrasound is used to guide the physician as a needle is inserted through the abdomen into the amniotic sac. Approximately an ounce of the fluid is withdrawn for laboratory analysis. Fetal cells are cultured and analyzed, a process that takes 2 to 3 weeks. AFP levels are also measured in the amniotic fluid itself.

When amniocentesis is done in early pregnancy, its purpose is to detect hereditary diseases, neural tube defects, and genetic disorders. In late pregnancy, amniocentesis can determine if the baby's lungs are developed enough to allow survival outside the womb. (Insufficient lung development is a risk factor in pregnancies of diabetic mothers.) When Rh factor is a concern, the amniotic fluid can provide information about the severity of the problem, and can help determine the need for a blood transfusion for the fetus prior to birth or the necessity for early delivery after other viability indicators are evaluated.

Miscarriage is considered the major risk of amniocentesis. Therefore, the risk/benefit ratio must be evaluated. It is generally recommended for "older" mothers—those over age 35—or for those thought to be at high risk for birth defects and genetic disorders.

When done in early pregnancy, the preparation for amniocentesis is the same as for standard ultrasound. However, in late pregnancy, a woman will be asked to empty the bladder to significantly lessen the risk that the needle will puncture the bladder.

Chorionic Villus Sampling (CVS)

CVS is performed between the eighth and twelfth weeks of pregnancy. Its purpose is to detect genetic defects, and involves removing a small sample of the villi on the chorion, the tissue that surrounds the early placenta.

During the procedure, ultrasound is performed to guide the physician, who places a catheter or a hollow tube through the vagina and cervix and into the uterine cavity. It may also be performed by inserting a needle through the abdomen and into the uterus. In either method, a sample of the tissue, which has the same genetic make-up as the fetus, is suctioned out. The chromosomes in the fetal cells are analyzed for hereditary disorders, such as Down's syndrome and Tay-Sachs disease. Reports are usually received in a week or so, allowing time for a first-trimester abortion if that is the parents' choice.

CVS is considered to have about the same risk to both mother and fetus as amniocentesis, the primary one being miscarriage. The procedure itself may cause cramping, leakage of fluid, or minor bleeding for a few days after the test.

Because the risk for chromosomal defects rises with age, pregnant women over age 35 are likely to have this testing recommended to them. Women who have previously had a child with a genetic disorder or who have a family history of hereditary conditions—hemophilia, for example—are also candidates. CVS is also used when both mother and father carry a recessive trait for Tay-Sachs disease.

Preparation for CVS is the same as that for a routine ultrasound. There may be momentary discomfort when the catheter or tube is moved around in the uterus or when the needle moves through the abdominal wall.

Electronic Fetal Monitoring (EFM)

EFM is a system that records the heartbeat of the fetus, and also measures contractions of the mother's uterus. It is done to ascertain the health and strength of the fetus at the time of testing. EFM is done to help judge the ability of the fetus to handle normal labor. It is also done during labor in order to detect possible fetal distress. The monitoring may be done externally or internally.

External monitoring is performed by strapping two belts around the mother's abdomen. One belt uses ultrasound to detect and monitor the fetal heartbeat. The other belt contains an instrument to measure uterine contractions. (There is a newer device that contains both instruments in one belt.)

Internal monitoring can be done only after the amniotic membranes have been ruptured. An electrode is attached to the head (scalp) of the fetus, and this electrode monitors the heartbeat. A tube or catheter is also inserted into the vagina to measure uterine contractions.

Both types of monitoring send information to a machine that produces a "tracing" of the fetal heart rate and uterine contractions. The tracings yield information about the fetal heart rate: variability, acceleration (a temporary rise in the heart rate), deceleration (slowing of the heart rate), variable slowing and quickening, or delayed deceleration of the heart rate. Changes in heart rate may or may not indicate a problem, although some changes are considered a sign that the fetus is not receiving enough oxygen. Intervention may then be necessary.

There are no known risks of the monitoring itself. However, misinterpreted results may lead to inducing labor and an unnecessary early delivery. On the other hand, EFM results may be reassuring and prevent unnecessary intervention.

In high-risk pregnancies, nonstress testing (NST) and contraction stress testing (CST) may be used in late pregnancy to check on the condition of the fetus. In NST, the external heart monitor measures the fetus' response to its own movements. For example, the heart rate usually accelerates when the fetus moves. NST is painless and generally takes 20 to 30 minutes.

When CST is used, the response of the fetus to stimulated contractions is measured. A contraction is sometimes induced by stimulating the mother's nipples with a warm towel or with her hand.

If manual stimulation does not work, oxytocin, a hormone that triggers uterine contractions may be used. This method employs an intravenous line to administer the oxytocin. The heart monitor then records reactions to the stimulated contractions. The results of CST provide information about how the fetus may respond during actual labor. CST can take 20 minutes to two hours. Although contractions can be quite intense, particularly when oxytocin is used, CST is generally not too painful. Breathing techniques are used if the contractions prove to be uncomfortable.

NST has no known risk associated with it. However, CST can result in hyperstimulation, meaning that contractions are close together and last longer than 90 seconds. This can result in delayed deceleration of the fetal heart rate, which can be dangerous to the fetus. Testing is stopped, but if the heart rate shows continued signs of distress, intervention may be needed. A labor-inhibiting drug may be given or an emergency delivery may be considered necessary. Therefore, CST is generally not used unless a high-risk situation already exists.

Fetal Activity Monitoring

All women notice their baby's movements inside the womb and usually find the fetal activity reassuring. In high-risk pregnancies, fetal movement may be more systematically monitored and charted, particularly during the third trimester. A certain number of movements during a thirty-minute period is considered reassuring, and women at high risk are told to monitor fetal activity three times a day for thirty minutes each time.

The obstetrician or midwife will tell a woman which signs may indicate a need for further testing to determine if the fetus is in jeopardy (e.g., fewer than ten strong movements in a twelve-hour period or no movement in the morning).

Some health care professionals believe that fetal activity monitoring can increase anxiety rather than lower it. However, decreased movement can signal the need for induced delivery. Further testing might produce reassuring results. In general, fetal activity monitoring is a more precise and formalized method of doing what women have always done; that is, notice changes in fetal activity as pregnancy progresses. In high-risk pregnancies, the actual charting can provide additional information upon which to base important decisions in late pregnancy.

Fetal Biophysical Profile

This test combines both EFM and ultrasound scanning. It is done to check a fetus's breathing and movements, as well as obtaining information about muscle tone, heart rate, and the amount of amniotic fluid. A score (2 = normal, 0 = abnormal) is assigned for each characteristic. Total scores of 8 to 10 are considered normal, although in the higher ranges scores are more subject to interpretation. Very low scores indicate fetal distress.

In high-risk pregnancies, a fetal biophysical profile may be done to help determine if and when early delivery should take place. If scores are normal, the pregnancy may continue. If scores begin to drop, intervention may be necessary.

Fetal Echocardiography

This test uses highly advanced ultrasound technology to detect heart defects in the developing fetus. Because structures must be large enough to be seen clearly on the sonogram, the test is performed after the eighteenth week of pregnancy. It is a painless procedure and does not put either the mother or the fetus at risk.

Fetal echocardiography is generally performed when there is increased risk of heart defects indicated by such things as family history; exposure to certain drugs, such as lithium; or the presence of particular diseases in the mother (diabetes or lupus, for example). Depending on the findings, special prenatal care can be arranged prior to delivery, and birth can take place in a setting that specializes in high-risk pregnancies and deliveries.

Ultrasonography (Ultrasound)

Ultrasound is widely used in pregnancies regarded as normal, as well as in those considered high-risk. (See entry for explanation of the procedure.) There are numerous reasons for performing it, especially in high-risk pregnancies. Among the most important is the fact that it can establish gestational age, which is crucial in the timing of other prenatal tests. It can also monitor the rate of growth and establish the number of fetuses, if this is in question. In addition, ultrasound can detect serious birth defects.

Ultrasound is often used in high-risk pregnancies to augment or confirm other information. For example, if AFP levels are high, ultrasound may be used to evaluate possible neural tube defects. Because it is considered relatively safe, ultrasound can be used to evaluate serious problems in pregnancy (e.g., suspected ectopic pregnancy, excessive or insufficient amniotic fluid, or separation of the placenta from the uterine wall).

A full bladder helps create a clear image of the uterus, and a woman may be asked to drink several glasses of water prior to the test. The pressure of a full bladder and the slight pressure of the transducer moving across the abdomen may be slightly uncomfortable, but ultrasound is essentially pain-free.

While generally considered a very safe procedure, ultrasound is seldom performed more than once a month, even in high-risk pregnancies.

APPENDIX II
Employment Testing

Testing job applicants for attitudes, aptitudes, interests, motivation, and personality traits is a standard practice among today's employers. For the most part, however, adolescents are not tested extensively, mainly because the types of jobs high school students are qualified for do not require complex skills. Therefore, preemployment testing is usually restricted to establishing basic skills. An employer might, for example, ask a young person to take a typing test when applying for a clerical position. Nowadays, many clerical positions require knowledge of particular software programs and an employer might test an applicant's computer skills. Basic math competence might be tested for a cashier's position. These tests are usually similar to those encountered in a school setting.

The second type of testing your teenager could encounter is that which measures particular attitudes, and is sometimes referred to as integrity or honesty testing. Once done primarily to assess attitudes toward work values such as reporting to work on time and the ability to cooperate with co-workers, attitude testing has expanded in recent years. Employers have become more concerned with theft and damage done by employees, as well as other irresponsible behavior.

At one time polygraph (lie detector) was used extensively to assess the integrity of job applicants. However, federal law currently allows polygraph only for jobs considered high-risk or security sensitive (transportation and nuclear power plant positions and so on). It is unlikely that your minor would be considered for jobs for which polygraph is allowed. If your child tells you he or she is scheduled for polygraph testing as part of the hiring process for a fast-food, convenience store, or retail clerk position, the test would most certainly be illegal. Drug screening tests that require urinalysis or blood samples are in all likelihood illegal as well. State law varies, however, and also changes rapidly.

Paper-and-pencil employee screening is legal. It is becoming quite common because it is inexpensive and meets fair employee selection guidelines outlined by the Equal Opportunity Employment Commission (EEOC). It may seem odd that employers would bother with such testing for minimum wage retail jobs or when hiring a counter clerk in a convenience store. Employers often go through this trouble because, statistically at least, young people are considered high-risk employees, meaning that as a group, teenagers tend to have casual attitudes toward theft of cash and merchandise. Some of the tests also screen for attitudes toward safety consciousness, drug abuse, customer relations, and a tendency to violent reactions and behavior, all of which contribute to liability risks and loss of profits.

Employee testing is considered valid—and legal—only if the tests are job-related. In other words, your teenager should not be tested for clerical aptitude if the job does not require clerical tasks. The sophisticated measures of management style are not appropriate for convenience store jobs. General measures of work values and integrity are considered job-related when the position requires handling money and merchandise, interacting with customers, and adhering to a work schedule. Testing is not meant to replace the interviewing process or reference checks, but rather to augment the traditional employee screening measures. These tests are usually in a multiple choice or true/false form, or a combination of formats. Basic literacy (sixth- or seventh-grade reading level) is assumed. There are many attitude tests available, but the most common ones used in low-skill, low-wage jobs are the following.

Personal Outlook Inventory (POI). A basic integrity test designed to predict a candidate's potential to steal cash or merchandise.

Personnel Selection Inventory (PSI). A preemployment screen covering many work-related issues, including honesty, nonviolence, safety consciousness, drug avoidance, and loyalty and tenure, meaning the likelihood that the person will stay with the company a reasonable length of time once hired. (The latter, of course, may not be relevant when hiring teenagers.) The tendency to loyalty would be considered the important factor in this scale. The test takes 30 to 40 minutes. There are many versions of this test, each designed for use in specific industries—banking, for example. The PSI is available in Spanish and French.

Reid Report. A test that specifically assesses the likelihood that an applicant would steal if given the opportunity. Some questions ask for information about theft on previous jobs and current and past alcohol or drug abuse. This test is available in five languages, including Spanish.

The Stanton Survey and the Stanton Survey, Phase II. Two tests that assess attitudes and social behavior, including alcohol and drug abuse and gambling. The two versions of the test are similar, but the Stanton Survey requires biographical data. This section is omitted in the Stanton Survey, Phase II.

Trustworthiness Attitude Survey (T.A. Survey). Measures attitude and personality characteristics that indicate trustworthiness for a job requiring handling money or products.

GLOSSARY

Ability: The capacity or talent to do or learn particular skills.

Abnormal values: The term used in some medical tests for results that fall outside of normal range. However, the result does not necessarily establish the presence or absence of a disease or disorder.

Achievement test: One way to measure what a person has learned after having been taught in the subject area.

Age equivalent/age score: The name given to a particular score on a standardized test in which age norms are used as one way to report a score.

Age norms: A norm that reports the average age of the children who got the same number of correct answers on a test. This is then used to derive the age-equivalent score.

Alternate form reliability: The concept of judging test reliability, involving a correlation coefficient between two comparable (equivalent) forms of a test.

Anchor test: A term associated with a method of establishing a grade equivalent or other scale. Representative groups are given tests judged appropriate for the grade. Certain items in each test are common, and by comparing results of these items, it is possible to design a standardized scale.

Aphasia: See Dysphasia.

Aptitude: The degree of natural ability to learn in particular academic areas.

Assessment: A group of procedures used to give a profile of a child in many areas. It can include developmental, educational, and psychological testing, and sometimes medical testing, interviews, and observations. An assessment implies a team approach to evaluating a child and making decisions based on the body of information compiled.

At risk: A term used to describe children who, on the basis of screening, observation, and testing, are likely to encounter problems in an academic setting. This term is also used in a medical setting. For example, a premature baby is considered at risk for developmental difficulties. A child with a parent who developed juvenile diabetes would be considered at risk of developing the disease, and parents and the physician would closely monitor the child.

Attention Deficit Disorder (ADD): The name given to a condition characterized by a short attention span, distractibility, emotional swings, and impulsive and unpredictable behavior. ADD can exist with or without hyperactivity, and the term is replacing hyperactivity as a single diagnosis. It may or may not be linked with learning disabilities; it can't be automatically assumed that a child with ADD is learning disabled. Because the condition has so many variations and symptoms, a child thought to have it may well be given numerous tests in a variety of settings. Medications may also be used, depending on the philosophy of the physician and others on the assessment team.

Attribute: A characteristic or trait either absent or present to some degree in the person being observed.

Auditory perception: The ability to identify and organize external sounds such as music, speech, and those classified as environmental, as well as comprehend their meaning.

Autism: A disorder characterized by abnormal responses to stimulation. Autism often shows up in early infancy, although it may not be diagnosed until much later. An autistic child is sometimes said to live in a world of his or her own, in that he or she is unresponsive to and even rejecting of physical interaction and touch, as well as verbal interaction.

Band: Scores that are presented within a range of scores rather than at one specific point. This is done to avoid comparison of close scores whose difference may be statistically insignificant.

Basal: The first age level or place within a test at which all the questions are answered correctly or the required tasks are performed correctly. This is sometimes expressed as the basal age, and some testing formally begins after the basal age has been established.

Battery: A group of tests or subtests designed for a specific purpose (to assess overall academic achievement, personality and behavior, a source of psychological or educational difficulties, and so on). The results of the battery may then be used in establishing diagnoses, planning an IEP, and so on.

Bilateral integration: The ability to coordinate sensorimotor functions on both sides of the body in activities requiring movements of both hands or both legs.

Ceiling: The opposite of basal, representing the highest level a student achieved on a test.

Chromosomes: Tiny strands of genetic material (DNA) present in the nucleus of every cell. Chromosomes carry the genes, which in turn determine hereditary characteristics.

Chronological age (CA): Age expressed in years and months (7 years, 5 months, for example).

Classroom tests: The tests, quizzes, and other tools that classroom teachers devise to measure progress in a particular skill, as opposed to the tests developed and mass-produced by professionals and test publishers.

Cognition or cognitive ability: Refers, in a general way, to intellectual processes and the abilities associated with various types of thinking, such as reasoning, problem solving, organizing, and remembering ideas and images. Cognitive abilities are sometimes broken down into *directed* and *undirected cognition.* Undirected cognition refers to the process and content of the inner life: dreams, daydreams, and general free flow of thought. Directed cognition describes the thought processes involved when concentrating on a specific task: solving a problem, learning to read, retelling a dream, discussing the past or future, and so on.

Completion questions: Test items that require a student to furnish missing information, as in "fill in the blank."

Congenital: A term used to describe conditions present at the time of birth, both those that are inherited and those that are caused by a prenatal event or during the birth process.

Correlation coefficient: A statistical term used to measure the relationship between two variables. The value range is -1.00 (perfect negative correlation) to +1.00 (perfect positive correlation). Methods that establish a test's reliability (e.g., test-retest or split-half reliability) will assign a correlation coefficient to describe how well the test performed; that is, how reliable it showed itself to be.

Criterion-referenced test (CR): Test that measures what a child has mastered based on specific objectives. Results are not compared to others in a group or to national norms. The score is not assigned a percentile rank or a stanine band.

Cumulative record: A school record maintained over many years. Test scores, grades, attendance records, and behavioral reports are generally included in cumulative records.

Derived score: A score that has been converted from a unit on one scale into units on another, thus allowing results of a student's test scores to be expressed and compared in a different way. Percentile rank and grade equivalents are examples of derived scores.

Developmental lag: Delayed maturity in one or more areas. It implies that the delay is temporary and that the child will "catch up," sometimes with specialized help.

Developmental milestones: A term used in pediatrics and early childhood development to refer to particular abilities universally considered signs of normal growth (i.e., sitting alone, social smile, walking, speech sounds, and so on).

Developmental scales: General guidelines and assumptions about infant and child development; a child's performance is observed and compared to other children of the same age. Motor skills, speech, sociability, and responsiveness are among the many areas of development for which developmental scales have been established.

Deviation IQ: The degree to which a child's performance on an IQ test is either above or below that of others in the same age group.

Diagnostic test: A procedure or tool that identifies a particular problem and its severity. It may also attempt to discover its source. This type of test is used in many disciplines. In medicine, for example, a diagnostic test might be recommended after a screening tool has revealed that a problem *may* exist. Because important decisions may be made on the basis of a diagnostic test (i.e., special-education placement, recommendation for medication or other treatment, and so on), only highly skilled examiners in the specific fields should score and interpret test results.

Domain: An area of development or a skill, attribute, behavior, or condition that is tested. An intelligence test measures functioning in the cognitive domain; a motor skills test measures functioning in the sensory domain.

Down's syndrome: The name given to a specific congenital condition characterized by certain physical signs and deficiencies in mental functioning. At one time, the term *mongoloidism* was used to describe Down's syndrome because of the characteristic slanting eyes associated with the syndrome. Other physical characteristics include poor muscle tone, short stature, and a smaller than average skull size. The degree of mental retardation varies greatly, and many

Down's syndrome–afflicted infants and children can learn self-care and vocational skills.

Dysfunction: An abnormality or impairment in any organ of the body. The term is also applied to other concepts or systems (i.e., dysfunctional family, dysfunctional behavior, and so on).

Dysgraphia: A difficulty in the visual-motor sphere, often resulting in an inability to "translate" the mental vision of a figure, number, or letter, for example, into its written form.

Dyslexia: The term used to describe difficulty in learning to read. It is often associated with specific characteristics that can be measured (letter reversal, missing letters or words, and so on). The term is not meant to include difficulty with reading that results from lack of motivation, psychological difficulties, or deprivation of basic needs (such as inadequate food, shelter, or medical care). Nor does the term refer to children who are simply taking a bit longer to learn to read than other children of the same age.

Dysnomia: A difficulty naming objects or in recalling or remembering words, and, therefore, an inability to retrieve the word at the time it is needed. However, if a word is unfamiliar in the first place, the term would not apply.

Dysphasia: Weakness in the ability to learn the symbols of a language. It includes such things as an inability to understand spoken language or to speak. Generally, dysphasia is caused by damage to the speech centers of the brain through illness or injury or by inherent dysfunction. The term *aphasia* may be used, which implies that the weakness is severe.

Dyspraxia: Difficulties in planning and carrying out tasks involved with particular skills. Oral dyspraxia involves an inability to use the physical systems involved in forming speech sounds, even though the physical structures appear normal. Motor dyspraxia means that there is difficulty in performing new motor tasks, although those that are familiar can be performed adequately.

Echolalia: Repetition of words or phrases without understanding their meaning. Echolalia is a normal part of speech development, and it is generally outgrown between the ages of two and three years. Mentally retarded or autistic children may not, however, outgrow this behavior.

Educational age (EA): A score derived from the average chronological age of children obtaining each score on a test, sometimes called a learning age (LA).

Educational objective: Goals or milestones developed for a child to achieve within a given period of time based on specific instruction during that period.

Educational prescription: Activities designed to help a child meet specific objectives.

Educational quotient (EQ): The relationship between the chronological age of a child to his or her educational age.

Education for All Handicapped Children Act: Passed in 1975, this law guarantees special education to all children who need it. It also mandates that decisions about special education should be made free of bias. For example, the law specifies that tests used must be racially and culturally nondiscriminatory, and that children be tested in their first language if they are not proficient in English. It further specifies that decisions will not be made on the results of a single test, that the tests selected must be validated for the purpose used, and that test administrators must be qualified as described by the author/producer of the test. The law also dictates a multidisciplinary approach; that is, specialists in a number of fields must be part of the diagnostic team.

Other provisions of the law call for placement in the most "normal" environment possible—one that allows for maximum interaction with children in the same age group who are not receiving special-education services. The law also provides for "due process," in that placement, changes in placement, or challenges to placement must follow certain procedures. Parents also have the right to have their children evaluated by an independent team. The results of that evaluation must also be considered. There must also be a written IEP (Individualized Educational Plan).

Equivalency method: A way of standardizing a new test. The scores on the new test are compared with raw scores on a test that has already established norms, referred to as the anchor test. (It is assumed that both tests measure the same thing.)

Equivalent forms: Also called alternate forms. These are parallel forms of one test that measure the same thing. Equivalent forms are sometimes used to retest a student or to measure progress at a later time.

Examiner: The person who administers a test; often, but not always, the same person who scores and interprets the results.

Expressive language: A child's ability to use words and language conversationally and in writing. As children develop language skills, they are expected to have a command of all parts of speech when expressing themselves.

False positive/false negative: The terms used to describe a situation in which a medical test indicates the presence of a condition or disease when it does not exist (false positive), or "misses" the presence of a condition or disease that does exist (false negative). These terms are used in other fields—education for example—when a test fails to spot deficiencies or difficulties or suggests that they are present when they are not.

Fine motor skills: One of the categories of visual-motor skill groups, meaning small movements of the hands and fingers where precision and speed are more important than strength.

Floor: See Basal.

Formal tests: A term generally applied to standardized tests in which the scores are reported in grade equivalents, percentiles, and the like. Any norm-referenced test is considered a formal test.

Frequency distribution: A count of the number of individuals receiving the same score on a test.

Gross motor skills: One of the categories of visual-motor skill groups, meaning large body movements for which strength is required.

Hard sign: When used in neurology, this refers to a clear and easily identified problem, such as the absence of a basic reflex, for example.

Hearing vocabulary: The ability to recognize words as they are spoken and to connect them to the correct object or concept.

Hyperactive: A clinical term meaning nondirected behavior, extreme distractibility, and excitability. Both medical and psychological reasons are often cited for hyperactivity. In popular use, the term can be used to describe boisterous, active children with so much energy that they can be difficult to "manage." However, this is not clinical hyperactivity, a condition requiring careful diagnosis.

Individual Educational Plan (IEP): A provision of the Education for All Handicapped Children Act, an IEP is a document that describes recommended instruction and specifies short- and long-term educational goals. The IEP is developed after assessments have been performed by a team of specialists, who recommend various instruction and placement. There is also a provision in the law for periodic evaluation of the IEP.

Informal tests: A term used when the test score is not norm-referenced, often meaning that the examiner is free to modify the test formats, choose and analyze individual items, and so on. These tests are often designed by a classroom or special-education teacher to identify areas in which further instruction is needed. Informal tests may also be used to monitor progress when a child is placed in a tutoring or remediation program.

Intelligence: In standard educational practice, intelligence is defined by looking at many types of functions in a global way. The functions generally included in an overall measure of intelligence include cognitive skills, abstract numerical and verbal reasoning, comprehension and memory, and the ability to learn new information, solve problems, and grasp concepts. This is one standard definition, but by no means is it accepted as inclusive of all types of human ability and functioning.

Intelligence quotient (IQ): The way mental abilities are indexed or scored on an intelligence test, usually resulting in a number that places a person above or below the score considered average, most often 100.

Interpreter: The person who reviews the score or results of a test and establishes its meaning in a larger context. The interpreter may or may not be the examiner. For example, the radiologist (an M.D.) interprets an x-ray series that a technician may administer.

Interscore reliability: The degree of correlation between the same test samples when scored by two examiners.

Inventory: Generally a questionnaire, an inventory lists behavior, attitudes, and interests. Noting the presence or absence of these characteristics is a common way to answer inventory questions, often with a way to establish frequency, degree, and so on.

Kinesthetic, kinesthesia: The perception of the body in movement and the ability to choose direction and speed of body motion.

Learning age: See Educational age.

Learning disabilities: Considered a catch-all term for conditions that interfere with school performance, although home and social skills may also be involved. Learning disabilities may have a variety of causes, ranging from slow development in some areas to physical and psychological disorders.

Learning quotient (LQ): The score on a test that compares the number of questions answered to the scores of the average child in the norm group taking the same test. An LQ is a form of IQ.

Learning style: Particular characteristics that either facilitate or interfere with various learning tasks—a long or short attention span, for example.

Linguistics: Refers to the field of study that examines the form and function of language and language concepts.

Mainstreaming: The integration of exceptional children into standard classrooms. For example, a child with learning disabilities is mainstreamed when he or she is given special, individualized instructions within the regular classroom setting as opposed to a special-education classroom.

Mastery test: One designed to establish that a student has learned a skill previously taught. It is a term associated with criterion-referenced testing in that results are not compared with other children's scores on the same test. For example, if a second grade student has difficulty learning to add and is receiving special tutoring, a mastery test would be given to measure progress. When one skill has been mastered, another learning goal would be set. This same child might later be given a standardized test along with other children in the same grade. However, the score on that test would not accurately reflect the progress the student had made.

Mean: The arithmetical average of all scores on a test. The mean is established by adding the scores of all people taking a particular test and then dividing the total by the number of test-takers.

Median: The term used to describe the middle point in a set of scores. By definition, there are the same number of scores above and below it.

Minimal brain dysfunction (MBD): A term that replaced "minimal brain damage" as a catch-all term associated with many conditions: learning disabilities, developmental lags and deficits, hyperactivity, attention deficit disorder, and so on. The term is used because actual brain damage often cannot be demonstrated. This label is now going out of use in some professional circles and is being replaced with the more specific conditions previously listed.

Mode: The term for the score that occurs most frequently in a distribution of scores.

Morphology: The aspect of linguistics concerned with the way in which words are formed by using particular rules.

Motor planning: The ability to plan, and then execute, unfamiliar motor tasks that use already acquired motor skills.

Neonatal: The period immediately after birth up to the first month. An infant may be referred to as the neonate in medical reports.

Nonverbal: Tests or test items that do not require a verbal response. The term is also used when referring to a child who is not able to use language to communicate.

Norm: A particular way to "translate" a score into a comparative measure so that one individual's test score can be compared to a group considered comparable. Grade equivalents, percentiles, standard scores, and so on are by definition derived from using norms. Norms can be established on a national basis, within a school district, or for groups with the same disability or descriptive diagnosis. Although not part of parents' report forms, the groups used to establish norms on a given test are usually those cited in professional literature that discusses and critiques tests. Test publishers generally include information about norms in their catalogs and other promotional material. When tests are revised, new norms are established.

Normal curve: Sometimes referred to as the bell-shaped curve, the normal curve graphically shows the distribution of scores on a test and establishes the normal levels.

Normal level: The average level.

Normal values: A term used to describe the results of a test for which the findings fall within a generally accepted normal range. The normal values for any given test may vary from one culture to another and may also change as attitudes or information changes. For example, levels of lead in the blood considered normal in one country might be judged abnormal in another. Some physicians have begun referring to "reference values" rather than normal values.

Normative group: The representative group of people whose performance has been used to develop and standardize a test. The group's scores are then used as the yardstick by which to measure the scores of others taking the same test. The stanine, age, grade equivalent scores, percentile, and so on are derived by comparison to the group(s) who took the test. Theoretically, the normative group must be representative of those for whom the test is designed. For example, if a language test is normed on 300 English-speaking children, the norms would not be useful for a child who is just learning English. The test might be a way to measure progress, but the grade or age equivalents and so on would not adequately reflect the abilities of that child. Teachers and clinicians often interpret scores in different ways for different populations and their specific needs.

Norm-referenced tests (NR): Tests in which the results are compared to a representative group of children of the same age or grade. Standardized achievement tests are norm-referenced.

Objective testing: Refers to the way a test is scored; that is, theoretically, no question can have more than one correct answer. Generally, these tests can be scored mechanically and a raw score achieved without subjective judgment. This term does not, however, mean that the test design itself is free of bias.

Percentile, percentile rank: One method of expressing the comparison of scores of a group of people taking the same test. It indicates the percentages of people who scored above and below a particular score. For example, a percentile rank of 75 means that a person scored at or above 75 percent of the people taking that test.

Percentile band: A range of scores in which a "true" score is likely to be. This is used to compensate for the error factor inherent in all tests.

Perception: The way in which the brain recognizes and makes sense out of incoming sensory stimuli.

Perceptual-motor: See Visual motor.

Phonology: The actual sounds made in any spoken language.

Pragmatics: The way language is used in the context of communication. It refers to the ability to carry on a conversation, take turns speaking, respond to a topic, and so on.

Praxis: Another term for motor planning.

Predictive value: The degree of correlation between a test score and actual future performance.

Prognostic test: Designed to help predict future performance in a particular skill or the future course of a disease or illness.

Projective test: A test in which a person is asked to respond to material that is nonstructured (sometimes referred to as "ambiguous material"). The person creates a response based on the material presented, "projecting" his or her own perceptions and thoughts on the material. There are no right or wrong answers, and the person's responses are said to reveal certain aspects of personality.

Projective tests are done individually, usually in an office setting. These tests generally take considerable skill to give, and licensed clinical psychologists are the only qualified examiners for many of the standard projective psychological tests. More than one test is needed before a diagnosis can be made.

Psycholinguistics: A field that studies the correlation between the psychological processes and those involved in language and communication.

Public Law 94-142: See Education for All Handicapped Children Act.

Ratio IQ: A score that, using a specific formula, reports mental age in relation to chronological age.

Raw score: The number of correct answers on a test. For example, in a test with ten questions, the range of possible raw scores is 0 to 10.

Readiness testing: Generally associated with reading readiness or readiness for kindergarten. Readiness tests are generally given to children before and after kindergarten, with the intent of screening for problems that may interfere with learning to read or to do basic arithmetic. This is considered one of the most controversial testing categories, especially when young children are either held back, placed in special classroom settings, or otherwise grouped solely on the basis of the test result.

Receptive language: The ability to process and understand spoken or written language. It involves the ability to both listen and read.

Reliability: The degree to which a person would get the same results if he or she took a test again. Test publishers use various methods to establish reliability, including alternate form reliability, interscore reliability, split-half reliability, and test-retest reliability. (See individual entries.)

Remedial: A common term used in education to describe extra teaching required to help a child learn a skill. It also implies that the child is performing below his or her grade level in that skill, and that help is needed for him or her to make progress. Remediation is sometimes used when discussing the need to go back and reteach basic skills to older children who have been passed from grade to grade without acquiring an adequate foundation of skills to keep up with more difficult academic demands. For example, some community colleges offer basic skills classes to students to prepare them for college-level work, and these are sometimes referred to as remedial classes. Remedial is usually not used when describing the special teaching required for a child with learning disabilities.

Risk factors: In the context of medical testing, this term refers to the possible dangers or potential harm involved in performing a test. It also refers to conditions that put a person at high risk for particular illnesses or disorders.

Scatter: The extent of the variation of scores on the subtests in one test or among many different tests. Wide discrepancies do not automatically suggest a problem, however.

Screening: Testing or observations that may identify areas of weakness or deficiency, as well as areas of strength. Children are screened for possible vision or hearing problems, for example. A screening can determine that a problem may exist, but it does not diagnose the problem. In-depth evaluation usually follows when a problem is identified in a screening.

Semantics: The meaning of language elements and their relationship to thinking and behavior.

Sensory discrimination: The ability to notice differences among various stimuli. Auditory discrimination involves the ability to differentiate between sounds. Tactile discrimination involves the degree to which a person can notice the similarities and differences between objects using only the sense of touch. Visual discrimination is the ability to differentiate visual symbols such as designs and letters. Some professionals consider these abilities important for establishing learning styles and, therefore, placing children in environments in which the most valuable instruction can take place.

Sensory integration: The brain's ability to organize incoming sensory stimuli.

Separation anxiety: Although this sounds like pathology, the term actually refers to a normal stage of development wherein a child is afraid to be apart from a parent or the primary caregiver. It becomes a problem requiring attention when a child doesn't "outgrow" it or when a trauma has occurred that makes the reality of separation extreme—the death of a parent, for example.

Social age (SA): An age equivalent score on a test that measures social skills of young children (e.g., playing in a group, interacting with others, or the ability to cooperate).

Soft sign: When used in psychological testing, this term refers to findings that suggest minimal neurological disturbances or impairments—mild memory or speech problems, for example. (See Hard sign for comparison.)

Spatial: Associated with the ability to see relationships between shapes or objects in an environment. Spatial orientation refers to how a child perceives himself or herself in relationship to the surrounding environment. Poor spatial orientation may result in left-right confusion or a poor sense of direction.

Split-half reliability: A method by which a test is split in half, often by separating odd- and even-numbered questions. The results of each half of the test are compared to determine a correlation coefficient. Numerous educational, developmental, and psychological tests use this method as a way to determine reliability.

Standard deviation: The measure of the degree of variation of scores around the established mean.

Standard error of measurement: Also expressed as standard error, test error, and SE, it is the term that indicates the degree to which chance errors may cause variation in a score if the test were repeated any number of times. For example, if the SE is 3, there is a 2 to 1 chance that a given person's score will be in a range of three points. Hence, a "true" score of 93 on a test with an SE of 3 would fall between 90 and 96.

Standardized test: Refers first to uniform conditions under which a test was developed that resulted in a standard of performance. It is implied that a representative sample of children (i.e., economically diverse, coming from all races and ethnic groups, both urban and rural, and so on) was used to determine reliability. The term also implies that the tests are administered uniformly; that is, the instructions are given in exactly the same way each time, the same time limits are used in all test settings, and so on.

Standard score: A derived score based on the mean and standard deviation. Comparisons can then be made of a child's scores on a number of tests.

Stanine: A ranking derived by dividing all test scores into nine parts; hence, the range of stanine scores is 1 (low) to 9 (high). The average stanine is 5. The majority of standardized achievement tests include a stanine score.

Subjective testing: Refers to scoring based on the judgment and attitudes of the tester or scorer. In academics, the essay test is considered subjective. In psychology, projective tests are sometimes considered subjective.

Subtests: Sections of a test, usually measuring a particular skill or attribute.

Syntax: The system in which a language is correctly used (i.e., grammar, the function of each word in a group, the ordering of words, and so on).

Tactile perception: The ability to recognize and understand stimuli received through the sense of touch.

Test misuse: A general term used to describe many situations in which testing and/or test results are used incorrectly. Choosing the wrong test, scoring errors, making specific diagnoses based on too few tests, violating student privacy, predicting future performance on the basis of a test not intended for that purpose, and repeating the same test too often are examples of misuse of tests and testing.

Test-retest reliability: Administering the same test twice to the same group of students and then establishing the correlation between the two scores.

Timed test, speed test: A test in which the amount of time allowed to complete it is specified. Therefore, with few exceptions, the speed with which a student works is important to the final score.

Underachiever: A term used to describe children who generally perform below the level of ability they are thought to have. It does not, however, automatically follow that these children lack motivation. Learning disabilities, physical problems, and various emotional difficulties may be among the reasons for underachievement.

Validity: The extent to which a test actually measures what it is designed to measure. Validity is discussed in the context of a test's value for measuring specific skills and traits, as well as its ability to predict performance. Thus, if scores on a test of mathematical ability consistently conform to the actual performance of those taking it, the test would be said to have a predictive validity.

Vestibular system: The way in which we control and adjust to body position and balance as we carry out movement.

Visual-motor: Also called perceptual-motor, psychomotor, or sensorimotor, the ability to coordinate hand-eye movements. It also refers to items on a test that measure a child's ability to coordinate vision or perception with physical movements. Various researchers have named and classified specific movements that constitute visual-motor skills—finger dexterity, for example.

INDEX

A

AAMD Adaptive Behavior
   Scale (ABS), 284
Ability, 299
Abnormal values, 299
Academic achievement test,
   193–94, 217–19
Accountability debate,
   195
Achievement Identification
   Measure (AIM, AIM-TO).
   See Group Achievement
   Identification Measure
Achievement tests, 197, 206,
   230, 234–36
 debate over, 5–6
 defined, 299
ACT (American College
   Testing Program)
   Assessment 162–64

ADD-H Comprehensive
   Teacher's Rating Scale, 234
Admission Testing Program
   (ATP), 208
Advanced Progressive Matrices.
   See Raven's Progressive
   Matrices
Age equivalent/age score, 299
Age norms, 299
AGS Early Screen Profiles
   (ESP), 183–85
AIDS (acquired immune
   deficiency syndrome), 71
Alcohol screening, 76
Allergy testing, 21, 22–25, 28
Alpha Fetoprotein (AFP)
   Screening, 288, 289, 294,
   308
Alternate form reliability, 299

Thyroid Screening tests, 47
Timed test (speed test), 315
Tine test, 78–79
Toe Walking, 64
Toeing In, 65
Token Test for Children (Token Test), 152–54
Torticollis, 64
Total hemoglobin, 36
Toxicology Screening, 76–77, 83, 87–88
Toxoplasmosis Tests, 49
Tracking, 12, 159, 175, 180, 222
Trichamonas vaginalis, 74
Trustworthiness Attitude Survey (T.A. Survey), 297
T3 uptake, 47
Tuberculosis Skin Test (PPD, Tine Test, TB Test), 20, 78, 79
Turner's syndrome, 35
2-Hour Postprandial Blood Sugar (2-Hour PP), 40

U

Ultrasonography, 18, 79–81, 288, 289, 294
Underachievers, 186, 315
Unmanageability, severe, 9
Urinalysis (urine test), 18, 19, 20, 21, 28, 31, 57, 82–88
Urine culture, 50, 57, 87
Urobilirubin, 83, 86
Utah Test of Language Development, 154

V

Vagina, discharge from, 72
Vaginal culture, 53
Vaginal itching, 66, 72
Vaginitis, 53
Validity, 315
Venipuncture, 30
Vestibular system, 315
Vineland Adaptive Behavior Scales (The Vineland), 277–78
Viral cultures, 50
Viruses, 51
Vision Screening, 224–27
Vision tests, 4, 14, 20, 106, 121–22
Visually-impaired, 261, 279, 285
Visual-motor integration skills, 106, 241, 315
Visual perception tests, 99, 136, 145

W

Walker Problem Behavior Identification Checklist, 236
Wepman Auditory Memory Span Test (AMST), 154
Wepman Auditory Sequential Memory Test (ASMT), 154
Wepman Auditory Visual Memory Test (VMT), 154
Weschler Adult Intelligence Scale, Revised (WAIS-R), 279–81